contemporary Spain

MANCHESTER
UNIVERSITY PRESS

For my dear mother
and for all the girls and boys

Women in contemporary Spain

Anny Brooksbank Jones

MANCHESTER UNIVERSITY PRESS
MANCHESTER and NEW YORK

distributed exclusively in the USA by St. Martin's Press

Copyright © Anny Brooksbank Jones 1997

Published by Manchester University Press
Oxford Road, Manchester M13 9PL, UK
and Room 400, 175 Fifth Avenue, New York, NY 10010, USA

Distributed exclusively in the USA by
St. Martin's Press, Inc.,
175 Fifth Avenue, New York, NY 10010, USA

Distributed exclusively in Canada by
UBC Press, University of British Columbia, 6344 Memorial Road,
Vancouver, BC, Canada V6Y 1Z2

British Library Cataloguing-in-Publication Data
A catalogue record for this book is available from the British Library

Library of Congress Cataloging-in-Publication Data
Jones, Anny Brooksbank
        Women in Spain / Anny Brooksbank Jones
            p.   cm.
        Includes bibliographical references (p.   ).
        ISBN 0 7190 4756 0 (cloth). — ISBN 0 7190 4757 9 (pbk.)
            1. Women—Spain—Social conditions. 2. Women—Employment—Spain.
        3. Women—Spain—Economic conditions. 4. Women in mass media—Spain.
        I. Title.
        HQ1692.J66   1997
        347.41'012—dc21   97-20797

ISBN 0 7190 4756 0 hardback
        0 7190 4757 9 paperback

First published 1997

01   00   99   98   97   10   9   8   7   6   5   4   3   2   1

Typeset in Joanna
by Koinonia Limited, Manchester
Printed in Great Britain
by Biddles Ltd, Guildford and King's Lynn

Contents

Preface and acknowledgements

IN A RECENT BBC radio programme on Spanish lifestyles, feminist philosopher Victoria Camps observed that her countrywomen and men could not get through the day without an after-lunch nap. Minutes later, sociologist Salvador Giner was declaring that the 'siesta' had virtually disappeared in Spain. In this contradiction lie the pains and pleasures of writing a book on women in contemporary Spain. The pains are mostly related to the need to be selective – which is particularly trying for those who believe (as I do) that every detail signifies. Despite the rapidity of democratic modernisation, for example, Spain did not spring fully formed in 1975 from the ashes of the dictatorship and, even in a relatively short study, this can only be demonstrated with reference to the Franco years. Sociologist Luis Garrido has gone so far as to posit two biographies for Spanish women: a traditional one, associated with women formed under Franco, and a modern one, associated with those who have grown up in the transitional and democratic periods. From this perspective, Camps might be said to speak from a traditional position, and Giner from a more modern one. No study of Spanish women can avoid this binary, which structures the analysis of many workers in the field. But binaries notoriously polarise terms and mask heterogeneity. Despite her views on the siesta, for example, Camps' biography has very little of the traditional about it. And just as women who grew up under Franco have not remained untouched by the democratic period, so some younger women may lead relatively 'traditional' lifestyles away from (and sometimes within) urban centres.

The figures of Camps and Giner are used here to conjure up two quite different approaches to women's lives, however, both of which have their advantages and shortcomings. The empirical sociological perspective, for example, has difficulty avoiding 'la falacia agregada', averaging out its data across a larger group in a way that rarely corresponds with any living individual, and distilling them into figures that create an often misleading sense of exactitude. This may be especially true in Spain, where the department responsible for collecting statistics has been very close to central government during the democratic period and the presentation, if not collection, of data has been widely politicised. Gender-differentiated statistics can be particularly hard to come by: 1996 essays on women's education, for example, are still partly reliant on figures dating back to 1989. Where they are available, they have usually been commissioned for the national, and more recently regional, Institutes for Women for their own purposes. In the absence of alternatives, these data circulate widely and are factored into other analyses – including my own – where any inaccuracies or questionable assumptions risk being compounded. Even where they manage to avoid leading questions and forced choices, sociological surveys designed to give insight into individual opinions are at best a snapshot of a selection of individuals at a particular moment, and at worst an opportunity for respondents to posture, anticipate or even deliberately mislead researchers. A series of such snapshots is a shaky basis from which to infer changes and trends. On the other hand, the more personalised 'Camps-type' perspective of an individual or small community within the larger group is always partial and may be completely atypical. And a series of interviews with different small groups would be shaped by structural and interpersonal dynamics not so very different from those of mass surveys.

Neither of these approaches can unlock the 'truth' of Spanish women. There isn't (only) one. But juxtaposing the two can bring into relief the patchy and often contradictory nature of socio-cultural change as it affects women, and in a broader frame than has previously been available to anglophone readers. This study bears the traces of all the individual Spanish women I have known while living, working and researching in and outside of Spain, but it is particularly indebted to the insights of feminist sociologists and other academics there. The questions raised and the positions taken are presented broadly on their own terms (not least because a comparative study would require much more space) and the different emphases of each chapter acknowledge the discourses dominant in each field. This is not to suggest that Spanish women in some way speak for themselves in this text. An author's power to select and represent sources can be played down but it cannot be surrendered and to claim otherwise would be foolish or disingenuous. More importantly, it would expose a wide-ranging volume like this one to charges of weak, uncritical pluralism or incoherence. With this in mind and for reasons of personal politics the authorial framing of source material is consistently engaged; empirically-focused chapters are underpinned by a critical concern for the subjectivity of the women discussed; and cultural studies chapters insist on the material circumstances of cultural production.

One clear organisational advantage of a critical source-led approach is that it eases the problem of selection, since little has been written in Spain about women's art, for example, or music. Conversely, high-quality English-language studies of women's writing are plentiful, and my more general observations in chapter 6 reflect this fact. To facilitate the volume's use by non-Hispanists, specialist knowledge of Spanish literary and other contexts is not assumed. Given the need to introduce these contexts economically over the course of the study, sources of statistics are supplied throughout but references elsewhere are kept to a minimum. Language difference is a key contextual feature. Although all translations (unless indicated otherwise) are my own, some terms present particular problems. The term 'gender' is a case in point. Spanish academics have not tended to use its Castilian equivalent, 'género', partly because of the less theorised nature of much early feminist work, and partly because 'género' also means 'genre' and its use can lead to ambiguity. In recent years, however, rapid social change and the growth of academic feminist theorising have destabilised the terms 'woman' and 'man'. This in turn has helped to popularise the distinction between women as bearers of particular biological features (sexed) and as bearers of the social meanings attributed to those features (gendered), and with it the use of the term 'género'. Since biological differences are less self-evident than this opposition suggests, however, its English equivalent is used sparingly in the pages that follow.

Despite all the foregoing, I hope readers will find the difficulties of this project less in evidence than its many pleasures. Chief among these are the contacts with old and new friends in Spain, the UK and the US, some of whom generously supplied copies of published and unpublished material, not all of which could be credited in the necessarily restricted bibliography. I am particularly indebted to the following for their comments, support and encouragement while absolving them of responsibility for any errors on my part: Carmen, Angela and Toñi; Concha and Beatriz of Asamblea Feminista de Madrid; Catherine Davies; Judith Drinkwater; Peter Evans; Linda Gould Levine; Helen Graham; Inés and Antonio; Alec John; Vanessa Knights (whose impressively-researched Ph.D. thesis I was reading as I drafted my final chapter); Alex Longhurst; Bernard McGuirk; María Antonia; Roger Mills; Rikki Morgan; Hilary Rollin; María Pereda Pérez of Presencia Gitana; Carmela Sanz Rueda; Ana María Segura Graiño; Paul Julian Smith; Monica Threlfall; the staff of Madrid's Dirección General de la Mujer, and of the Women's Departments or Institutes in Madrid, Navarre, Andalusia, Asturias and Catalonia. This book could not have been written without research support and funding from Nottingham Trent University. But thanks most of all to John Tomlinson, for the occasional clerical assistance and endless cups of coffee that kept the cold woman in the attic at her labours.

1   Versions of activism

I N THE LAST thirty years Spanish women's lives have changed
beyond recognition. Twenty years ago they lived under a dictatorship: today the Spanish parliament boasts four women
ministers and, proportionally, more than twice as many women
deputies as the UK or the US. But this increased involvement in
formal politics, like many other gains in the democratic period,
would not have been possible without women's informal feminist
and other activism. This chapter looks at the often tense relationship
between formal and informal politics, and assesses their role in the
transformation of women's status in today's Spain.

Spanish women were latecomers to formal politics. Suffragism did
not gather momentum until the 1920s, impelled by liberal men,
conservative women and the Catholic Church (Scanlon 1986).[1] And
when, in 1924, the dictator Primo de Rivera granted certain women
voting rights it was not because he was persuaded by suffragists'
insistence on women's rationality, but because he believed them to
be instinctive allies of the right and the Church.[2] Seven years later, for
largely the same reasons, the Constituent Assembly of the Second
Republic denied women the vote, while allowing them to stand for
election. After another six months of heated debate the right to vote
was finally extended to all women in October 1933 (Instituto de la
Mujer (hereafter IM) 1995b).[3] Despite this, their assumed conservatism would continue to condition party responses to women voters
well into the 1980s.

Like most other advances won for women during the Second
Republic, opportunities to exercise this right were quickly curtailed
by the Civil War. During the conflict the mobilisation of nationalist
women was co-ordinated by Sección Femenina de Falange (SF)
(Women's Section of Falange). With the nationalist victory, SF
became the focus for all issues relating to women, which it officially
remained until its dissolution in 1977 (Alted Vigil 1991). In this
capacity it helped to prepare women for their new role as rebuilders

of the Spanish nation, the dedicated, self-denying heart of the Catholic family and mainstay of Franco's deeply authoritarian patriarchal regime (Gallego Méndez 1983; Sánchez López 1990; Graham 1995). This role legitimated their restricted access to public life, educational opportunities and key legal entitlements, and was in turn legitimated by their correspondingly lower expectations and possibilities. Although their right to vote was not actually withdrawn, opportunities to exercise it were extremely limited during the regime and political participation was discouraged as unfeminine. Just 13 'procuradoras' (women procurators or deputies) participated in the ten Franco legislatures.[4] Four of these were appointed directly by Franco, including the longest-serving one, Pilar Primo de Rivera. Their interventions during the 1940s and early 1950s were negligible, but became more significant as new socio-economic circumstances made the regime's demands on women increasingly complex and contradictory.

In the immediate aftermath of World War II, Spain's isolation allowed little in the way of alien ideology to unsettle the regime's vision of women as repository of the nation's spiritual values.[5] But by the late 1950s this isolation had become increasingly unsustainable. From 1957 the regime's tightly-regulated 'national economy' began to be dismantled and new policies were introduced to promote rapid industrial growth within a market economy open to Western capitalism. By the end of the 1960s, the Opus Dei technocrats who had spearheaded the modernisation process saw their efforts rewarded. However, it was soon clear that the desired international recognition would also require a measure of socio-cultural liberalisation. Though fumbling and superficial, these developments were resisted tooth and nail by the Catholic hierarchy. From the earliest days of the regime it had fought to preserve women from Hollywood movies and other cultural influences that were deemed to 'inhabilita[r] o menoscaba[r] la futura consorte y madre con prácticas exóticas que la desfeminizan y tornan descentrada del hogar' (to disable or discredit the future consort and mother with exotic practices that make her less womanly and distract her from the home) (Nicolás and López 1986: 375). But by 1960 the Church's moral authority was in decline and this tide had become a flood. New values took root quickly in the period of intense social and demographic change associated with industrialisation, the rise of consumerism and tourism, and the convergence of thousands of rural families on the cities in search of paid work. Younger urban women in particular found themselves caught between their official role as centre of the home and the demand for an enlarged work-force. These competing pressures made the shift from a traditional to an (at least superficially) modern society an extraordinarily rapid and contradictory process. With the crisis of the regime's family-centred social model, conflict was taken into the heart of individual households. As one contemporary survey indicates, even apparently 'modern' young women exhibited a mix of deeply traditionalist and more liberal attitudes (Campo Alange 1967). Yet by questioning their mothers' lifestyles – the educational and employment discrimination, the demands made on them by the Catholic Church, their subordinate roles at home – and by identifying with images of women's more liberal lives elsewhere, these young women helped to undermine the patriarchal authoritarianism of the regime.

Initially at least, few recognisable political channels were available to them. In the immediate post-war years some women whose Republican relatives and partners had been imprisoned by the regime participated in 'pro-preso' or prisoner support groups, many of which were linked to the Partido Comunista de España (PCE) (Spanish Communist Party). Both the development of women's solidarity and their tradition of political activism on behalf of others can be traced back to this experience. The only officially-tolerated women's groups were those which – like the nationwide Asociación de Amas de Casa (Housewives Association) and Asociaciones de Vecinos (Neighbourhood Associations) – were closely linked to SF. Until the clampdown of the late 1960s, the regime's historic link with the Catholic Church made it relatively tolerant of progressive Catholic organisations. One such, the Seminario de Estudios Sociólogicos sobre la Mujer (Seminar for the Sociological Study of Women) was founded in 1960 with the aim of modernising women's place in society and ending discrimination through education. Although its early appearance, its publications and the work of individual members (especially María, Condesa de Campo Alange) have given the Seminar a high profile in the history of the Spanish Women's Movement, its particular brand of liberal feminism did not flourish. A more direct challenge to the regime were women members of groupings like Hermandad Obrera de Acción Católica and Movimiento Apóstolico Social (Catholic Action Labour Fraternity and the Apostolic Social Movement) as well as young workers' groups. At a time when the official Falange-led union organisation had few female members these women worked alongside communists and socialists of both sexes in Comisiones

Obreras (CCOO) (independent Workers' Commissions). Particularly after CCOO was banned in 1967, these women played an active role in some of the most focused and persistent opposition to the regime. Partly through its leading role in CCOO, the Communist Party was able to establish itself as the strongest and best organised of the opposition groupings and base for some of the most influential women activists of the time. In 1965 a group of Communist and Catalan Socialist women convened the first general meeting of the Movimiento Democrático de Mujeres (MDM) (Democratic Women's Movement). At a time when SF and the Church dominated almost all women's organisations it spread quickly across the northern half of Spain. It was the first grouping to fight – albeit ambiguously at first – for recognisably feminist as well as broader socio-political ends. This double emphasis – or 'doble militancia' as it became known – caused tensions with fellow party members, some of whom were concerned that feminist issues might distract attention from what were seen as more immediate political priorities. Reservations were strongest among older women who had been active in the first generation of prisoner support groups, for which party concerns had always come first. By contrast many of MDM's leaders had been active in the second 'pro preso' generation, which had engaged in clandestine neighbourhood activism and broader support for women, with the result that party and feminist priorities had tended to become more blurred. Yet despite the anxieties of its critics, MDM's activities at this stage were still very largely party-led.

Throughout the 1960s SF continued to dominate women's lives in Spain though, like the Church-led organisations, it was obliged to liberalise superficially along the lines proposed by the Second Vatican Council. But at the same time a new generation with no memory of the war years was rising through SF's ranks, some of whom defected to opposition groups. Meanwhile, the neighbourhood and housewife associations it had established were growing stronger and increasingly independent. Despite increases in women's informal activism the participation of married women in particular in formal local politics continued to be discouraged, on the grounds that it might threaten domestic harmony. By the late 1960s, however, the level of independence enjoyed by married women – though still very limited compared with most other European countries at the time – had increased as the Church's moral and political influence declined. In 1968 SF steered through changes to the 1955 Ley de Regimen Local

(Local Regime Law), allowing married women to vote and stand in local elections.[6] By 1971, however, Spain boasted only six women provincial deputies, while at the time of Franco's death, women amounted to 62 of the 8,635 mayors and 1.38 per cent of all local councillors (Franco Rubio 1986).

But by the mid-1960s women with a very different view of Spain's future and the regime's phantom political choices were mobilising more openly. In 1964 a feminist lawyer from Barcelona published the first in a series of key texts designed to make women who were used to focusing on their obligations think instead about their rights and possibilities. These texts made Lidia Falcón one of Spain's best-known and most controversial feminist theorists. During the early 1960s, groundbreaking texts from the US and Europe were also beginning to reach Spain, including Simone de Beauvoir's *Le Deuxième Sexe* and Betty Friedan's *The Feminine Mystique*. Texts on women's history – a history that was only now beginning to be charted – became available and helped to ground the discourse of women's liberation at a time when the Women's Movement as such had yet to emerge.

When it did emerge, the movement was profoundly marked by the oppositional political culture that had nurtured virtually all of its leading figures, and the parties did not hesitate to exploit this fact as they sought to extend their spheres of influence. At a time when the necessarily clandestine nature of its activism was restricting its development, the MDM sought a legal base by infiltrating the officially-sanctioned Housewives Association. When this proved unsuccessful they formed their own Asociación de Amas de Casa Castellana (Castilian Housewives Association) and, through it, contributed significantly to women's mobilisation across Spain. In 1969, split increasingly around the question of party influence on its activities, MDM's presence in Catalonia collapsed. However, it persisted in Madrid and other PCE strongholds, where it remained subject to party priorities. It was not until 1974, when the letters MLM (Movimiento para la Liberación de la Mujer or Women's Liberation Movement) were added to its name, that the organisation became more clearly feminist in orientation.

Like most other feminist groups of the period, MDM-MLM was attacked by critics on the left for promoting what they saw as a bourgeois distraction from class politics, and by critics on the right as a communist-backed challenge to traditionalist visions of womanhood, and thus 'anti-woman' and anti-regime. Dual activists were themselves increasingly divided on the desirability of single-sex groups. For some they were a space from which to challenge the patriarchal assumptions of many fellow party members; for others, single-sex groups tended to marginalise women's activism, or to divert attention from mainstream party work. The degree of autonomy accorded women's groups within parties would also remain a vexed question. But the early imbrication of the Women's Movement and the left was arguably inevitable, and not only because many of the most active women were already party members. By severely restricting the space for legitimate social action the regime had pushed the Women's Movement and other embryonic social groups into the arms of the clandestine parties and virtually ensured that their demands could only be expressed as conflict. As noted above, in the late 1960s and early 1970s there remained virtually no channels for formal political participation and the profound contradictions within the regime were becoming increasingly evident. The intense rate of growth had allowed no time to establish appropriate structures for collective action and the welfare state was still no more than a promissory note. In this context, oppositional – and particularly neighbourhood – groups were the only effective mouthpiece for citizens' demands for goods and services.

By the early 1970s, as opposition to the regime became more open, wives of striking workers, prisoner support groups, women lawyers, university and other women's organisations, feminist and other activists all organised to demonstrate their solidarity with the opposition agenda, and to ensure that it included their own demands. Although independent women's groups were still clandestine, SF could no longer ignore their existence and sought to enhance the international profile of the regime and its own 'liberalising' credentials by organising, in 1970, the Primer Congreso Internacional de la Mujer (the First International Women's Congress), and this initiated an (albeit limited) exchange between SF and certain national and international women's groups. Meanwhile, the feminist texts filtering into Spain from the US and Britain had, by the mid-1970s, become a flood. The debates it generated were prompting some dual activists to reflect more systematically on the discrimination they experienced within the parties, and in particular to challenge the overriding claims of solidarity with others' struggles. As Monica Threlfall notes, the parties of the left tried to bring dual activists back into line with arguments about political priorities, backed up by dogmatic analyses that women's liberation was a deviation from the more urgent task of building democracy and socialism. Most feminists were sensitive to the fact that without a complete overhaul and renewal of the political system, the deeply ingrained structures of sex discrimination would not begin to be eradicated. [Debate] centred on the notion of the specificity of women's oppression, over and above the division of class, and on the need for an autonomous organisation independent of the political parties. (Threlfall 1985: 46)

As Threlfall goes on to observe, Spanish feminists seeking political legitimacy were hampered by the absence of a strong feminist tradition, the lack of a democratic culture sympathetic to the idea of equal rights, and the disinclination of many progressive women to return to sex-segregated activities after the years of Catholic-run, single-sex schooling.

The first major milestone for contemporary feminism came in 1975, when International Women's Year provided the impetus for the Primeras Jornadas Nacionales por la Liberación de la Mujer (First National Conference for Women's Liberation). Though held in secrecy two weeks after Franco's death the conference attracted 500 delegates. Among the exceptionally diverse positions represented there, a number of broad tendencies emerged. Very schematically these were: dual activism, with party links and (usually) party priorities; socialist feminism, advocating dual activism but independent of the parties; radical feminism, which rejected dual activism. High levels of commitment and energy, and the relative efficiency and influence of their party organisations helped to make dual activists the dominant force. Although in 1975 most left feminist activism was still associated with PCE, it no longer had the field to itself. The rise of independent socialism and the emergence of Trotskyist and Maoist groups opposed to what they saw as PCE's betrayal of orthodox Marxist-Leninism diverted the attention of party hierarchies, and measures to contain women's dual activism became less stringent. In fact, as the profile of the Women's Movement grew some parties began actively to exploit dual activists' efforts. In 1975, PCE out-manoeuvred its left opponents by formally declaring itself the party of women's liberation. Two years later it set up a women's committee, which found more support among the leadership than the rank and file. By contrast the women's group of the Partido Socialista Obrero Español (PSOE) (Spanish Socialist Party) had been set up by activists a year before and largely ignored by the leadership.

Many members of the second, 'socialist feminist', tendency had
themselves experienced anti-feminism and exploitation within the
parties. While some retained their individual party membership, all
insisted on the need for group autonomy. In the case of the Madrid-
based Frente de Liberación de la Mujer (FLM) (Women's Liberation
Front). This extended to denying men membership. Like socialist
feminists, members of the third, 'radical feminist', tendency were
often younger than dual activists, less closely identified with the
historic opposition struggle, and alienated by the left's increasingly
high-profile quarrels and crises. Although some radicals held views
close to those of their US namesakes, others elaborated a different,
peculiarly Spanish, version of radical feminism which was at times
very close to socialist feminism.[7] Schematically, the first type held that
men and women are opposed as sexual classes, and focused on issues
around sexuality and reproduction. The second held that men and
women are opposed as social classes, and focused on women's role in
the production and reproduction of material life. Both types had
diverse inflections. For example, the Partido Feminista (PF) (Feminist
Party) was a separatist group of the second type, but members of the
Seminario Colectivo Feminista (Feminist Collective Seminar) from
which PF had split in 1976 rejected its exclusive focus on class
domination. Instead they linked women's subordination to additional
sexual, economic and legal factors. By contrast, US-style radical
feminists tended to take their lead from such theorists as Shulamith
Firestone and Kate Millett. They saw patriarchy – however defined –
as broadly related to women's denial as a subject under male
domination and rejected all party politics as tending to perpetuate
women's oppression. Although they too were oriented towards social
transformation, and saw themselves as a renovating force in feminist
theory and practice, much of their activity was structured around self-
help groups which (as one influential commentator has noted)
enabled them to analyse women's oppression while offering little
insight into the structural or other means by which it might be
addressed.[8] Their focus on the personal and principled rejection of
fixed hierarchical structures made US-style radicals very wary of
collaborating with institutions and this restricted their growth while
shielding them from many of the negative – as well as the more
positive – effects of feminism's progressive institutionalisation under
PSOE. By the late 1970s, however, aligned with representatives of the
emerging 'difference feminist' tendency, they would challenge the

dominance of party-based feminists and accelerate the fragmentation of the Spanish Women's Movement.

By the time of the Primeres Jornades de Catalunya (First Catalan Conference) in 1976 questions of sexuality were already higher up the agenda and there were also more delegates from neighbourhood associations and other sectorial groups. One influential account observes that 'the congress agreed on a position of "socialist feminism" or "class-struggle feminism", and this has remained constant in Spanish feminism' (Durán and Gallego 1986: 209). But the Madrid and Barcelona conferences saw the emergence of many new women's groups of different types, both locally and nationally. And in 1977, they were followed by the first democratic general elections for 41 years. Both events contributed to an unprecedented surge in women's political activism. Over 300 parties contested the 1977 elections and the high profile of women's mobilisations ensured that the election manifesto of many made some concession to women's demands. Since these demands emanated from neighbourhood, housewives and other cross-class organisations, as well as single sex, feminist or left groups, right and centre parties also took part in this bidding process. The right acknowledged the need for greater equality of opportunities for men and women in its educational and cultural policy, but focused particularly on support for the family. This Francoist conflation of women's concerns with family policy (which has persisted up to and including the 1996 general elections) was also evident in liberal and social-democratic manifesto pledges. By contrast, socialists and communists backed most of women's demands for equality in all spheres, including the socialisation of domestic work, equal opportunities for paid work, and an end to educational and legislative discrimination. Activists' campaigns also incorporated certain radical feminist demands around sexuality, most notably the provision of contraception through social security, the legalisation of abortion, and an end to discramation against lesbians and prostitutes. These campaigns helped to produce mobilisations around key issues and a general raising of political awareness among younger women, especially in the main urban centres.

The fact that only 27 of the 690 women candidates for Senate and Congress actually gained a seat in the 1977 elections suggests that any concessions regarding women's position on the electoral lists were minimal (IM 1995e). The return of 22 women deputies to Congress (6.3 per cent of the total) was nevertheless seen as reasonably encouraging for dual activists. But the final results did not give the victorious Unión de Centro Democrático (UCD) (Union of the Democratic Centre) an overall majority, and this forced its leader Adolfo Suárez to include representatives of more conservative interests in his government. The resulting political tensions helped to make UCD's more liberal manifesto pledges effectively unrealisable and exacerbated divisions among women activists. The negotiations and lobbying that accompanied the drafting of the new Constitution were particularly divisive. The energies of feminists and other women activists focused particularly on the legalisation of divorce and abortion, the sale of contraceptives, and the ending of 'patria potestad' (the statutory authority of the male head of the household) and – at least where dual militants were concerned – were concerted up to a point. However, as negotiations became more detailed splits along party lines and conflict between dual and single activists became increasingly evident. As Threlfall notes, tensions arose partly from the fact that voting on the Constitution obliged women to act either as citizens or as members of an oppressed group or class (Threlfall 1985: 50). Those who chose the first supported the constitutional text, which was by European standards a fairly progressive one. Those who felt that citizenship was either withheld from women and/or undesirable as currently constituted voted against the Constitution. Radical feminists who saw party politics as irredeemably patriarchal tended to reject the text as 'machista', while most dual activists gave it qualified support. As the detailed and painstaking incorporation of constitutional principles in law got under way, however, earlier levels of concerted activism and mobilisation proved impossible to sustain. Outside of the parties too the promised coexistence began to look increasingly unrealistic, as the loss of focus encouraged the proliferation of single activist groups and a corresponding dispersal of energies.

The results of the 1979 general elections seemed to bear out radical feminist scepticism regarding institutional politics, as women's representation in Congress actually fell from 22 to 21 (6 per cent of the 350 seats) (IM 1994d). Although virtually all activists for women's rights were on the left of the political spectrum, Suárez's centre-right UCD boasted most women voters, as well as the majority of women deputies and senators (11 and 4 respectively) (IM 1994d). Within PSOE, an unwillingness to increase institutional support for its dual activists – for example, by placing women higher on electoral lists – helped to slash its women deputies from 11 to 6. Figures for women senators were lower, but stable, at 6:4 representing UCD and the remainder the Socialists (IM 1994d).

PSOE's gains in the 1979 municipal elections enabled its feminist activists to extend the network of municipal women's information centres that would provide the basis for later contraception and other women's advice centres. Elsewhere, however, the complexity of social and political change, the economic crisis, and tensions between and within dual and single activist groups were all contributing to the fragmentation of the Women's Movement. The (albeit partial) satisfaction of some less contentious equality demands, the difficulty of mobilising around the remainder, and in particular the ongoing tensions around party priorities were leading some dual activists to abandon the parties. These tensions came to a head at the Granada Jornadas Feministas (Feminist Conference) of 1979. The 3,000 women who attended this chaotic event saw the familiar distinction between single and dual activism redrawn around the axes of equality and difference. In particular the dominance of dual activists was challenged by younger women influenced by the work of leading French and Italian feminists such as Luce Irigaray and Carla Lonzi. Like radical feminists, these women were alienated by what they saw as the androcentric, universalising values underpinning formal politics and proclaimed themselves 'independientes', autonomous from the parties.[9] Difference feminists were alienated from orthodox left politics not just pragmatically but in principle: they rejected the masculine, supposedly universal values that underpinned them. Believing that the eradication of social and economic inequalities would not, of itself, mean the end of the patriarchal system, these women adopted a focus that was at once broader and narrower. They demanded active participation in the construction of knowledge and saw personal, lived experience as the only legitimate starting-point. From this perspective, dual activists' attempts to promote programmatic and organisational change within the parties was misguided, and led inevitably to the activists' own transformation and co-optation. Unlike dual activists – who had seen expectations whipped up in the late Franco years evaporate in a climate of horsetrading and expediency, as parties turned to what they saw as more immediate priorities – these younger women exuded confidence and energy. They were prepared to approach questions in new and sometimes playful ways and to celebrate precisely the everyday, marginalised aspects of women's lives that party feminists were seeking to transform. But difference feminism was controversial chiefly for its rejection of institutionalised politics. For independent feminists of all persuasions, party politics was enshrined in inflexible hierarchical structures that compromised women's political and personal auto-nomy and blocked the development of their gendered specificity. Arguably the most uncompromising rejection of androcentric politics came in 1979, in Barcelona, with the founding (and two years later the legalisation) of the Partido Feminista by Lidia Falcón and others. Although its attempts to separate women's political future from male politicians' (more or less) enlightened self-interest found some early support, it was unable to extend this base.

One persistent strand in Falcón's thought (and in independent feminism more generally) has been a questioning of dual activists' qualifications for representing other women: first, on the grounds that party feminists seek to enter what they themselves admit is a deeply patriarchal culture; second, because once inside they adapt too readily to its norms. In 1979 formal political participation was still a relative novelty, and many feminists who joined parties did so in the belief that major advances could be made simply by manipulating the political game from within. If today fewer (party and other) feminists place their faith exclusively in formal political activism this is partly as a result of independent feminist activism. But it has also, crucially, been fuelled by the inability or unwillingness of successive governments to respond effectively to dual activists' demands. And it has been compounded by the institutionalisation of these demands in what has become known as democratic feminism. Like the fragmen-tation of the Women's Movement, this institutionalisation process accelerated under the early PSOE governments, although both have their roots in the previous decade. The massive popular mobilisations of the early 1970s proved impossible to sustain once the Transition got under way. As the decade progressed, their increasingly close links with the Administration began to condition the strategies and priorities of locally-based mass movements like the Neighbourhood Associations. They became more stable but less flexibly organised. The work of the supporters – including many thousands of women volunteers – became more bureaucratically mediated. More paid workers were recruited, almost all of them male and many with government connections. These changes accelerated a shift towards pragmatism which ensured certain political gains while neutralising much of the spontaneity and individual commitment that had sustained the early mobilisations. Levels of affiliation and support began rapidly to decline.

This decline was exacerbated across many sections of society by a mounting disenchantment with formal politics, as political leaders failed to meet often unrealistic expectations produced by the transition process and fuelled by their manifesto pledges. By 1980 tensions in the ruling UCD had brought the party to the verge of collapse. Meanwhile, far left groups that had played key roles in the last years of the dictatorship found themselves marginalised by an electoral system which favoured larger parties. The Communist Party, by some way the strongest of these, had worked hard to build consensus and a new political system after Franco's death and it was the only party to improve its previous electoral results in the 1979 elections. But the party's own generational and ideological tensions made its relations with the Women's Movement increasingly strained, while pressure on dual activists increased. And when internal and external strife tore apart smaller far-left groups, their associated feminist organisations collapsed with them. The socialists too had been split during the early years of the Transition as, helped partly by the electoral system, the younger, renovating strand staked its claim to represent democratic socialism, and began working to replace UCD as the centre ground of Spanish politics. A number of key activists left the party during this period, but without provoking the type of crisis experienced by PCE. PSOE's feminists were caught up in this ideological regrouping and (like the reluctance of the party hierarchy officially to support feminist activism, and the deepening crisis of the Women's Movement) it diverted considerable energy. But it did not prevent them from working in their national, regional and local bases towards the implementation of Constitutional provisions relating to women. Unsurprisingly in this context, their achievements were sometimes ambiguous and invariably partial. Yet the energy and commitment of these activists has been a major factor both in the rapid transformation of women's legal status in post-transitional Spain, and in the dominance of democratic feminism today.

These women received a major boost from PSOE's landslide victory in the 1982 general elections. In the previous legislature UCD's 11 women deputies had represented just over half of the total, but from 1982 women's national political fortunes were tied even more closely to a single party. The number of women deputies rose from 6 per

Table 1. Proportion of women deputies to total deputies in Congress, by party and legislature (from the General Elections of 1979 to May 1996)

Party	1979 to 1982			1982 to 1986			1986 to 1989			1989 to 1993			1993 to 1996		
	Total	Women	%	Total	Women	%	Total	Women	%	Total	Women	%	Total	Women	%
UCD	166	11	6.6	12											
PSOE	120	6	5	202	18	8.9	184	13	7.1	175	34	19.4	159	28	17.6
CP/AP/															
PP	9	1	11.1	108	2	1.9	105	8	7.6	107	10	9.3	141	21	14.9
CIU	8	1	12.5	12			18	1	5.6	18	1	5.6	17	1	5.9
PNV	7			8	2	25	6			5			5		
PCE	23	2	8.7	4											
CDS				2			19			14					
IU							7			17	2	11.8	18	4	22.2
Others	17			2			11	1		14	4	28.6	10	1	10
Total	350	21	6	350	22	6.3	350	23	6.5	350	51	14.6	350	55	15.7

Source: Adapted from Instituto de la Mujer (1995e). For abbreviations, see Appendix.

cent (in 1979) to 6.3 per cent of the total – 22 in all, of whom 18 were aligned with PSOE (IM 1995e). As is usual, women's representation in Senate was significantly lower (4.3 per cent) but here too 10 of the 11 women were PSOE representatives. Three years earlier UCD had received over a quarter of all women's votes, compared with under a fifth for its nearest rival, PSOE (Ortiz Corulla 1987). But in 1982 UCD's share plummeted to under 7 per cent, while PSOE's rose to over a third (Ortiz Corulla 1987). Although the mobilisations of the intervening years had clearly moved a significant number of women towards the left, the only slightly less dramatic rise of the right (see Table 1) highlights the limits of this apparent radicalisation (Ortiz Corulla 1987). So too does the contribution of women voters to the 1982 electoral collapse of PCE. Around half of communist voters in the 1979 general elections had thought of themselves not as ideological communists but as centre-ground fighters for democracy. But by 1982 PCE was no longer seen as the only – or the most credible – alternative to dictatorship. Largely as a result, its electoral support collapsed, with women's contribution alone falling by two-thirds to less than 2 per cent of the total (Ortiz Corulla 1987). Its activist support also fell away during this period.[10]

As PSOE's star ascended, PCE's was not the only one to decline. By 1982 extra-institutional activists were also in the grip of mounting disillusionment. The efforts of dual and single activists had helped to secure the legalisation of divorce and contraception and the rapid expansion of women's educational and labour opportunities. As the decade progressed, however, the persistent gap between the constitutionally-enshrined principle of equal rights and the social reality gave rise to mounting concern. The stresses of combining paid and domestic work and rising unemployment levels were hitting the female workforce particularly hard, while abortion rights and certain other key feminist demands from the 1970s had yet to be met. At the same time, channels for expressing demands and disquiets continued to contract. By mid-decade the parliamentary parties and the two largest unions all had a women's secretariat, committee, caucus or spokesperson, each active to different degrees on institutional women's issues. This institutional activism was a crucial focus for the Women's Movement, but at the same time its successes made the reopening of channels to extra-institutional activists seem less pressing. The resulting narrowing and institutionalisation of left politics had a profound effect on the development of the Women's Movement during the 1980s. And so too did the marginalisation of non-party (and increasingly non-PSOE) women's activism.

This process accelerated from the early 1980s, with the move of many of the protagonists of early feminist mobilisations into national, regional and local government and other public offices. These were the women of what Monica Threlfall has termed 'the socialist-feminist current' who tried in their different ways, to 'work the system for women, and to use all the possibilities offered by the Left's positions in local, regional and central government to extract specific concessions and benefits for women' (Threlfall 1985: 54). As well as advancing feminist aims, they sought to change the institutional culture. While this culture would prove more intractable than many supposed, over the decade their efforts helped to produce a social climate broadly sympathetic to egalitarian feminist aims.[11] While these efforts did not go unchallenged by non-party feminists the balance was clearly in favour of self-styled 'democratic' feminists, who supported the demands of other activists only where they fitted the institutional agenda. Critics have highlighted this containment or minimal satisfaction of feminist demands as a factor in the decline of participative democracy in Spain during the 1980s (Astelarra 1990b). By contributing to the prevailing mood of political disenfranchisement, institutional feminism indirectly encouraged the spread of pragmatism and *ad hoc* campaigning among independent groups. And this in turn accelerated a tendency towards atomisation and individualism, and a dispersal of the early utopian energies.

From its establishment within the Ministry of Culture in 1983, the Institute for Women was a key force in this institutionalisation process. By mid-decade, there were reportedly around 700 women's organisations in existence, of which around 150 were feminist (Threlfall 1985). In 1987, however, some 600 responded to the IM's national survey of women's organisations, of which only 60 characterised themselves as feminist (IM 1990a). Most of these had no single ideological focus or were explicitly pluralist, and their objectives were often short term and usually single-issue oriented: non-sexist education, for example, or abortion rights. Among the non-feminist organisations were socio-cultural clubs for dressmaking and similar activities – often organised by the Church and most common in rural areas – but also labour and civil rights groups concerned with women's issues from a broader perspective. Given the importance of regional differences in the Spanish Women's Movement, independent feminists' commitment to flexibility and diversity, and a widespread suspicion of the conservative and bureaucratic tendencies of mass organisations, even if these figures were accurate they were not necessarily negative. Many independent feminists nevertheless interpreted the IM's survey as an attempt to undermine extra-institutional feminism by reducing its status to that of one pressure group among many (Pineda 1988). Others seeking to promote broad, politically-aware feminist groupings were unsurprised by these figures, but worried by the loss of a wider forum for debate. By the end of the decade it was clear that '[s]i la existencia del movimiento feminista ha de ser valorada a partir de una presencia masiva en la calle o en grupos permanentes y amplios, es obvio que éste ha perdido peso' (if the feminist movement is to be judged on the basis of a massive presence in the streets or large, stable groups, then clearly it has lost ground) (Cervera *et al.* 1992: 42).

By mid-decade, some influential extra-institutional feminists were openly acknowledging that diversity could be a source of functional weakness as well as philosophical strength and that a measure of co-ordination was essential if demands were to be heard in national forums. Given independent feminists' principled rejection of bureaucracy and hierarchies, debate around this issue was heated. Today, although some form of feminist co-ordinating committee exists today in all large and some smaller cities (most of them affilitated to the Coordinadora Estatal, or National Feminist Co-ordinating Body) this debate is ongoing. Like the weakness and fragmentation of their grassroots support, these tensions are common across Spain's social movements and undoubtedly restrict extra-institutional lobbying potential. But they have not prevented certain women's groups – most notably pro-abortion campaigners – from mobilising large forces when the occasion demanded.

One side-effect of this atomisation process was a growth in women's publishing, as activists sought to work through their positions and differentiate themselves from other groups. As in the UK and the US during this period, the loss of political impetus was also accompanied by a growth in academic feminism and associated research. In 1980 María Angeles Durán and others set up the Seminario de Estudios de la Mujer (Women's Studies Seminar) at Madrid's Autonomous University, and it was not long before others followed suit. Approaches have tended to focus on the socio-political and philosophical dimensions of feminism (usually from a left

feminist perspective), and questions of gender, sexual difference, and
the elaboration of discourses based on women's experience (informed
by aspects of radical and difference feminism). Their research and
public working through of feminist issues increased opportunities for
ideological hybridisation and, as the far left regrouped, as PSOE
worked to transform the social bases that had brought it to power,
and as the IM sought to convert politico-juridical pronouncement
into social fact, independent concerns around sexuality, identity and
diversity moved up the feminist agenda. The independent emphasis
on individual self-realisation did not displace party feminists'
emphasis on the broader social context and nor did tensions between
the two tendencies dissolve overnight. But attitudes towards these
tensions have changed. As increasingly concerted independent
feminist demands became more difficult to ignore, and as the
dominant political, socio-economic and cultural discourses became
less socialist and more liberal in tone, state feminist policy began to
reflect these shifts. The IM's second major policy statement, for
example, refers to 'libertad' as well as 'igualdad', to 'la pluralidad y
diversidad existente en el mundo femenino' and 'los valores
femeninos' (liberty as well as equality, the plurality and diversity of
the world of women, women's values), while terms like 'corres-
ponsabilidad' (co-responsibility) take precedence over 'solidaridad'
(solidarity) (IM 1993a: 33, 79). At the same time, while in 1983 the
IM was virtually the only official channel for women's demands – and
as such was a focus for womens' groups from across the ideological
spectrum – by the early 1990s it had begun to redistribute many of
its powers and responsibilities to regional and local government
bodies. This devolution was, in one respect, part of a wider process
driven by the demands of autonomous governments. It has
nevertheless led to a significant increase in the involvement of local
and regional groups in policy-making around women's issues. Like
levels of commitment and funding among regional and local
governments, the results of this increased consultation are variable.
Yet most independent activists would agree that the climate of
increased accountability and access is wholly positive. Combined
with the increased representation of women at national government
level it helped to transform the political culture of the early 1990s.

Partly in response to the lobbying of dual activists, the 1980s had
seen increased efforts to raise levels of women's formal political
representation. Despite this, increases have been generally limited and

patchy, and in 1993 an IM survey suggested that 53 per cent of of the voting population remained unhappy about women's continuing under-representation in the national political sphere and wished to see it redressed (IM 1995e). Until the late 1980s, women's representation in both Congress and the governments of the Autonomous Communities had fluctuated around 6-7 per cent – although with considerable variation in the regions (Ortiz Corulla 1987) – and around 3-6 per cent in the Senate (IM 1994d). The general elections of 1989 saw the first significant increase at national government level. They took the proportion of women in Congress to almost 15 per cent, and in Senate to nearly 11 per cent (IM 1995e). Two years later this was repeated in regional parliaments, where their representation doubled to over 14 per cent (IM 1994d). And in the 1993 general elections women's representation in Congress rose again to almost 16 per cent, with almost 13 per cent in Senate (Table 2).

These were still relatively small numbers, however, and far fewer attained high office. It is worth recalling at this point that, for women who both want and manage to enter politics, winning a seat is only the first hurdle. It is usually (but not always) by entering the homogenising structures of the workplace and discussing the inequities of those structures with colleagues that women begin to perceive their situation in political terms. And though they are in many cases particularly sensitive to these inequities, women politicians are not exempt from them.[12] The experience of persistent under-representation in senior positions is routinely compounded by unequally distibuted responsibilities at home, especially where there are children (IM 1994c). But even when they are more equally distributed, domestic and childcare responsibilities do not fit easily around punishing parliamentary schedules and extended sittings. This institutional failure to acknowledge the claims of childcare and domestic responsibilities has important professional implications for aspiring women politicians. Men tend to be socialised and politicised chiefly through their work, including party work and those professions (notably the law) which produce most politicians. Prospective women candidates also tend to be socialised through paid employment, often party work and increasingly, too, work within the legal and other professions. But in many cases they are also socialised within the family, through childcare and affective relation-ships which carry no professional status and which are either ignored or adversely interpreted when mentioned on CVs. Yet at the same time, it is widely

Table 2. Proportion of women senators to total senators, by party and legislature (from the General Elections of 1979 to May 1996)

Party	1979 to 1982			1982 to 1986			1986 to 1989			1989 to 1993			1993 to 1996		
	Total	Women	%	Total	Women	%	Total	Women	%	Total	Women	%	Total	Women	%
UCD	119	4	3.4												
Socialists	70	2	2.9												
CP/AP/	3			68	1	1.5	75	2	2.7	90	7	7.8	106	10	9.4
PP															
PSOE				157	10	6.4	149	12	8.1	128	18	14.1	117	21	17.9
IU							1								
CDS							2			7					
CIU							9			11	1	9.1	14		
PNV							11						6		
Others				28			4			15	1	6.7	13	1	7.7
Total	208	6	2.9	253	11	4.3	252	14	5.6	251	27	10.8	256	32	12.5

Source: Adapted from Instituto de la Mujer (1995e). For abbreviations, see Appendix.

accepted that many male politicians in Spain (and elsewhere) would be unable to function without the domestic, secretarial, political and other services rendered by many woman partners. To this extent, while the participation of women representatives is widely acknowledged to be essential for the legitimation of the political process, key aspects of that process continue directly or indirectly to inhibit their participation.

The first senior woman politician after Franco was the UCD Culture Minister Soledad Becerril. Between 1982 and 1993 PSOE appointed two others: Matilde Fernández (Social Affairs Minister) and Rosa Conde (Government Spokeswoman). From 1993-96 3 of the 16 ministers were women: Angeles Amador (Health), Carmen Alborch (Culture), and leading feminist Cristina Alberdi (Social Affairs). Although four had been promised, this was a significant advance for activists, and one which enabled the PSOE government to enhance its modernising profile nationally and internationally with minimal cost in organisational terms. The assignment of these women to the so-called 'ministerios María' ('women's ministries') was compensated to some extent by the qualities of the women concerned and by the wider range of responsibilities covered by the five women Secretaries of State (in Justice and the Home Office, Prisons, Housing and Environment, and the President's Office) (IM 1995a). The May 1996 elections brought centre-right Partido Popular (PP) (People's Party) to power with a record four women ministers – some of them in supposedly 'men's' ministries: Loyola de Palacio (Agriculture), Esperanza Aguirre (Education and Culture), Isabel Tocino (Environment) and Margarita Mariscal (Justice). Unlike PSOE's ministers these women have no feminist credentials and cannot rely on the support of active party women's sections. Their largely cosmetic role – designed to deflect calls in and outside of PP for positive discrimination – is underlined by the complete absence of women at the level of Secretary of State, and their rarity at Sub-Secretary level.

Since Spanish politicians today are not required to be members of the party in whose government they serve, feminists who decline to join a political party do not necessarily forgo a role in institutional politics. Moreover, the publicity that party support and campaigning can bring is rendered much less crucial than in the UK or the US by Spain's 'closed, blocked list' electoral system.[13] Under this system, rather than voting for an individual, electors vote for a political grouping or party, each of which prepares a list containing as many candidate names as there are seats available in that particular voting ward. Seats are awarded according to the number of votes obtained by that grouping or party and the order of names on the party's list. This is positive in so far as the political focus is generally less oriented towards personalities, and women do not have to endure the lengthy and often harrowing selection procedures experienced in some other countries. Less positively, candidate selection remains in the hands of (national, regional, provincial or local) party managers who have not always seen the value of placing women on their list, much less at or near the top of it. In most cases this reluctance seems to stem as much from pragmatism as simple prejudice: it reflects internal divisions within parties, for example, and the perceived demand for male electoral 'stars'. And it reflects the fact that, as recently as 1993, 43 per cent of Spaniards between 18 and 50 (and 55 per cent of those over 50) reportedly believed that 'a la hora de votar inspira más confianza un hombre que una mujer' (when the time comes to vote a male candidate inspires more confidence than a female one) (Abad 1994: 45). In 1986, under 22 per cent of candidates for Congress were women. However, when parties with little chance of actually winning seats – and which often have a significantly higher proportion of women candidates – were extracted from the total the figure was closer to 14 per cent (IM 1995a). Since then, this has risen steadily on the left and the right, largely in response to the demands of women activists. But the total number of women candidates is less important than their place on electoral lists: 10 per cent of women candidates at the head of their lists will produce more representatives than 50 per cent placed lower down. In June 1993, for example, Madrid boasted the largest proportion of women candidates of all regional parliaments, with an all-party average (including fringe groupings with minimal chance of winning a seat) of 33 per cent (Sal 1993). But when the electoral dust settled, women parliamentarians made up under a quarter of the total.

This figure is high in national terms, but helps to explain why the issue of quotas and of positive discrimination generally has given rise to heated debate on the left. Supporters tend to see quotas as the only way of moving a patriarchally-structured system towards a more equitable one, and point to the significant rise in women parliamentarians following the introduction of PSOE's quota in 1988. Detractors (who include many women) see them as unjust, patronising or ineffective, and note that those gains were not maintained.[14] Although Catalan socialists introduced a 12 per cent quota for all women in internal and public posts as early as 1982, PSOE activists needed three attempts before its 1988 Party Congress finally supported a quota. Although this support amounted to nothing more binding than a commitment to 25 per cent representation for women in party posts at all levels and on electoral lists, it implied significant increases in certain bodies. In the elections that followed, PSOE's deputies rose from a previous high of under 10 per cent (in 1977) to around 19 per cent (IM 1994d). However, a fall to under 18 per cent in the 1993 general elections suggested that activists could not raise the necessary momentum behind women's increased representation by voluntary measures alone, and in 1994 this commitment became an obligatory minimum on electoral lists and on all managerial and decision-making bodies, including the Party Executive. Although Izquierda Unida (IU) (United Left) had introduced its 35 per cent quota in the same year as PSOE, a year later it had only two women deputies in a total of 17 (under 12 per cent) (IM 1994d). After the 1993 elections, however, this rose to four out of 18 (over 22 per cent), the largest proportion in the legislature (IM 1995e).[15] IU policy currently includes a commitment to a 40 per cent minimum on electoral lists, and to a 40 per cent minimum and 60 per cent maximum for both both sexes at all administrative levels, including most senior posts (Sal 1993). These commitments are broadly in line with the European Union's (EU) promotion of 'representación paritaria' (equal representation) in politics, and take their lead from progressive practice in parts of Northern Europe (IM 1994c). PP, meanwhile, has rejected out of hand the idea of a quota system. But this does not mean that the right cannot deliver specific advances for women by a process of policy competition. Such processes start with activists' demands which are usually ignored or a response deferred until their weight becomes irresistible. Or, more usually, until other factors combine to make party hierarchies respond pragmatically with positive action or discrimination. This helps to consolidate women's position and leads in turn to more radical demands. Joni Lovenduski has noted three characteristic party responses to women's demands for increased representation. Schematically, they are: rhetorical strategies (women's claims are accepted on campaign platforms and frequent reference is made to the importance of having more women in office); positive affirmation strategies (special training and considerable encouragement is offered to aspiring women, and targets are set for women's inclusion); positive discrimination strategies (places are reserved for women on decision-making bodies, on candidate slates, and on shortlists) (Lovenduski and Norris 1993). While parties on the left are more likely to opt for positive action or discrimination strategies, party competition can lead parties on the right to follow or even outbid them – as the current level of ministers indicates. Under PSOE, national government policy (as articulated by the Institute for Women) has included a range of positive affirmation measures to increase women's participation in national party politics: special guides and publications, for example, seminars, workshops and training programmes designed to stimulate associationism, and to promote research into factors determining women's political behaviour (IM 1993a). Such programmes are unlikely to continue under the new government, and not only because they have been closely identified with PSOE. Although appeals to women are part of PP's modernising strategy – and appear to have paid dividends[16] – senior women members of the party have repeatedly rejected what they characterise as special treatment for women.

But the democratic representation of women's interests implies not only their equitable incorporation in policy-making forums, but also their full participation in the election of their representatives. By effectively precluding both, the experience of the Franco years seriously weakened Spain's participative culture and it is in this context that the Institute for Women has promoted research into women's ideological positioning, political culture and voting behaviour. By the late 1980s, two broad tendencies could be detected in these studies. The first suggests that women's political participation is not so different from men's – for example, by challenging particular sets of statistics or their interpretation. The second (which, interestingly, is sometimes used to supplement the first) reinterprets and affirms gender differences and in particular women's different political culture. This divergence highlights the extent to which the discourse of democracy which underwrites these votes is itself contested – for example, by radical or difference feminists who see representative democracy as a factor in the subordination or marginalisation of women by men. Yet it is a mark of Spain's political trajectory, its recent politico-economic crisis, and the advances of democratic feminism, that most women would probably demand more rather than less democracy. For sociologist Judith Astelarra, women want not only increased institutional representation but also recognition of their changing political culture and priorities

(Astelarra 1986, 1990a). Despite the surge in political activism in the last years of Francoism and of interest in formal politics during the Transition, in 1977 less than a quarter of Spaniards saw themselves as on the left of the political spectrum (De Miguel 1993). From 1982, however, certain socialist and feminist assumptions began to be appropriated within more liberal social groups and by 1986 the majority of women and 56 per cent of the population as a whole characterised themselves as on the left (Ortiz Corulla 1987; De Miguel 1993). Combined with the expansion of tertiary education and their increasing incorporation in the workforce, these shifts have helped to make women an increasingly active and vocal section of the voting population.

They appear to have begun from a low base, however. Many of the women and men who took part in the 1977 national elections were voting for the first time, and pre-electoral surveys recorded high levels of inhibition – as measured by the incidence of 'No saben/No comentan' (Don't know/no comment) voting survey responses – among both sexes. This was repeated in 1979. The fact that women's inhibition levels were significantly higher on both occasions testifies in part to the persistence of Francoist ideology among older female voters. But inhibition cannot be read off simply as an index of conservatism. It also reflects women's more restricted opportunities in education and public life at that time, since the greater an individual's knowledge of and interest in an issue, the more ready and equipped she is to articulate an opinion regarding it and to do so in terms that will be recognisable to the questioner. This gender difference in inhibition levels recurred in 1982 pre-electoral surveys. This time, however, when figures for women who described themselves as housewives were extracted they showed inhibition rates of 42 per cent, while those for working women (at 31 per cent) were barely distinguishable from men's (33 per cent) (Ortiz Corulla 1987). By the time of the 1986 general election campaign these figures had fallen overall by 10 per cent, with the biggest reduction (of around 12 per cent) in the housewife category and the smallest (around 5 per cent) among women in extra-domestic employment (Ortiz Corulla 1987). This underlines the increasingly blurred distinction between the two groups: today the enormous majority of women who have paid employment also do housework; some women do paid work at home; others combine unpaid domestic work with part-time employment (at home or outside) or with study; an increasing number who are unable to combine more demanding paid employment with unpaid domestic labour employ other women as surrogate 'housewives'. These figures nevertheless appear to suggest a broad tendency towards decreasing variation among women as a whole as the number of women who retain traditional views on the primacy of family over career, for example, is diluted by women returning (permanently or temporarily) to the home to raise children.[17]

Partly because readiness to express an opinion on certain socio-political issues does not amount to an active interest in politics, levels of voting abstention among women have not fallen as rapidly as inhibition levels. Apart from a significant fall (to around a quarter) during the major political mobilisation of 1982, women's abstention levels have hovered around 33 per cent – although with significant age and geographical variation – since 1979 (Goetze and Solé 1994). Between 1994 and 1995, however, De Miguel recorded a fall in the proportion of avowedly apolitical women from 33 to 23 per cent of the total (De Miguel 1995). The fact that 70 per cent of the newly politicised women had migrated to his right or centre-right categories appears to support the view that apoliticism correlates with conservatism. Yet the speed and extent of this shift suggests a rather different explanation. The least politically-engaged sectors of Spanish society could hardly ignore the crisis of the party most strongly identified with the Spanish left/centre-left throughout the democratic period. Meanwhile PP, the only major party on the right, had been less concerned with setting attractive new agendas than with evicting PSOE from office. To this extent, the flight to the right registered by De Miguel reflected PSOE's alienation of sectors of Spanish society previously indifferent to national party politics – including younger middle-class groups (Valenzuela 1995) – rather than the triumph of the right. This alienation should not be overstated, however. As late as 1994, 61 per cent of women described themselves as on the left or centre-left , and PP's unexpectedly narrow election victory underlines the remarkable persistence of PSOE's identification with democracy (De Miguel 1995).

In an influential 1986 essay, sociologist Judith Astelarra cited IM survey data which suggested that women interested in politics were less likely than their apolitical counterparts to be practising Catholics, and more likely to be single, aged between 25 and 34, middle class, divorced or separated, in paid employment, educated to upper secondary or tertiary level, and on the political left. 'Es un grupo que se puede caracterizar como "moderno"' (It is a group which can be characterised as 'modern' (Astelarra 1986: 11)). She found that the least interested group tended to be housewives or Catholic (usually both) living in rural areas.[18] But if, in 1986, women with an interest in politics were 'modern', the intervening decade has confirmed that simply being modern is no guarantee of political interest. Indeed, it is increasingly argued that late modernity (in some analyses, 'post-modernity') is characterised precisely by the 'aversión [...] del ciudadano de a pie por la actividad política, o bien su indiferencia, o la creencia de que se habla de algo que no le atañe en absoluto' (dislike or indifference on the part of ordinary citizens where political activism is concerned, or the belief that it has absolutely nothing whatever to do with them) which is common to both men and women and is not restricted to Spaniards (Román 1995: vii). Since most surveys of women's voting behaviour and associationism have been linked to equality feminist programmes (designed ultimately to bring women's political participation into line with men's) the fact that men are themselves increasingly uninterested in formal politics is significant. Because men's status as citizens is rarely questioned, a lack of interest in politics can no longer be interpreted simply as evidence of civic immaturity; it increasingly figures as a (more or less rational) response to a party political culture perceived as alienating. Olga Salido Cortez has suggested that the dominant model of the political leader – as rational, authoritative and manipulative – is grounded in masculine stereotypes that are at odds with the personal and professional values of most women (Salido Cortez 1994). Similarly, while women with little interest in politics may respect female politicians for their achievements they tend to see them as rather contradictory. They are characterised as atypical of the women they are taken to represent, as having forsworn the domestic sphere in favour of exclusiveness, aggressiveness, competition, abstraction and stress within the male-dominated public political space, and as having become 'cabezas de hombre' (women with men's heads) in the process (Gispert 1990: 242).[19]

Yet, despite these reservations, many of the harshest critics of women politicians continue to demand equal representation. This reflects the continuing dominance of equality discourse in Spain and in particular the view that, while increasing the number of women politicians will not of itself 'sexuar la política' (en-gender politics), it

will produce the democratic parity on which women's full citizenship
depends (Valcárcel 1994: 47). Once again, these tensions reflect the
difficulty of converting key politico-juridical advances into sustained,
material improvements in individual women's lives. As one
democratic feminist commentator has noted, these advances have
enabled women to enter workplaces where they experience
inequality in new forms, while at home a certain discourse of
difference justifies further inequalities (Paz Benito 1993). At the heart
of these tensions is the speed with which many of these changes have
occurred, and the inevitably slower pace of cultural and mental
adjustment to them. In its second major policy statement, the IM
accepts that genuine equality will not come until this readjustment
process is further advanced and has been co-ordinating efforts to ease
and accelerate it through educational, media-oriented and other
initiatives. But social change is a heterogenous and contradictory
process, and these initiatives are interacting with the epiphenomena
of other cultural, political, economic and labour market shifts. And
while some activists have tried to adapt their strategies to changing
conditions in order to achieve outstanding goals, other women have
been more inclined to retain the strategies that made earlier gains
possible. Tensions between the two orientations were highlighted by
the 1993 annual conference of the state Coordinadora de Organizaciones
Feminstas (Co-ordinating Body for Feminist Organisations). Its
Madrid spokeswoman, Justa Montero, stated that the militant
radicalism of the 1960s and 1970s was an essential, affirmative first
stage of feminism but observed that now was the time for 'el nuevo
feminismo' (new feminism) (Cristóbal 1993: 21). This she linked to
the rejection of oppositional activism by many feminist groups in
favour of '[una] lucha fundamental ... contra las ideas estereotipadas
y normativas' (a profound struggle against stereotypical and normative
ideas) (Cristóbal 1993: 21). Against a background of broad politico-
juridical equality, Montero gives the recognition of differences a new
emphasis which rules out the wholesale condemnation of men as a
class.[20] But there are other women – particularly feminists active in the
transitional years – who see attempts to subordinate the goals of unity
and equality to the demands of plurality and difference as non-
feminist. In a response to Montero, for example, Carmen Rico-
Godoy insisted that the old adversarial feminism cannot be abandoned or ghettoised just because some people – notably men – find it
uncompromising and uncomfortable (Rico-Godoy 1993). In her

novels, Rico-Godoy wittily dramatises the realities of professional women's lives, and the difficulties of combining extradomestic with domestic responsibilities. She is particularly concerned about the rising generation of Spanish women who have yet to experience these competing demands, and who think of equality as already, inalienably theirs rather than as something to be won. For other commentators, however, the broad social acceptance or naturalisation of certain feminist assumptions among younger women is activists' greatest achievement (Alba Pérez 1993; Puleo 1994).

Although feminist assumptions are less broadly and homogeneously accepted in Spanish society than such claims imply, the gap between equality feminists and women generally is no doubt smaller than it has ever been. Yet very few women today would describe themselves as feminist, and a signficant number actively reject the term.[21] This is due partly to its demonisation, particularly in right-leaning media. But it also reflects a resentment among some older women of what they see as feminists' blanket condemnation of women who do not conform to their models (Vilchez Fernández 1994). At the same time, however (as Rico-Godoy notes), there are many young women who now take key politico-juridical gains for granted, and while some share Montero's respect for feminists' contribution to these gains, others see feminism as a kind of reverse machismo, grounded in discredited stereotypes and linked to battles which arose in very different social, political and economic circumstances and retain little or no contemporary relevance. Put otherwise, the appropriation of certain feminist notions as part of democratic, modernising currency, has meant the displacement of others. Today, younger women are less likely to feel the need or obligation to assess themselves (as equal or different) in relation to men, and are less likely to support policies which discriminate in their favour or otherwise single them out for special treatment. But this reportedly does not prevent some from exploiting sexual differences for specific ends (Gil Calvo 1990; Méndez 1995). Feminists like Rico-Godoy are suspicious of such pragmatism, since it relies on advantages like youth, energy and enthusiasm which tend to have a short shelf-life, and could rebound on women if 'el neomachismo' (new machismo) continues to gather momentum (Ramírez 1996b). However, as some younger feminists have noted, when women are confronted with concrete inequities − in the workplace, for example − this pragmatism may encourage them to recognise the non-ideological value of feminist organisations (Col.lectiu de Dones joves Desobediencia 1994).

Despite its basis in principles of justice and equality, democratic feminism itself exhibits a strong pragmatic tendency. This has been highlighted in recent years as a result of the devolution of powers from central to regional, provincial and municipal institutions. All but three regional parliaments (as well as some larger municipalities) now have a women's office, department or institute, most of which have produced their own Equality of Opportunity Plans in line with those of the national Institute for Women. The existence of local focuses for women's issues is particularly important because – despite their often very limited resources – the municipalities remain 'el marco por excelencia de la vida ciudadana' (the optimal setting for civic life) (Sampedro 1993: 93).[22] Local activism can provide women with ideological satisfaction, flexible opportunities for public service and broader social contacts (Astelarra 1986). And, particularly for women with domestic or caring responsibilities, it can function as something like a bridge between national party politics – widely perceived as the maximum and most exclusive expression of the public sphere – and the domestic sphere. This preference for local activism began to emerge from 1977, when many women who had been active in feminist or other oppositional social groups, and who identified strongly with their locality, did not offer themselves as candidates for national government. Instead they became involved in local government initiatives relating to women's rights and information services, healthcare and (to a lesser extent) cultural activities such as adult education classes. With the expansion of state provision under PSOE, emphasis shifted away from welfare support towards the materialisation of women's wider rights. In the 1990s, local activism has been increasingly determined by the devolution of certain previously centralised responsibilities. Resources to meet these new commitments have been limited and difficult to deploy, since links with other sectors of municipal and regional government often remain weak or unclear (Sampedro 1993). This is particularly true of smaller municipalities, as funding is in proportion to population and underfunded initiatives continue to rely heavily on the goodwill and commitment of individual workers. One of the more positive effects of underfunding has been to encourage municipal government to involve non-governmental organisations (NGOs) and local pressure groups in policy formulation and implementation. In this context, extra-institutional women's groups have achieved a measure of protagonism, while in some places co-ordinating bodies have evolved to maximise the effectiveness of smaller groups, enabling alliances and a measure of solidarity to emerge around specific campaigns.[23] In 1993, for example, Mujeres Jóvenes (Young Women) had reported a membership of 7,000, while the Asociación de Mujeres Progresistas (Progressive Women's Association) boasted a total of 40,000 nationwide (Cristóbal 1993).

Bodies like these have contributed directly to a greater tolerance of diversity among groups, in the process further destabilising the equality/difference dichotomy. Since the mid-1980s, for example, Astelarra has not only questioned the liberal goal of equal partici-pation in current party politics as tending to divest women of their sense of identity; she has also rejected the radical extra-institutional search for a non-patriarchal alternative, on the grounds that a focus on identity to the exclusion of all else leads to political marginali-sation and devaluation (Astelarra 1986, 1990a). Independent women's groups cannot make sustainable advances without institutional support, she insists, and institutional politics must be prepared not only to negotiate with these new groups but to promote them. And since the existence of a strong and diverse range of women's groups is crucial for the advancement of women's interests in a democratic frame, it is argued, this must not be done selectively or on the basis of apparent commonality of concerns. Throughout the 1980s insti-tutional feminism was widely perceived as hegemonic, but in recent years its leading representatives have openly acknowledged the need for wider and more diverse women's activism. Leading democratic feminist Carlota Bustelo – who through her work with the IM has been a leading contributor to the institutionalisation of one form of feminism – has underlined the extent to which women's field of action is restricted by party membership. In her view, truly radical ideas can only come from groups outside of institutions, or at their margins (Bustelo 1994). This has been recognised in formal institu-tional initiatives to promote the role of women's groups as social agents and as genuine participants in social dialogue and democratic decision-making (Senado/IM 1994). The impetus for these initiatives has come largely from NGOs themselves, either in consultation with the IM, regional women's offices and women's groups, or via EU consultative bodies.

Informal and more formal pressure groups are a key feature of contemporary political culture, and the motor of 'democracia directa' (direct, rather than representative, democracy).[24] One increasingly high profile form is 'feminismo sectorial', which encourages strategic 'networking' across the ideological spectrum between women with specific professional interests: lawyers lobbying for legal changes, for example, doctors arguing for an extended abortion law, or housewives campaigning for increased nursery provision. Although early forms have been in existence since the 1960s, its rapid growth in the 1990s reflects encouragement from women's groups within the European Parliament, as part of their campaign for women's increased social protagonism. But despite the rather broad claims sometimes made for it, direct democracy is not a panacea for all the ills of contemporary political culture. While the degree of directness is unquestionably greater than with representative democracy, pressure groups' demands continue to be mediated by policy-makers working to party or other priorities. And while in principle it allows minority or marginal groups to be given a measure of social protagonism – particularly, but not exclusively at local level – relatively small numbers of well-organised, clearly-focused and articulate individuals can still achieve disproportionate influence. Some commentators go further, seeing extra-institutional (and particularly single-issue) politics as symptomatic of a contemporary social malaise, the replacement of a general sense of collective social action by a consumerist rights culture (Alvárez Junco 1994; Foessa 1994). However, the rise of women's pressure groups or feminism cannot be read off as a lamentable side-effect of supposed socio-political fragmentation. As an innovative and pragmatic response to conditions that have brought representative democracy to crisis – and in particular as a response to and a contributory factor in the emergence of 'los nuevos valores' (new values) in Spain from the 1970s – women's activism is inextricable from those conditions, but not wholly determined by them.

These post-materialist new values – often markedly eclectic and pluralist, and with a focus on personal fulfilment and quality of life – lie at the heart of certain forms of associationism. And they have very particular resonances for women active in the Catholic Church. Recent weak and ambiguous statements on women's changing social roles notwithstanding, John Paul II has presided over a conservative, bureaucratic hierarchy that has actively compounded Catholic women's marginalisation in Spain and elsewhere. Although women have become much more active in the Church in recent years, women priests remain prohibited, and the hierarchy is exclusively male, despite the fact that women Catholics have long outnumbered men (Bellosillo 1986). Contraception is forbidden, along with abortion: as Opus Dei founder José María Escrivá famously observed, the proper state for married women is pregnant. Yet despite doctrinal hardening or at best ambiguity at the highest levels in the face of social change, there is some evidence at lower levels of attempts to accommodate the newer anti-hegemonic perspective of feminism and ecologism (Díaz Salazar and Giner 1993; Guerra Gómez 1993). It is emblematic of these tensions that while only 1 per cent of Spaniards profess a faith other than Catholicism – most of them European-style Protestants, including many gypsies – the majority no longer describe themselves as practising christians (De Miguel 1993, 1994). A significant majority of those who do is made up of women, and while many of these are rural or older women who do not work outside the home some are younger women who are trying to transform the Church from within. Since the early 1980s the growth of base communities, charismatic renovation groups, parish communities and movements like 'Comunión and Liberación' (Communion and Liberation) has testified to the pluralism and the new vitality of non-traditional Catholicism (Bellosillo 1986; Toharia 1989). Women who find their traditional roles too restrictive are usually able to participate more fully in these groups. And they can increasingly count on the support of bodies like Teología Feminista (TF) (Feminist Theology), a feminist umbrella organisation for christian groups which promotes the full participation of women in all areas of the Catholic Church and ministry. While some, more charismatic, groupings tend to focus on the group 'spirit', most express a concern for broader social change as well as self-realisation (Pina et al. 1994). TF's own focus on recovering the body repressed in traditional Catholicism, its emphasis on the achievement of pleasure and balance for themselves and those nearest to them, and its rather unfocused sense of solidarity towards those further away all attest to its New Age influences. Although in principle a subjective tendency need not detract from its transformative potential – expanded subjective experience may become intersubjective, for example, and feed back into institutions via a presiding nun or priest – as with independent feminists the risk of ghettoisation is never far away.

The Church is not the only focus for the working through of

these new values, however. During the late 1980s, environmental
and pacifist pressure groups enjoyed fairly high levels of support,
particularly among women, and more recently there have been
signs of growing support for animal rights (Olivares 1994). In
1992, half of Spain was reportedly opposed to nuclear power, and
among women this figure reached 65 per cent (De Miguel 1993).
Despite this, women's groups in one of the most influential environmental co-ordinating bodies – AEDENAT (Asociación Ecologista de
Defensa de la Naturaleza, or Ecological Association for the Defence of
Nature) have tended to address women primarily as consumers to be
mobilised around environmental issues (Grupos de Mujeres de la
AEDENAT 1994). There are signs that this is beginning to change,
however, in response to developments elsewhere in the green
movement. In 1994 what would, in other parties, have been called
the women's groups of Los Verdes (The Greens) split off to form
Spain's first registered ecofeminist group. The founder members, who
had organised a number of ecofeminist group meetings in 1993-94, are
active in mixed ecology (as well as left) groups. Although its position
is still evolving, the new group is oriented towards the emancipation
of both women and men, through the analysis of women's social
situation and efforts to secure structural socio-political change.
Similarly oriented towards social change is 'Feminismo ecologista o
ambiental' (ecological or environmental feminism). This tendency
focuses more directly on the broader material dimensions of
environmentalism and feminism – including the appropriation of the
planet's resources by the exploitative few – with a view to
transforming relations between men, women and nature (Asamblea
de Mujeres de Bizkaia 1994). Arguably better known than either of
these, however, is 'ecofeminismo cultural' (cultural ecofeminism).
To the extent that it attempts to revalue the negative overtones of
women's conventional asssociation with nature this owes more to
difference than socialist feminism, while global (or local) environmental concerns tend to be secondary to a New Age concern for
personal health and fulfilment. It aims to challenge the mechanistic
rationality which grounds the patriarchal devaluation of nature, to
revalue what are characterised as women's displaced spiritual and
ethical dimensions, and to reinforce their links with nature (Sendón
de León 1994a, 1994b). As articulated by Spain's best-known
exponent, Victoria Sendón de León, cultural ecofeminism has
been consistently criticised by left feminists. By aligning men's

domination of women with their domination of nature, it has been argued, Sendón essentialises and homogenises the three key terms; and by restricting women to (supposedly natural) nurturing functions she perpetuates their subordination in the public sphere (Amorós 1986). More recently environmental feminists have taken issue with its focus on the ideological factors in women's subordination at the expense of material ones, a focus which they see as actively undermining attempts to counter environmental degra-dation (Alvarez Durante 1994). These are largely warranted criticisms. Yet Sendón remains one of the very few feminists of the 1970s whose work is read by younger women today – and in particular by the growing number who combine elements of quasi-religious sensibility with a belief in horoscopes and other forms of esoterism. In 1993, De Miguel reported that around half of Spaniards believed in fate, while around a quarter believed that the stars affected their lives. A signficant majority of these were women. While younger ones tended to be more convinced by horoscopes, older women who defined themselves as housewives were more likely to believe in destiny – perhaps reflecting a less developed sense of personal auto-nomy than among women in paid employment.

This combination of religion, magic, esoterism and the pseudo scientific is often associated with the approaching millennium, rapid social change and the advance of technological materialism. Like demands for fuller and more harmonious lives in the face of fragmentation and routine, its traces can be found in a wide variety of popular and other social discourses. But it has not displaced informal environmental and other activism, any more than informal activism has dis-placed party politics. In 1993, for example, the Mesa Confederal de los Verdes (Green Confederation Conference) demanded 50 per cent participation for women in formal politics, in the belief that this would contribute to a change in political culture and, in turn, make dual militancy more productive (Barrio Rodríguez 1993). Conversely, even parties on the right have had to reflect the rising profile of green issues and a more general green sensibility in their policy-making, and the resulting expansion of political options for the environmental lobby has meant greater competition between the parties.[25] In turn, where environmental or other issues are incorporated into policy – usually, but not always, in a diluted form – non-party proponents either become more radical or turn their attention elsewhere.

As this chapter has demonstrated, a similarly complex dynamic has enabled formal and informal activism by women to challenge Spain's formal political culture. But as Teresa Gallego has noted, before this challenge can be followed through some persistently blocked communication channels need to be opened up – between members of the male and female political elites and women's groups, but also between and within the groups themselves (Gallego 1994). The democratic feminist campaign for representational parity (50 per cent representation for women in formal political forums) acknowledges the importance of clearing these channels if women's formal and informal activism is to get the equitable institutional support it needs (IM 1994c). It remains to be seen whether the new party of government, averse as it is to anything resembling positive discrimination, will support these aims.

Notes

1 The history of Spanish feminism and 'proto-feminism' goes back much further. María de Zayas y Sotomayor (1590-1661?), Sor Juana Inés de la Cruz (1651-95) and Josefa Amar y Borbón (1753-?) have all been claimed for the second category. Notable nineteenth- and early twentieth-century feminists include influential suffragist Concepción Arenal (1820-93), Cuban-born Gertrudis Gómez de Avellaneda (1814-73), Emilia Pardo Bazán (1851-1921) and essayist María de Maeztu (1882-1948). I am indebted throughout this chapter to Monica Threlfall, and particularly for her generous comments on an earlier draft, though we do not always reach the same conclusions.

2 The Estatuto Municipal of 8 March 1924 granted voting rights to single and widowed women at municipal level. The right of the same women to vote at national level was recognised in the Royal Decree of 12 April 1924.

3 The victory of the right in the 1933 national elections was attributed – by Victoria Kent, one of Spain's first women deputies, among others – to the female vote. On the suffrage debate and women's political and social gains during this period see Scanlon (1986), Folguera (1988), Instituto de la Mujer (1992), and Graham (1995).

4 The regime's Cortes (or Parliament) was an advisory body, unable to control the government and unrepresentative of society at large. Business was conducted through a number of commissions. On these sat the 'procuradores' (procurators) – national councillors, and representatives of the official unions, the municipalities, university rectors, senior judges and other officially-sanctioned interest groups – many appointed by the Executive and some by Franco himself (Franco Rubio 1986).

5 I am indebted in this chapter to a wide range of sources, and in particular: Alvarez et al. (1977), Gould Levine and Feiman Waldman (1980), Threlfall (1985 and 1986), Borreguero et al. (1986), Durán and Gallego (1986), Amorós (1986), Roig (1986), Moreno Sardá (1988), Folguera (1988), Scanlon (1986, 1988b), Astelarra (1986, 1990b), Roig (1989), Rubio (1990), Falcón (1992), Grau Biosca (1993), Brooksbank Jones (1994, 1995b, 1995c) and IM (1991, 1992, 1994a, 1994d and 1995e). In the interests of economy, they are specified in the text only when cited directly.

6 Local councillors ('concejalías') and those able to elect them came equally and exclusively

from three groups: male or female heads of family; representatives of official unions; and representatives of economic, professional and cultural organisations in the municipalities. Holders of the more senior posts of mayor and provincial deputy continued to be appointed rather than elected.

7 This second form of radical feminism has no direct equivalent in Anglo-American (radical or other) feminism and many of the women concerned would emphatically not want to be associated with the more familiar US-influenced form (Amorós 1986). I have nevertheless followed the widespread Spanish use of 'radical' here, since to do otherwise would simply compound the confusion.

8 See Rubio (1990). I am grateful to Vanessa Knights for bringing this useful article to my attention.

9 At this stage the term 'independiente' covered women of many different tendencies. From 1980 to 1986 its adherents held annual conferences in an attempt to establish some form of common ground. These attempts had borne little fruit by the 1984 conference, at which point two relatively clear strands emerged – one more ludic, the other more socially committed (Threlfall 1985). Notable exceptions like Victoria Camps apart, however, the socially committed tendency has never been strong, with the result that Lidia Falcón is not alone in opposing difference to political feminism (Falcón 1992). The term has never enjoyed much popularity in Spain, and women with all the characteristics of difference feminism are more likely to call themselves independent feminists. Fanny Rubio has attributed this to uncertainty surrounding the precise nature of difference feminism rather than to a rejection of what it stands for (Rubio 1990).

10 The negotiations accompanying the drafting of the Constitution had at times led PCE to adopt more ambiguous and less radical postures than PSOE. While this had won it increased national support in the 1979 elections it had alienated many dual activists. And as it became clear that the promised rewards for their forbearance would not be forthcoming there were many defections (Pardo 1988).

11 They began from a very low base. To the extent that debate around the Constitution had reflected feminist demands, they were those of a relatively limited number of energetic activists. In 1978, for example, at the height of the feminist mobilisations around the Constitution, a Metra Seis survey indicated that only 18 per cent of women publicly identified themselves as feminist (Folguera 1988). However, a relatively high proportion of these women were active campaigners.

12 The end of 1994 saw a striking example of a cross-party woman's alliance, when a group of senators objected to the omission of women's names from a list of candidates for a senior post and (apparently encouraged by then Social Affairs Minister Cristina Alberdi) disobeyed the voting instructions of their respective parties (EV [sic] (1994b). Broadly speaking, however, PP's women representatives tend to think of themselves as elected on the basis of personal qualities and speak for society as a whole. This reflects the greater individualism, different selection procedures and absence of (acknowledged) quotas on the right. Left representatives are more likely to see themselves as elected in part because of their gender, and speak more readily on women's issues.

13 The electorate cannot add names to this list nor alter the order of names on it, hence its name. On the implications of this arrangement and on the d'Hondt formula by which seats are distributed, see Román (1995) and Heywood (1995). On the desirability for women of open lists – in which the elector can (according to the model used) alter the order of candidates, add names or combine names from different lists – see Abad (1994).

14 Quotas have also been criticised as a very partial response to the problems of women's unequal parliamentary representation. During the 1993 election campaign, for example, independent Cristina Alberdi noted that women entering government as a result of PSOE's 25 per cent quota had tended to end up in the places where they were already traditionally over-represented, such as Social Services. 'En cambio, se cuentan con los dedos de la mano las mujeres promocionadas en Defensa, Interior, Justicia o Exteriores' (On the other hand,

women promoted in the Defence, Interior, Justice or Foreign Ministries can be counted on the fingers of one hand (El País, 14 May 1993)). Her own appointment two months later as Social Services Minister underlined this point.

15 At the time of writing the breakdown for the May 1996 elections remains unavailable.

16 In 1992, women reportedly made up 26 per cent of PP membership, compared with 23 per cent of PSOE (IM 1994d). By 1993, the PP figure reportedly exceeded 35 per cent (Foessa 1994). Even allowing for the Institute's tendency to underplay PP affiliation, and PP's own broad definition of 'member', this is a significant increase. Formal membership of organisations is not a strong tradition in Spain and this is also reflected in union membership. In 1992, women reportedly made up around 20 per cent of members in the two largest unions, and around 12.5 per cent of their senior staff (IM 1994d, 1995e). De Miguel suggests that in 1994 22 per cent of working women and 30 per cent of working men were either union members or sympathisers (De Miguel 1995).

17 The surge of support among women for PP in May 1996 and data from the UK (on women who have moved from left to right in recent general elections) suggest an alternative interpretation of this trend as a passing effect of women's political pragmatism (The Guardian, 9 September 1996; The Independent, 10 October 1996). To the extent that men too (and especially younger men) are, reportedly, increasingly pragmatic where politics are concerned, this can be seen as reflecting broader social change rather than an inherent characteristic of women (Instituto de la Juventud 1993; De Miguel 1995; Valenzuela 1995).

18 For example, the abstention rate for women in Galicia (traditionally an area of high abstention for both sexes) was almost 54 per cent in the 1986 elections (Ortiz Corulla 1987). It reflects, in part, the persistence of Francoist ideology in an ageing rural population, many younger voters having migrated to urban centres.

19 In the 1989-93 legislature, a typical male deputy was a 44-year-old graduate, married with three children. By contrast women deputies were over twice as likely to be single, almost half had fewer than two children and only one described herself as a housewife (García de León 1991).

20 For a powerful and comprehensive discussion of the relations of difference and equality feminisms in Spain see Gil Ruiz (1996), which came to my attention only after this study had gone to press.

21 A 1991 central government survey found that 67 per cent of 18-25 year olds and 51 per cent of 26-40 year olds surveyed thought feminist groups a very or quite good thing (CIS 1991). Despite this exceptional figure – the highest ever recorded – feminist affiliation levels reportedly remained very low, with the highest figure (3 per cent) in the 26-40 age group and the lowest among the over 41 year olds (CIS 1991). At the time of writing, another official survey reports that 55 per cent of women and 45 per cent of men are in favour of full sexual equality (CIS 1996, cited Aguilar 1996).

22 This does not mean that women are particularly well represented in formal local politics, though there has been significant growth in recent years. In 1994, 11 per cent of the approximately 65,000 local councillors were women (compared with 7.3 per cent in 1987) along with just under 5 per cent of mayors (IM 1995e; Sánchez Mellado 1995). In 1994, women made up under 15 per cent of regional deputies (with Madrid boasting the highest proportion at 23.8 per cent and Cantabria the lowest at 5 per cent) and only one regional government (Murcia) had a female president (IM 1995e). For breakdowns of these figures see IM (1995e) and El País (1996).

23 A recent and highly selective guide gives details of some 200 NGOs operating in Spain (De Felipe and Rodríguez 1995). By contrast the Institute for Women reported the existence in 1993 of 2 women's confederations, 17 women's federations, 76 national women's associations and two foundations (all of them supposedly nationwide) (IM 1995e). The enormous majority of the individual associations were reportedly feminist (1,364), followed by housewives and consumer organisations (595), widows (265) and

socio-cultural organisations (257), with single mothers (17), rape victims (6) and divorcées and separated women (28) bringing up the rear. For reasons that are not made clear, this breakdown does not tally with the figure of 2,290 that the Institute gives for women's NGOs at regional, provincial and local level.

24 Interviewed in 1994 on the role of social collectives in securing enhanced rights, PSOE's Elena Vázquez rather surprisingly observed that these collectives 'son los absolutos protagonistas de los intereses que representan. Nosotros, lo único que podemos hacer es estar a su lado' (they are the absolute protagonists of the interests they represent. All we [politicians] can do is stand by their side' (Alonso and Hernández 1994: 18)).

25 The contradictory effects of this are already being felt. Within a week of taking office, PP had resolved to the satisfaction of campaigners a high-profile environmental dispute that had raged for months under PSOE. It had also given Environment separate ministerial status and placed a woman – the pro-nuclear Isabel Tocino – at its head.

2   In and out of the public sphere

I N ITS ROLE as state promoter of women's equality of opportunities, the Institute for Women has been a major force in the
campaign for democratic parity, and in many other initiatives
touching Spanish women's lives. Every chapter in this volume
testifies to advances won for women through – and occasionally in
spite of – its efforts. Here, the gains and the controversies are placed
in the context of a wider discussion of Spanish women's changing
relation to the state. This discussion begins with a critical account of
the IM's establishment and evolution. It concludes with an assessment of women's constitutional and welfare rights, with particular
reference to healthcare and education.

Today, most Spanish women have formal, direct contact with the
state when they seek welfare entitlements such as education or healthcare, pensions or social security and, less often, through the justice
system. During the Franco years, however, women's formal contacts
with the state were minimal. National Catholic ideology made them
the mainstay of the regime on the condition that they restricted their
activities to the private sphere. As wife and mother, for example, they
were expected to provide all welfare care, which was deemed to be
paid for by their husband's wages. During the democratic period,
however, the rapid development of Spain's (still fledgling) welfare
state as more women entered the workplace, and the introduction of
equality legislation, have transformed women's relation to the state
and the IM has been a key factor in this process. Modelled on the
French Ministry for Women's Rights, it was established in 1983 with
a brief to promote the conditions for genuine equality of the sexes, in
accordance with Article 9.2 of Spain's Constitution.[1] Rapid changes to
women's role and status in the 1960s and early 1970s eased the way
for the inclusion in the 1978 Constitution of the principle of sexual
equality before the law. After Franco's death, the UCD government
had acknowledged these changes with the creation of a government
Subdirección General de la Condición Femenina (Subdirectorate for

Women's Condition). Although some feminists were numbered among its ranks, the Subdirectorate was structured along the lines of Falange's Women's Section. In the same year, PSOE's Mujer y Socialismo (Women and Socialism) study group began to take shape. As a recruiting point for the party's feminist sympathisers, it has been credited with preparing the ground for the establishment of the IM after PSOE took power, and for the introduction of the Secretaría de la Mujer (Woman's Secretariat) within the National Executive in 1984 (Threlfall 1985). The transition from Subdirectorate to Institute for Women was managed by the IM's first Director General, feminist activist Carlota Bustelo. Although not all of those involved in its establishment were PSOE members, like Bustelo herself all were active in the Womens' Movement and brought their feminist commitment and broad international perspective to the task of setting up the new body. At a time when the PSOE government had little knowledge of or interest in women's issues and many battlefronts elsewhere, these women reportedly enjoyed a degree of autonomy unimaginable today (IM 1994a).

The IM's publicity material describes it as an autonomous body – independent of the ministerial hierarchy rather than of PSOE – charged with 'la promoción y el fomento de las condiciones que posibiliten la igualdad social de ambos sexos y la participación de la mujer en la vida política, cultural, económica y social' (the promotion and encouragement of the conditions necessary for the social equality of the sexes and women's participation in public, cultural, economic and social life) in accordance with the Constitution. Located initially (as the Subdirectorate had been) within the Ministry of Culture, a move to the newly established Ministry for Social Affairs in 1988 enabled it to take a much broader role in the development of what would become known as democratic feminism. In particular it benefited from the support of two feminist ministers: Matilde Fernández to 1993 and Cristina Alberdi to May 1996. Immediately after its establishment, it began to promote the development of a nationwide network of community and local women's centres, building on the work of PSOE activists. From 1986 (when Spain joined the then EC) it became responsible for the harmonisation of Spanish laws relating to women with EC law, and for monitoring their observation. It has also co-ordinated the implementation of compulsory Community Action Programmes relating to women. The evolution of the IM's priorities and strategies from this time to 1993 are evident in its first and second Plan[es] para la igualdad de oportunidades de las mujeres (Women's Equality of Opportunities Programmes, hereafter Plan I and Plan II (IM 1990b, 1993a).

Plan I was based on the European Council of Ministers' Action Plans and on the IM's own 'Informe sobre la situación social de las mujeres' (Report on women's social situation), which incorporated data collected since its inception (IM 1990b). Designed as a framework for inter-ministerial co-operation on women's issues, it was the IM's first attempt to set out its priorities, and the specific actions it saw as necessary to achieve them, in an integrated and co-ordinated framework. Negotiations with some ministerial representatives around early drafts were reportedly difficult, and some measures proposed by the IM were rejected outright by its Consejo Rector (Ruling Council) (IM 1994a).[2] Key areas of concern were the law, education, employment and health. First came legal measures to promote equality of opportunity, including key reforms to the Civil Code and supplements to Article 14 of the Constitution. This focus on women's legal and juridical relation to the state was the most important and productive area of the IM's early work. It included measures to adapt financial provisions to changing family patterns – for example by protecting women's interests in the case of divorce, separation or abuse, and under the tax and social security systems. Measures on educational and broader cultural issues sought to: reduce unwanted pregnancies among the young by introducing sex education in schools; address sexism among teaching staff and in their teaching materials; promote equal access to the full range of educational opportunities and recognition of women's historical role in the development of culture. There were also measures to discourage sexism in advertising and the media; to promote women's access to stable paid employment with a range of educational and juridical initiatives, particularly within public administration, agriculture and technology; to prevent prostitution while protecting women caught up in it; and to prevent discrimination in all aspects of labour relations, particularly in relation to salaries and working conditions. A further section focused on women's healthcare rights and provision, including the standardisation of family planning and abortion facilities. And in almost every case, the measures proposed reflected an awareness of related developments in other parts of Europe, above all Scandinavia, France and Italy (Gispert 1990; IM 1994d).

Despite the involvement of cross-ministry commissions in the formulation of Plan I, it was given negligible support at Cabinet level. Moreover critics observe that it is often vague, short-term and voluntaristic in its approach, with little indication of how the stated aims are to be achieved or financed in practice (Valiente 1995). On the IM's own assessment, however, 116 of the 120 proposed measures had been successfully implemented by the publication of Plan II (Ministerio de la Presidencia 1994). Where amendments to the Constitution were concerned, or the harmonisation of equal rights with EC legislation, this success is readily quantified, as are the published results of IM-sponsored research. The same cannot be said for many of the other measures, and in particular the early consciousness-raising initiatives. Support for the principle of sexual equality has unquestionably grown since the late 1980s, but there is considerable debate around whether this is attributable chiefly to the efforts of the IM, to the ongoing work of extra-institutional feminists, to the national repercussions of EU politics, or to the effects of broader social change (Alba Pérez 1993, Cervera *et al.* 1992).

As this suggests, although the IM's remains the most influential discourse on contemporary women's issues in Spain it has not gone unchallenged. This was particularly true in the early years, when it was caught up in growing tensions in and between forms of independent, radical difference and socialist feminism (Izquierdo 1988). One general criticism of the IM's founders by some former fellow-activists was that they were power-seekers whose defection to institutional feminism weakened the morale and membership of the broader Women's Movement (IM 1994a: 41). Critics from other left groups were more concerned about the IM's relations with PSOE, and (prior to its reform) by the non-representation on the Ruling Council of extra-institutional groups. They were not reassured when, in 1988, Carlota Bustelo left the IM for the Social Affairs Ministry.[3] The IM has also been attacked for its reformism, its tendency to sideline the movement's more radical claims with a funding policy which prioritises the creation of groups sympathetic to its own objectives and policy line (Pineda 1988).[4] Some have seen this as part of a deliberate policy to 'domesticar el movimiento y hegemonizar la política y la sociedad' (domesticate the movement and achieve political and social hegemony), which actively compounded the marginalisation of these groups and encouraged a drift towards essentialism (Forum de Política Feminista 1992: 89). Meanwhile, independent feminists castigated institutional feminism for failing to

meet its commitments to women, for purporting to speak on behalf
of women who did not share its priorities, and for colluding with
patriarchal capitalism through measures that were themselves
potentially oppressive (Uría 1987; Cervera et al. 1993). At the same
time, some pro-institutional critics lamented the fact that the institutionalisation process had stopped short of a Ministry for Women.

From 1988, the IM was able to deflect some of these criticisms,
and dramatically increase the scope for women's initiatives at ground
level, by devolving certain equal opportunities responsibilities to
regional (and through them provincial and local) government. Most
of the newly created women's offices and departments have
produced their own plans, broadly in line with the national model,
although each reflects the political colour and priorities of its
sponsoring government. As the national IM's feminist pioneers have
moved on and gradually been replaced by bureaucrats, this devolution has provided new institutional opportunities for committed
feminist activism at ground level. As a result, several hundred women
are now professionally involved in promoting women's interests –
one of the largest such bodies in Europe (Threlfall 1996). At the
same time, by distancing itself from the harsh realities of policy
implementation and opening up spaces for activism the IM has
retained a high public profile, unhindered by a widespread conservative opposition. A survey it commissioned in 1991 reportedly found
78 per cent of men and women positively disposed towards it
(Valiente 1995). This comes at a time when economic crisis and
political exhaustion were compounding a sense that the era of major
politico-juridical advances for men and for women was over. In this
context, and in the light of the EU's Third Community Action
Programme (which promotes changes in social attitude as the only
way of achieving lasting advances for women), the IM has focused
increasingly on the materialisation of what were, in many cases,
merely formal rights for women. This shift of focus from 'igualdad
legal' (equality before the law) to 'igualdad ... real' (real-life
equality) is made explicit in its Plan II, which covers the period from
1993 to the 1995 Beijing Conference (IM 1993a). Much less ambitious
that the first, this focuses primarily on measures to raise awareness
and to eradicate prejudice and stereotypical assumptions in the
workplace, advertising, the school, and the home (Brooksbank Jones
1994, 1995b; Valiente 1995). The earlier emphasis on encouraging
women to seek work is gone, reflecting a further narrowing of the

gap between women and men employees and rising unemployment among men and, especially, women. Instead there is a new emphasis on practical measures – such as training in CV preparation and job applications – to help those seeking work to do so more effectively. There are proposals to address sexism in language, on which the IM had campaigned strongly for some years, and to address the unequal distribution of domestic reponsibilities, which is characterised as the main cause of women's inequality. Unlike its predecessor *Plan II* also acknowledges differences between women, with proposals to combat forms of social exclusion and marginalisation by integrating sex workers, ethnic minorities, single mothers, immigrants and the extreme poor into mainstream provision, for example, while permitting them to retain their personal autonomy.[5] The promotion of interaction and debate among women has a central place, and grant aid and other measures to extend women's political participation also figure. At the same time, references to greater openness in the allocation of institutional funding and support go some way towards deflecting earlier criticisms, as do measures to promote and support the exchange, reflection and debate it had been accused of inhibiting in the past. Once again, however, the tone is often vague and voluntaristic.

This vagueness is linked partly to the fact that the IM entered the new decade with a new, more advisory role, as a consultant to government and ministers, a promoter of research into women's issues and co-ordinator of regional equality initiatives (IM 1994a). But from May 1996 it has been negotiating its responsibilities in an increasingly uncertain context. Critics of institutionalisation have long warned that a high profile and only quasi-autonomous body like the IM could see its gains rapidly reversed by a conservative government with disastrous effects for women. One of the first actions of the new PP government was to downgrade the Ministry of Social Affairs (to the status of a department within the new Ministry of Employment and Social Affairs) and to appoint Amalia Gómez as its head with a brief to focus her much-reduced resources on socially marginal women (Cañas 1996). Coming as it did after news that the EU is to downgrade its Equal Opportunities Commission, this will have done little to reassure those who have worked to promote women's wider interests. But while they are undoubtedly worrying, changed priorities and reduced funding do not necessarily imply a reversal of women's gains. The growing regional and local involvement in elaborating and implementing equality policy, the obligatory incorporation of (so far relatively progressive) EU equality legislation, pressure on the right to maintain a modernising national and international profile, and the higher expectations of women themselves all militate against such a reversal. So, too, do a range of constitutional and other legal safeguards many of which have been extended (where thought necessary by the IM) to reflect women's changing roles and expectations (IM 1994). While laws relating to specific aspects of women's lives are discussed in the relevant chapters, the Constitution merits separate attention as the broadest statement of women's rights in Spain.

The new Constitution, which came into effect in 1978, was a progressive one for its time. It was remarkable both for breaking with Franco's authoritarian legacy in a number of ways crucial for women – as late as 1973, for example, women were legally required to leave paid employment on marrying and to seek their husband's approval before accepting payment for work outside of the home (Franco Rubio 1986) – and for the consensus between the centre, socialists, communists, nationalists and the democratic right which made this break possible. Of all its provisions, the most significant and far-reaching for women is the principle of equality for all citizens before the law, established in Article 14.

Los españoles son iguales ante la ley, sin que pueda prevalecer discriminación alguna por razón de nacimiento, raza, sexo, religión, opinión o cualquier otra condición o circunstancia personal o social.
(Spaniards are equal before the law and there shall be no discrimination on the basis of birth, race, sex, religion, opinion, or any other personal or social condition or circumstance.)

Articles 32 and 35 relate this principle to the home and the work-place respectively.[6] The individual's rights and freedoms fall into six main areas:

1 'Derechos personales' (personal rights) relating to the moral and physical integrity of the individual, including freedom of ideology and expression and the right to privacy. The implications of the notion of 'the private' as it relates to women are discussed below.
2 'Derechos civiles' (civil rights), protecting the individual from the state and from other individuals. Provisions include the right of appeal to the Tribunal Constitucional (or Constitutional Tribunal, which enjoys equal status to the government on constitutional

matters), entitlement to legal aid in cases of need, and the presumption of innocence. This presumption is particularly significant in rape cases, where victims are all assumed to be liars in the first instance.

3 'Derechos políticos' (political rights), including the right to vote, to join with others to propose a law, to associate (peacefully) for political purposes, and to defend one's interests. Significantly for women, this is not taken to include the right to participate equitably in the articulation of those interests in Parliament.

4 'Derechos económicos' (economic rights), most importantly the right to one's own property, subject to circumstances. It was not until 1981, however, that the husband ceased to be the legal administrator of a couple's possessions (Pujol Algans 1992).

5 'Derechos sociales' (social rights), among them employee rights (the right to work, to organise, to withdraw labour) and welfare rights (the entitlement to welfare provision, including healthcare, accommodation, and state care for the elderly). Some of the most important advances for women in the last decade have been made in this area, and some of the most blatant discrimination against them remains here.

6 'Derechos culturales' (cultural rights), including the right to culture and cultural production, education and academic freedom. Compared with the years of censorship under Franco and the educational restrictions and discrimination associated with the regime, women's gains in this category have been some of their least ambiguous.

As indicated, there are certain key rights – in particular the right to equitable political representation – that are not recognised as such under the Constitution. And although the text eased the way for the introduction of the divorce law three years later, it did not envisage the legalisation of birth control and (most contentious of all) abortion.[7] At the same time, the ability – and in some cases the willingness – of the state to guarantee in practice all the rights theoretically granted in the Constitution is debatable (P. Román 1995). For example, while a judge can defend an individual's right to strike, she or he cannot insist that an employer give a woman (or a man) a job. More fundamentally, the application of Article 14 itself is hampered by the notorious difficulty of defining unequal treatment in practice.

As noted, the IM was established specifically to promote the
conditions necessary for the social equality provided for in the
Constitution, and Articles 14, 32 and 35 in particular involved
substantial changes to legislation then in existence. Two of the more
important amendments it steered through involved the decriminali-
sation in certain circumstances of abortion, and the introduction of
co-education in state-funded secondary schools (Pujol Algans 1992;
IM 1994a). In addition, and in accordance with Plan I, 1989 saw the
extension of maternity leave, the criminalisation of sexual harassment
and, importantly, the shifting of the burden of proof to the accused.
The next year saw reforms designed to bring the Código Civil (Civil
Code) into line with the Constitution's definition of socal rights –
most notably with a range of measures to ease women's return to
work if desired.

Partly because such changes intervene in a constantly changing set
of social and other relations, no legal framework is ever entirely
adequate to its context. New claims and demands – for example from
'parejas de hecho' (cohabiting couples) – are constantly being
thrown up. At the same time, even where newly drafted or existing
legislation succeeds in eliminating direct discrimination, it may be
ineffective against persistent (and often mutating) indirect forms that
are just as far-reaching in their consequences. In the early democratic
period, moreover, the interpretation of equality legislation lay in the
hands of a judiciary still largely identified with the regime (Delgado
1996). But even younger and more pragmatic judges may find that
simply plugging legal loopholes encourages the circumvention rather
than observation of a law, particularly in the workplace.

Some commentators argue that these inequities reflect women's
historical exclusion from full participation in the state by a notion of
citizenship that has been conditioned by men and designed to meet
their interests (Astelarra 1986, 1990a). But those who take women's
politico-juridical advances for granted are often more open to the
possibilities of sexual difference, in the name of what they see as a
broader equality. For Carmen Sáez Lara, for example, the root of
these inequities lies in the notion of equality itself (Sáez Lara 1994).
It lies in legislators' insistence on equality, and their disinclination to
recognise what she sees as immutable physiological differences between
the sexes. For feminist philosopher Victoria Camps, women's
exclusion from the public sphere has also meant the marginalisation
of values traditionally associated with women (Camps 1994). This

exclusion reflects the kinds of dichotomies around which the notion of citizenship is constructed, men's association with the public domain and women's with the private domain, the home and the family. From this binary follow others (between rationality and emotionality, for example) and in each case the term conventionally associated with women is accorded less value.

In practice, the public/private division has never been quite as clear-cut as this suggests. But with the increasing interpenetration of both spheres the distinction and women's relation to it have reached something like crisis, with potentially profound implications for lawmakers. This suggests that the need to make women equal to men in order to give them access to justice is a manifestation of the problem rather than a cure for it. As Sáez Lara notes, simply assimilating women's particularities to non sex-specific models – treating pregnancy in employment law as a disability, for example – is to counter one form of discrimination with recourse to another. More generally, she argues, to characterise women as equal or different is to persist in defining them in relation to men. Instead, she advocates a legal framework which privileges neither juridical equality nor difference, but is flexible enough to allow for equal treatment where appropriate while acknowledging (without over- or understating) crucial differences.

Sáez Lara's privileging of flexibility and her attempt to move beyond conventional paradigms are in line with a broader social tendency. They underline women's changing relation to the law and the state in what some commentators characterise as a period of social fragmentation, growing insecurity, and contracting economic and social rights. As noted in chapter 1, this haemorrhaging of confidence from state and juridical solutions has enabled new mediators to emerge, whose strategies and assumptions do not always privilege rationality and other features conventionally associated with politico-juridical thought. Moreover, their demands may be unfamiliar and may be articulated in ways contrary to the law or otherwise difficult for the state to respond to – as with the hunger strikes or direct action of certain animal rights campaigns. Few members see social movements as a substitute for the state of law and its basic guarantees, however: first, and despite the current political legitimation crisis, because memories of the recent past make the prospect of a potentially anti-democratic free-for-all among competing social groups deeply unattractive to most Spaniards; second, because most

Spaniards have an interest in preserving certain features of the state even as they challenge others.

For most Spanish women, the most enabling of these features has been the state welfare provision. Unlike the US (where the emphasis is on private provision) or the UK (where state services have progressively been devolved to the private sector) this provision remained oriented towards the satisfaction of social rather than individual needs under PSOE, on the grounds that those least able to obtain cover from private sector sources are generally those who need it most. For both ideological and pragmatic reasons this solidarity model is widely supported by feminist commentators. The welfare state has developed services that have generated jobs for women, absorbing many of their employment demands. At the same time, the services in question have enabled women to undertake this work by ensuring that tasks which have traditionally devolved to them may (in principle) be catered for in the public sector. The expansion of the welfare state has also equipped more women to enter and leave the workforce (permanently or temporarily) by enhancing their educational opportunities, healthcare, pension and related rights. And by taking up paid employment, women have helped to generate both a wider role for the welfare state and the funds to finance it.

One side-effect of this process has been to expose women to a wider range of lifestyles and worldviews and allow them increased access to the category of citizens. By enabling, in principle, the redistribution of responsibility for 'domestic' labour, and by acknowledging the discrimination and social inequality to which many women are subject, the welfare state has begun to include women in the social contract. Yet even its supporters concede that much of this potential remains unfulfilled. Women who are not in work, particularly poor and older women, continue to have low status as citizens. Moreover, women are significantly under-represented at senior levels of public administration and have thus tended to figure in practice more as recipients than formulators of welfare provision, as consumers rather than citizens. And while levels of social protection and support are appreciably higher in a welfare state than in a neo-liberal one, wages are not.

Some of these charges are undoubtedly serious. But to the extent that the welfare state, flawed as it is and shrinking, is the only existing framework for the more equitable division of labour between the family, the market and the state, its current crisis is widely seen as a crisis for women (Forum de Política Feminista 1994). It has come about through a combination of increased demands on the system (more women in work, for example, and an ageing population) and deteriorating political and economic conditions. The consequent reduction in social expenditure has led to some reprivatisation of welfare services, cuts in service sector jobs – including social security, unemployment cover and other benefits, at a time of high unemployment – and demands from some quarters that women withdraw from the workplace and resume their family welfare responsibilities (Montero 1994). But even if the restructured job market could survive without women's skills and much-debated flexibility, and if women were prepared or could be induced to return to the home in sufficiently large numbers, the stable full-time jobs in industry and construction with which most male bread-winners once supported their families have gone. Spain's welfare system is vulnerable today largely because it was conceived in political and socio-economic circumstances which it has itself since helped to transform – apparently irreversibly. Two aspects of this transformation with particular relevance for women have been in the areas of healthcare and education.

The state's responsibility to provide health protection and to organise services and resources, regardless of an individual's contribution to the scheme, is set out in Articles 43.1 and 43.2 of the Constitution. Back in 1982, 86 per cent of the population were entitled to health cover and those who were not could expect to be turned away from state hospitals, whatever their condition (Ministerio de la Presidencia 1994). The 1986 Ley General de Sanidad (General Health Law) and subsequent creation of the Sistema Nacional de Salud (National Health System) had reportedly extended this to 99 per cent of the population by 1993. The remaining 1 per cent were excluded by their high income (Ministerio de la Presidencia 1994). Under the 1986 law, the Health Ministry manages the distribution of public health funds, formulates general healthcare policy and seeks to ensure equitable provision across the regions, via the Instituto Nacional de la Salud (National Health Institute or Insalud). Mean-while, regional governments and municipal governments have responsibility for ground-level provision, detailed monitoring and health promotion.

The introduction of the National Health System has brought significant advances in Spanish healthcare, despite the fact that its funding is among the lowest in Europe. The speed of expansion since 1986 has inevitably meant that these advances have been uneven. Despite one of the world's highest ratios of doctors per thousand population, for example, the supply of hospital beds is limited and patchy, while around one-third are private (Zaldívar and Castells 1992; Ministerio de la Presidencia 1994). As demand continues to expand and public hospital hospital waiting lists grow, those who can afford it increasingly have recourse to private care, which tends to be concentrated in urban areas and to focus on technology-driven specialisms. This shift towards specialism reflects changing conceptions of health and healthcare in recent years – for health (like illness) is socially produced, and not only in the reconfiguring of random aches and pains as symptoms. When PSOE came to power, 'medicalist' approaches to health which focused on curing and repairing were the orthodoxy, and it was in this context that major extensions of provision were planned. But as demand continued to outstrip supply, risk and cost-benefit calculations were shifting the balance of healthcare decision-making increasingly from medical staff to administrators. And as the cost of technology- and drug-driven practices began to spiral, a different understanding of health-care began to develop, more sensitive to environmental factors and focusing on lower-cost preventive measures and rehabilitation. This has meant a continuing reliance on domestic care as an (invariably unpaid and less valued) supplement for institutional healthcare. In a pioneering study of women's domestic roles, María Angeles Durán and her collaborators noted that women are conventionally respon-sible for establishing conditions conducive to good health: the teach-ing and monitoring of personal hygiene and safety, for example, the nutrition of family members, and other forms of emotional and physical support (Durán 1988). They may also be involved in the long-term care of severely disabled or chronically ill family members whom the institutional system can or will no longer support. Durán also highlights women's special role in rites of passage (such as death and funeral preparations, particularly in more traditional households) and in general preventive healthcare: the recognition of an illness and the preliminary (and sometimes critical) decision as to whether to have it treated at home or institutionally; treatment with home medicines or traditional remedies; the redistribution of household roles to cope with resulting changes to the domestic routine; and the transfer of the sick person to the institutional system where necessary.

Whether or not they work outside the home, Durán notes, women remain the principal link between the domestic and the institutional healthcare systems; for example, some recent changes in the distribution of household roles notwithstanding, mothers are still significantly more likely to take sick children to the doctor than are fathers (De Miguel 1994). They are also more likely to manage the relationship between the domestic and institutional spheres by arranging medical appointments, obtaining prescriptions, and administering specified treatment as part of the cure and rehabilitation process. At the same time, women increasingly work within the institutional system itself, as health professionals at all levels, but particularly the more junior ones. And in the process they contribute through insurance and taxes to the functioning of the system.

Its immediate downgrading of social affairs and the resource allocation and management models it is adopting suggest that the new PP government will oversee an increase in women's involvement in home-based healthcare. But it will have to take into account some crucial changes in health patterns during the democratic period. Between 1976 and 1989, for example, Spain's perinatal death rate fell from almost 20 per cent to just over 8 per cent (IM 1994d). The maternal mortality rate has also dropped – from 11.03 per 100,000 live births in 1980 to 2.94 in 1989 (IM 1995e) – to one of lowest levels in the world. These figures reflect the extension of healthcare provision (particularly among higher-risk groups), improved obstetric care, and a generally higher standard of living. But they also testify to broader social change. If infant mortality has declined, for example, so too has Spain's birth-rate. Between 1965 and 1986 it fell by by 40 per cent in the 20-24 age group, and 60 per cent in the 40-44 group; from 2.86 children per family in 1965, it had fallen by 1994 to 1.2 children – second only to another Catholic country, Italy (IM 1995e; Alberdi 1996). The late 1930s and early 1940s saw huge areas of Spain depopulated by the Civil War and emigration, and the regime's repopulation policy included financial incentives to produce large families which remained in place into the 1970s. Under Franco, women were also expected and encouraged to produce children virtually up to the menopause. By 1986, however, their growing access to paid employment, the greater availability of contraception, changes in family structure, and higher levels of general education were beginning to alter this pattern (Alberdi 1996). Broadly speaking – since the trend is more marked in the north than the south of Spain – working women are increasingly deferring parenthood, while older women are tending to stop child-bearing sooner, leading to a radical foreshortening of the childbearing years and the possibility of a baby boom at the turn of the millennium (Longhurst 1991; Alberdi 1996). Only in the 15 to 19 age range has the birth-rate increased – by around 60 per cent – in line with the rising number of unmarried mothers (and girls who get married on becoming pregnant) to around 10 per cent of the total (Alberdi 1996).

There has been concern in political circles about the socio-economic implications of a birth-rate that has fallen below the replacement level of 2.1 children per family (Alberdi 1996). For some critics on the right it marks the final triumph of egocentric materialism (Rollin 1995). For many women, however, the falling birth-rate is an expression of their increased reproductive autonomy, a reflection of the decline or deferral of marriage in response to new job opportunities, and the cumulative effect of individual decisions by women who are exploiting opportunities unthinkable 25 years ago. But it may equally be conditioned by less positive factors: the need to pay for a flat, for example, or to support an unemployed partner. The debate is given an extra twist by the fact that birth-rates are not falling proportionately among poorer, immigrant and certain other marginalised women, and it may be that some of the more urgent calls for pronatalist measures are motivated partly by familiar subterranean anxieties about the swamping of the middle classes.

One area where women's advances seem more unambiguous is in their life expectancy. In 1900, for example, a Spaniard could reportedly expect to live for around 35 years (Ministerio de la Presidencia 1995). Yet by 1980 women's life expectancy had already surpassed the World Health Organisation target for the millennium, and a decade later it stood at a record 80 years – the second highest in the EU (IM 1994d).[8] The fact that women's lifespan is increasing faster than men's seems to support De Miguel's view that women are living longer as their lives become more like men's (De Miguel 1993). But the employment and educational opportunities that are making women's lives so much more like men's are much less marked in women over 50, and barely register in the most advanced age groups. By contrast, something of their effects on the health patterns of younger women can be gleaned from the female mortality rate, which in 1989 stood at 8.4 per 1,000 population (IM 1994d). The two major causes of death were cardiovascular illness, which accounted for almost half of the total, and cancer, responsible for almost a fifth. Although most illnesses tend to become more common with advancing age, the first of these was rarer in older women, suggesting a link with changing lifestyles. Similarly, while cancer-related death has decreased overall among women since 1970 (largely as a result of screening programmes and improved treatment) recent years have seen a rising trend (IM 1994d). In particular, breast cancer fatalities more than doubled between 1982 and 1989, and only around 62 per cent of Spanish women are surviving five years after treatment (IM 1994d; The Guardian, 17 May 1995). Equally revealing are figures for death from external causes, and particularly accidents. Among women, these have tended to occur in middle years or old age: among men, they are not only much more common – over 14,000 in 1989 compared with under 5,000 for women (De Miguel 1993; IM 1994d) – but also heavily concentrated in the 20 to 24 age range. Drug use, AIDS-related death and a rising suicide rate are also helping to swell the death rate among younger men (De Miguel 1993). And although women are more likely to attempt suicide, men have tended to be more than twice as likely to succeed. They become increasingly at risk with age, especially if they are unmarried. By contrast (and perhaps because many women find marriage a source of stress as much as support) single women fare better than married ones (De Miguel 1995).

Although the main cause of hospitalisation (and one of the main causes of death among women of childbearing age) remains birth complications, other factors are increasingly entering the calculations. In 1994, for example, 36 per cent of the population smoked, a large majority of them men (De Miguel 1995). But, as in so many other areas, this gender gap is shrinking rapidly. Today women, and especially younger women, form the bulk of new smokers – a trend which is evident in other parts of the EU and has been linked to dieting and stress reduction strategies – and this is increasingly reflected in changing health (including breast cancer) patterns and premature death. Recent figures suggest that over half of women under 45 currently smoke and according to De Miguel they are outnumbered by men only among the working classes (De Miguel 1995).

As noted, the traditional approach to women's health has tended to highlight their role as agents, rather than subjects, of healthcare. In recent years, however, women's increased social protagonism and the related fall in the birth-rate have helped to dislodge the long-

standing reduction of women's health to questions of reproduction.[9]
Their health patterns, particularly as they differ from men's, have
been determined largely by the different demands and lifestyles of
the sexes. By entering the paid labour force most women have not so
much assumed male lifestyles as combined a version of those
lifestyles (willingly or otherwise) with ongoing domestic responsibilities. As a result, their health priorities are not converging with
men's but becoming different from either of the traditional models.
The most striking manifestation of this is the development of
particular forms of physical and mental stress which affect women
workers at all levels but are more acute when that work is precarious
or poorly paid. Carme Valls-Llobet has linked these stresses to the
additional housework shift (to which little or no value is attached),
conflicting timescales and roles, a lack of free time, and the sexual
harassment experienced by many women in the workplace (Valls-
Llobet 1994). At the same time, women who do not work outside
the home are experiencing loss of faith in their self-worth, linked to
the devaluation of the domestic sphere, which is in turn leading to an
increased incidence of depression and medication-addiction.

But health is not only about the absence of disease. Even low-level
disability – poor balance, for example, or an inability to climb stairs
– can significantly reduce the quality of life, particularly among
women with low educational and income levels (De Onís and Villar
1992). Valls-Llobet's research bears out previous surveys which
suggest that women tend to visit doctors more often than men, are
given shorter consultations, and are more likely to be sent home with
medication (De Onís and Villar 1992). As a result, they may subsequently succumb to the illness that was not detected or become
increasingly dependent on the drugs prescribed. From this
perspective, preventive medicine has a key role to play. But the
medicalisation of their bodies – for example, through screening and
other generalised diagnostic procedures designed to improve health
levels – tends to encourage women to think of their bodies as a site of
potential pathology rather than satisfaction or pleasure. At the same
time it restricts their ability to make decisions about their own
bodies, adding indirectly to stress levels. Such stress can have economic
costs in terms of lost working days, as Valls-Llobet notes, but it can
also generate direct health costs by contributing to forms of stress-
related illness, as well as spontaneous abortions or premature births.

The IM's healthcare priorities for women are set out in its two

Plans. The first, drafted at a time when Spain's developing welfare state was coming under increasing pressure, focused on legal measures to ensure basic provision. By the time the second was drafted, emphasis had shifted from extending provision to the improved management of existing resources, including the mobilisation and co-ordination of NGOs working in women's healthcare. It is an indication of the IM's sensitivity to international work on women's issues that all the health objectives addressed in the UN Action Programme – the strengthening of preventive medicine and the promotion of research in the areas which most threaten women; the dissemination of information on women's health issues; the training of girls in health and nutritional matters; the promotion of women's sport and other physical activity – also figure in one or both *Plans*. The legal framework proposed in the first for the exercise of women's health rights includes the incorporation within the 1986 General Health Law of later family planning provisions, and measures to pave the way for the introduction of *in vitro* fertilisation techniques (IM 1990b). Planned increases in provision include the extension of the family planning service, programmes on maternity, sexuality and family planning (aimed primarily at adolescents), and health awareness campaigns targeting older and working women. In *Plan II*, these groups become the object of more specific initiatives designed to reduce adolescent pregnancy, to stimulate public understanding of the menopause and its ramifications, and to establish the causes of and pilot preventive measures in relation to women's work-related illness (IM 1993a). It also provides for the evaluation and co-ordination of earlier initatives for the prevention and detection of cancer, programmes designed to prevent the spread of HIV among high-risk groups, and specialised training courses for healthcare professionals.

The second key aspect of state welfare provision, and the one which has arguably done most to advance women's social protagonism in contemporary Spain, is the education system. As in the 1970s, the profound ideological conservatism of the Franco regime meant that most Spanish women were still educated separately, with different curricula and according to different criteria from men (Alberdi 1986; Folguera 1993a). This has changed dramatically over the last 25 years and Spanish women today have more 'educational capital' than ever before, reflecting and facilitating their greater integration into Spain's public culture in general and the labour market in particular. But while quantitative differences have become less pressing, key qualitative ones remain. As a result this educational capital, like women's access to public culture and the workplace, is not equivalent to men's. During the early years of the Franco regime, Falange's Women's Section had helped to educate women for a particular Catholic vision of motherhood and domesticity. But economic growth from the late 1950s required a more skilled workforce from which women could no longer be excluded. Four Education Ministers sought to adapt the educational system to the new demands being made of it during this period, with varying degrees of success. The reforms enshrined in Villar Palasí's 1970 Ley General de Educación (LGE) (General Education and Educational Finance Law) were ostensibly based on equality of opportunities regardless of sex, but did not mark a significant break with Francoist ideology. For example, it provided for a school curriculum 'bien diferenciado entre los ámbitos masculino y femenino' (in which male and female spheres were clearly distinguished) particularly in physical education (IM 1995a). Up to this point, however, pre-school provision for both sexes had been virtually non-existent; primary education was not universal; vocational training was restricted to industry; the Bachillerato (Baccalaureate) was available almost exclusively in private schools; and universities were accessible only to the privileged minority. To the extent that it reflected the need to address these shortcomings the LGE was in many respects a crucial plank in Spain's modernisation process. After Franco's death, this process continued under the transitional UCD government and in the drafting of the Constitution. Since then existing legislation has been modernised and brought into line with the Constitution, most recently with the 1990 Ley Orgánica de Ordenación General del Sistema Educativo (LOGSE) (General Educational Reform Law).[10] Like the LGE before it, this was designed to address deficiencies in the existing system, and to educate Spaniards for changing social and economic conditions – in this case, those produced by the rapid socio-economic restructuring of the late 1980s. It was the first piece of Spanish educational legislation explicitly to acknowledge the persistent sex discrimination within the educational system, and to affirm the anti-discriminatory role of education in general and of Educación Básica (Basic Education) in particular (IM 1993b; Pujol Algans 1992). Its preamble recognises the principle of 'efectiva igualdad de derechos entre los sexos [y] el rechazo a todo tipo de discriminación' (genuine equality of rights and the rejection of all forms of discrimination) in the educational system (IM 1993a). It goes on to state that primary education will seek to inculcate in both sexes the skills necessary for personal autonomy in the domestic sphere, that secondary education will develop students' respect for the principle of non-discrimination, that gender stereotyping in teaching materials will be addressed, and that educational administrators will be required to overcome discriminatory social attitudes when advising students (IM 1993a). The context for these aims – which were formulated in consultation with the IM – and the main obstacles to their achievement are discussed below.

At the time of writing, the phased transition from LGE to LOGSE is still in process. This chapter accordingly refers to both – although virtually all gender-differentiated data relate to the LGE period – and Figure 1 highlights their principal differences.

Compulsory education in Spain begins at six years of age. The privileging of the traditional family under Franco, combined with the relatively late development of the welfare state, has made publicly-funded education before this age a fairly recent phenomenon – although informal childcare is commonly arranged with relatives or neighbours. Despite this (and the fact that it has opponents on both ideological and economic grounds) pre-compulsory education is increasingly recognised as a key socialising experience for the children concerned, and a crucial support for the increasing number of families in which both parents or a lone parent work outside of the home. Under the LOGSE, a baby can, in theory, attend a crèche from 40 days old. In practice, demand for places for 0-1 year olds massively outstrips supply and virtually all places are in the private sector. Of day centres for 2-3 year olds, less than a quarter were wholly or partly dependent on public (mostly municipal or regional government) funding in 1989/90: the remainder were run privately, often by charities or larger employers (IM 1994d). In the absence of full statistics, the IM estimates that enrolment increased from under 10 per cent in 1981 to around 13 per cent (some 113,000) in 1989 (IM 1994d, 1995e). However, it attributes this not to increased provision but to a fall in applications as a result of the declining birth-rate.

Provision for nursery-school (3-4 year olds) and pre-school children (4-5 year olds) is significantly better, however. The most recent figures suggest that registration among both groups rose from

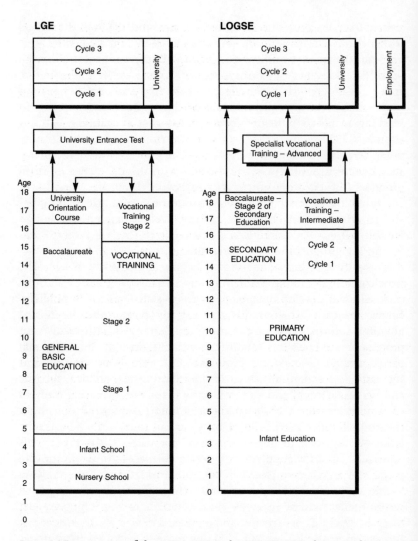

Figure 1. Comparison of the 1970 LGE and 1990 LOGSE educational systems

Compulsory education is shown in capital letters. Under the LGE (which is being phased out from 1991/92) those who do not study the Baccalaureate are required to undertake Compulsory Vocational Training.

Source: Adapted from Ministerio de la Presidencia (1994)

around 60 per cent to over 80 per cent over the 1980s (IM 1995e). Under the LOGSE pre-school education is free in public centres but, here too, demand continues to outstrip supply. In 1989/90, two-thirds of 4-5 years olds at pre-school centres were in the public sector, although girls were slightly more likely to attend a private centre (IM 1994d). Many of these private centres are Catholic-run and have tended to retain single-sex education against the trend elsewhere. At a time when co-education is obligatory in all new public educational centres this makes private centres particularly attractive to parents who oppose co-education on ideological or other grounds. The debate around co-education in Spain has been lively and protracted, and continues to resonate in discussions of girls' education today (Scanlon 1986; IM 1995a). Research elsewhere in Europe suggests that the tendency of many girls towards inhibition in the mixed classroom (particularly at higher levels, and even when they greatly outnumber boys) makes them more likely to develop their confidence and autonomy, and more likely to break away from traditional subject choices, in single-sex schools (Santos 1994b). The debate around these findings has made little impression in Spain, however, where single-sex schools are still associated with the profound traditionalism of the Franco regime. It is from this perspective that sections of the Women's Movement fought hard and successfully in the 1970s to put co-education on the political agenda, and against this background that the IM's continuing commitment to co-education needs to be seen (IM 1995a). This does not mean that feminist educationalists support co-education uncritically. Sociologist Isabel Alberdi, for example, has been questioning its tendency to reproduce masculine models for over a decade. More significantly, perhaps, the IM's own Head of Educational and Cultural Programmes has recently underlined the need to adapt educational paradigms to accommodate sexual difference (Alberdi 1986, 1996; Mañeru Méndez 1994). Elena Rodrigo indirectly acknowledges these tensions when she attributes Spanish girls' current tendency to outperform boys at all levels to the fact that

ellas son más listas, aplicadas, responsables, y *empollonas*. Participan menos en clase, les falta la iniciative masculina, pero son al final las que triunfan en los exámenes, las que más aprueban y las que obtienen mejores calificaciones en general, presentando, en consecuencia, una tasa de conflictos escolares y abandono mucho más baja que la de sus compañeros (cited De Miguel 1994: 608).[11]

(girls are smarter, more responsible, harder working, and *swots* [emphasis in original]. They are less likely to participate in class and they lack boys' initiative, but they are the ones who finally come top in exams, and achieve higher pass rates and better qualifications generally. As a result they experience fewer educational problems and are less likely to drop out than their male counterparts.)

By demonstrating the ability of many girls to match or outperform boys in educational terms, the large-scale introduction of co-education has overturned a certain discourse on girls' intellectual inferiority. Yet, as Rodrigo's words underline, the androcentrism that legitimated this discourse is powerful enough for its basic assumption to be turned on its head without apparent contradiction: once girls outperform men, it seems, performance ceases to be a primary value. This reversal is licensed by the rather adolescent assumption that being seen to work is a sign of weakness, and the traditional association of weakness with women. From this perspective girls are not intelligent or gifted. They are smart or diligent, 'empollonas' – a term usually translated as 'swot' but which has maternal overtones of chickens hatching eggs, and thus of reproduction rather than production or imagination. While ostensibly recognising girls' positive responses to more equitable educational opportunities, Rodrigo thus simultaneously devalues them. And she does so by replicating and legitimating the widely-documented tendency of boys to rate their abilities and understanding more highly than their performance warrants (Santos 1994b). Along with the relation between performance and ability, the stereotype of the studious male and frivolous female is thus reversed in an affirmation of boys' seemingly essential superiority.

The implications of tacit masculinist paradigms in the co-educational classrooms are underlined in a pioneering study of gender transmission in Catalan secondary schools by the current director of the IM, Marina Subirats, and her collaborator. Boys, they found, were more likely to use language to impose their will on their environment, to participate in class, to talk about their experiences, and to occupy central spaces, moving about and shouting if necessary to gain attention (Subirats and Brullet 1988). By contrast girls were less likely to participate or to transgress norms, they tended to move around the edges of the classroom, and used language to negotiate situations. These two forms of behaviour would be equally valid, the authors observe, were it not for the fact that one of them confers social power and the other does not. It is not clear from their analysis whether the authors see these differences as reflecting and reinforcing broader social tensions, or as inaugurating them. They also seem to suggest that, even when a measure of formal equality has been won, differences will invariably be interpreted to girls' disadvantage. Superficially at least Rodrigo's comments appear to bear out this pessimism, by illustrating the discursive manoeuvres through which stereotypical assumptions can be adapted to changing circumstances. A more optimistic reading might underline the extent of these manoeuvres, since the greater the contortion involved, the weaker the stereotypes in question become and the more likely they are to be displaced.

But for every girl whose family is concerned to see her develop her gendered autonomy in a single-sex environment, there are many more whose traditionalist parents see private education as an 'amortiguador moral' (moral shock-absorber) between the domestic and social spheres – particularly where family honour and reputation are foregrounded (Guerrero Serón 1996). This is linked to the persistence of a tradition established when girls were an educational minority, and thought to need closer monitoring for the sake of their modesty. Today some private centres have excellent reputations, but others do not. They are subject to fewer restrictions than public ones, and in practice can expect little in the way of official monitoring. Because of this, and because of their later development in Spain, mixed-sex nursery and pre-school education have been the object of relatively little gender-based research, and the bibliographies of influential publications testify to Spanish researchers' debt to work done elsewhere. This has begun to change over the last decade, however (García de Leon et al. 1996). In line with its brief to determine and eradicate the causes of sex-based discrimination across the educational system, the IM has been a key factor in this change, funding a number of important studies since the mid-1980s. These include the Subirats and Brullet study cited above, which suggested that while institutionalised discrimination had virtually disappeared across all age ranges, non-systematic discrimination persisted in teachers' expectations of and interactions with children – the so-called 'curriculo oculto' or hidden curriculum (Subirats and Brullet 1988: 138). The eradication of gender stereotyping among teaching staff subsequently became a central aim of the IM's anti-discriminatory programme (IM 1990b, 1993a). This focus was reinforced by the findings of another set of IM-funded studies published four years

later (Moreno 1992). As well as essays on factors conditioning girls'
representation and performance in sciences, technology, mathematics
and languages the volume includes a rare study of aggression in
Spanish children under 36 months. Though limited in scope, it found
no evidence of prevailing gender stereotypes in the subjects'
spontaneous behaviour, and concluded that they are derived later in
the educational process from the expectations and attitudes of
teaching staff, or from teaching materials (López Puig 1992). These
data resonate in the IM's measures to sensitise teaching staff to equal
opportunities issues and to promote the production of non-sexist
teaching materials, as set out in Plan II (IM 1993a).

Despite the current phased introduction of the LOGSE, at this time
gender-differentiated statistics are available only for the LGE system.
Under this, children enter compulsory Educación General Básica
(EGB) (General Basic Education) at six years of age and leave at 14.[12]
Girls made up just over 48 per cent of the five million EGB students
in 1989/90 (Guerrero Serón 1996). This slight preponderance of
boys reflects that of the population as a whole in this age group but
also, more significantly, the fact that fewer girls need to resit parts of
their EGB (2.6 per cent compared with 3.5 per cent of boys). As in
pre-compulsory schooling, girls also made up slightly over half of
private sector pupils (Guerrero Serón 1996).

Under the LGE, students completing EGB and opting not to leave
at 14 chose between vocational training and the Baccalaureate
(Bachillerato Unificado Polivalente or BUP) followed (if they wished
to go to university) by a pre-university course (Curso de Orientación
Universitaria or COU). Figures for 1989/90 suggest that girls were
around 4 per cent more likely to follow the more academic BUP or
COU route than boys, and by 1991/92 this gender difference had
reportedly tripled (Guerrero Serón 1996; IM 1995e). This is partly
because more girls pass EGB, and partly because parents have
historically been less preoccupied with daughters' immediate
employment prospects than with sons', and thus less likely to orient
girls towards vocational training. This highlights the extent to which
the education of girls still tends to be seen as a consumer choice by
more traditionalist parents, while the education of boys is perceived
as an investment (De Miguel 1994).

Although under the LOGSE the sexes are no longer required to
follow different educational programmes, the gender differences seen
under the old system are likely to persist (at least initially) in option

and Baccalaureate choices. Under the LGE, girls made up almost 54 per cent of the BUP humanities route in 1989/90, and under 45 per cent of Sciences (Guerrero Serón 1996). Figures for COU were even more differentiated, with girls making up 54-58 per cent of health, social sciences, and humanities and languages students, and only around 35 per cent on science and technology routes (Guerrero Serón 1996). While some educationalists reject the criticism and devaluation of so-called 'feminine' subject choices, others have shown a more pragmatic concern that early decisions (particularly on BUP type) condition future career possibilities – for example, that the science-based subjects preferred by many boys tend to lead to better paid jobs and more conventionally prestigious careers (Garrido 1993). Girls's reduced expectations of and access to traditionally male-dominated subjects like mathematics and technology have given rise to particular concern (Alvarez Lires and Sonreira Vega 1992; Busquets *et al.* 1992). The IM is co-ordinating attempts to address both the pragmatic and wider philosophical implications of girls' subject choices and the factors that condition them, by promoting equal opportunities training for careers guidance specialists and educational inspectors, as well as the development of a broader curriculum based on anti-discriminatory principles (IM 1993a).

One such conditioning factor is a persistent gender imbalance in sectors of the teaching profession itself. In 1984/85, some 94 per cent of pre-school, 61 per cent of EGB and 48 per cent of BUP and COU teachers were women, and these figures had remained virtually unchanged since 1970 (Alberdi 1986). By 1991/92, however, the EGB and the BUP/COU figures had both risen slightly (to around 65 per cent and 52 per cent respectively) (IM 1995e). As the educational level increases, however, the proportion of women teachers falls. For some commentators women's over-representation at the earliest levels offers young children a measure of continuity between the domestic and wider social spheres: others are uneasy about the instilling of the 'woman as carer' model in very young children, and the consequences of this imbalance for girls' later development (López Puig 1992). This unease is compounded by the fact that, despite their numerical disadvantage at certain educational levels, male teachers are consistently over-represented in science and technology and (partly because they tend to be promoted earlier) also in senior administrative posts across the educational system (IM 1993a). In its *Plan II*, the IM proposes positive action to promote

increased equality awareness in public teacher training (IM 1993a,
1995a). But such measures are unlikely by themselves to produce
major attitude changes in the short term, especially as they are
limited to the public sector.

Under the LGE, students who completed BUP but did not intend
to proceed to higher education undertook vocational training
(Formación Profesional or FP). Level 1 combined general education
and employment training for those leaving school at 14, while Level
2 was for those who had already achieved Level 1 or who had left
school at 16. FP has been widely criticised for its high drop-out rates,
outdated methods and materials, its under-resourcing, and the
narrow range of subject choices available in practice, and the LOGSE
seeks to address these shortcomings (Zaldívar and Castells 1992).
Given most girls' preference for the more academic route, FP is one
of the few areas of the Spanish education system that has remained
predominantly male. This has been changing over the last decade,
however, particularly in the face of spiralling youth unemployment
(Rollin 1995). In 1980/81 just under 17 per cent of women and
around a quarter of men in education were engaged in FP: by 1991/
92 the figure for both sexes stood at around 28 per cent (IM 1995e).
Although there is evidence of a shift towards hotel and catering,
chemistry, metalwork and other non-traditional subjects, administration remained the choice for over 50 per cent of women in FP (IM
1994d). Diversification is not encouraged by the fact that vocational
training centres have tended to give equal opportunities a low
priority. This reflects FP's historically male-dominated culture and
women's under-representation – around 40 per cent in 1989/90 – in
public centres (Guerrero Serón 1996). Private centres – which tend
to favour areas traditionally but decreasingly popular with women
students, such as administration, beauty therapy and health-care, as
well as unaccredited languages courses – are not obliged to adopt the
anti-discriminatory measures promoted in public centres, and their
activities have been subject to little official monitoring.

Partly because of the autonomy accorded it under the Constitution, areas of Spain's university system have also proved resistant to
equal opportunities measures. Despite this, university education in
general retains a key role in the acquisition of anti-discriminatory
values. And despite the effects of mass provision and high levels of
youth unemployment, it also continues to offer graduates in certain
subjects the possibility of enhanced socio-economic status and

employment prospects. More than any other sector, the universities have been the focus of Spain's educational modernisation. Since 1970 their number has more than doubled, while student numbers tripled between 1975 and 1990 (Ministerio de la Presidencia 1994).[13] Much of this increase reflects the larger number of women students in higher education. As late as 1981, 62 of every thousand men between 25 and 34 were in higher education, compared with 36 women (De Miguel 1994). From 1986/87 these proportions began to reverse throughout the country, and by 1991 the figures were 80 and 85 respectively (over half a million each in total), giving Spain one of the highest levels of female university attendance in the EU (De Miguel 1994). Significantly, this growth has not been in direct response to national or local policy or to measures co-ordinated by the IM. It is the unintended consequence of a complex of factors, including mothers who encourage their daughters to take opportunities they did not have themselves, the expansion of grant aid, the growth (until recently) of service sector jobs and the increasing need to compete for them, and the higher profile and accessibility of local universities, all compounded by the demographic growth of the 1970s (De Miguel 1994; Guerrero Serón 1996).

These increases are not across the board, however. In 1989/90 women made up just over half of students in Facultades and Colegios Universitarios (University Faculties and Colleges), and just under half in Escuelas Universitarias (Colleges of Higher Education) (De Miguel 1994). Despite campaigning work by the IM, they remain a small (though growing) minority in the conventionally more prestigious Escuelas Técnicas Superiores (Advanced Technical Schools) – 19 per cent in 1989/90 (De Miguel 1994; Guerrero Serón 1996). Over the last decade, however, women have come to form the overall majority in law and social sciences, and health sciences, and around half of the total in most areas of experimental science (IM 1995e). Partly as a consequence, health sciences in particular now rates high in unemployment statistics. Women also remain significantly over-represented in other areas of high graduate unemployment like education and particularly humanities, where they formed two-thirds of the graduate total in 1989/90 (IM 1995e). And while the number of women on primary education and nursing courses is currently declining, those studying languages, philosophy, journalism and medicine – hardly more favoured in employment terms – continue to increase.

It might be argued, of course, that higher education is not exclusively about jobs. However, in a period of high unemployment and social and economic instability – when grants are still not widely available, and when almost all students work to support their studies – Spanish students are increasingly seeing education in more instrumental terms. A widening sense that higher education is 'una fábrica de parados', an unemployment factory which takes crucial years from an individual's working career, is placing students under increasing pressure to take work where they can find it without waiting to complete their studies. But despite the fact that women with degrees are more likely to be registered as unemployed than those with only BUP or COU, their drop-out rate – in universities, as in elementary and secondary schooling – is consistently and significantly lower than men's (De Miguel 1994; IM 1995e). They are increasingly likely to postpone having children until they have finished their education, while those who do leave tend to return to their studies afterwards, despite the difficulties of readapting to university life (Garrido 1993).

It has long been recognised that one of the employment areas least open to women has been university teaching itself, where in 1989/ 90 they represented around a third of all staff, virtually all concentrated at the lowest levels (IM 1995e; Guerrero Serón 1996).[14] This gender differential – which has historically been highest in the prestigious Advanced Technical Schools – is an especially significant one, since it restricts women's participation in potentially far-reaching policy decisions. The universities are the site of most of the research on which future social and other policy is based, much of which will affect women's lives directly. The causes of this under-representation – indirect institutional discrimination and individual prejudice; the fact that the years of greatest activity clash with those of childrearing, which still falls largely to women; the weight of unexamined criteria and in some cases 'enchufe' (informal sponsoring or nepotism) in the recruitment and promotion processes – are addressed in the IM's Plan II. As noted above, this proposes various types of nationally and locally organised equal opportunities training for teaching staff at all levels (IM 1993a). Given the autonomous status of Spanish universities, however, this training is, of necessity, voluntary and likely to reach only the at least half-converted. More effective has been the IM's promotion of academic activity around women's issues. The IM-sponsored Libro blanco (White book), which registers the development of feminist research, Women's Studies Institutes and Seminars in Spanish university centres to 1993, is a key indicator of this growth and highlights the surge in demand for new materials – including, in 1996, Spain's first full-length sociological study of women (Ballarín et al. 1995; García de León et al. 1996). The growth of women's studies has enabled some Centres to offer inputs into broader teaching programmes. However, penetration so far has been patchy, particularly in the face of resistance from more conservative disciplines. This resistance will take on a different inflection under the new PP government, although established centres are likely to be cushioned against all but the most major policy changes (at least initially) by their integration in university structures, their national profile and their links with the increasingly powerful regional governments.

If the number and prospects of its graduates is often taken as an indicator of a nation's social-cultural capital, the same could equally be said for its literacy rate.[15] Illiteracy has historically been significantly higher among women then men in Spain, and while women's illiteracy declined by almost a third in the decade to 1992 (to around 7 per cent) this is still the case (IM 1995e). However, the existence of free and compulsory basic schooling, and the relatively high educational levels of young urban women in particular, means that illiteracy tends to be most common in older women and those from rural, ethnic minority, or other disadvantaged groups. In 1993, for example, it stood at almost 12 per cent in women over 45 – twice that of men in the same age group – while in the under 30s it was under 1 per cent, and virtually identical with male counterparts (IM 1995e). But at the same time the rural isolation in which some poorer Spaniards still live, the non-prioritising of (particularly girls') school attendance among gypsies and certain other communities, and the need in some cases for children to help with the family income were all contributing to persistent functional illiteracy in younger women. The state's proposals for making literacy and other key skills available to these and to all women who had not received basic education have been set out in the Plan de Educación Permanente de Adultas 1990-1995 (PEPA) (Continuing Education Programme for Adult Women). Promoted jointly by the IM and the Ministry of Education and Science, this proposed the development of information packs and awareness training courses for teaching staff, and teaching materials for women lacking basic skills, all with an equal opportunities

dimension (IM 1994a). Their marginalisation has nevertheless made
many of these women particularly difficult to reach. Partly for this
reason, the IM's Plan II includes a proposal for an outline agreement
with the state television channel for the promotion of greater equal
opportunities awareness in educational and other programming. This
led in May 1994 to a series of programmes on women's issues,
including employment, the double shift, and advertising. But while
this type of coverage can reach a relatively wide audience very
quickly, programming, economic and wider political factors make
opportunities to exploit it strictly limited. More enduring have been
the network of public adult education centres and similar private
centres for the teaching of basic literacy and numeracy skills, and the
'universidades populares' (people's universities) which were
introduced by municipalities to provide opportunities for greater
social and cultural contact among elderly and disadvantaged groups.
There are many other local, regional and national initiatives –
including Spain's Distance Learning or 'Open' University
(Universidad Nacional de Educación a Distancia or UNED) – through
which women can combine education with childrearing or paid
employment. One effect of this growing diversity of provision is that
women increasingly accumulate their educational capital in phases.
They are more likely than ever to complete their education after
having a family, for example; to combine study with full- or part-
time domestic commitments, or with temporary, part-time or full-
time work outside the home; or to undertake spells of vocational
training in the workplace. The contexts and some of the implications
of their decisions are discussed in chapter 3.

Notes

1 The IM's establishment was also a response to the 1979 UN convention to eliminate sex
  discrimination, the ratification of which by Spain (in 1984) was one of the new body's
  first successes.
2 This consists of 12 representatives from ministerial departments and 6 from women's
  NGOs. Until May 1996 its President was the Minister for Social Affairs; more recently, see
  below.
3 She was replaced by Carmen Martínez Ten, a gynaecologist, who was herself succeeded
  in 1991 by lawyer Purificacíon Gutiérrez. The present Director, educational sociologist
  Marina Subirats, took up office in 1993.
4 As Threlfall suggests, the tripling of the IM's budget (to the equivalent of £11.5m)
  between 1984 and 1992 reflects its continuing strategic significance. The fact that a
  reported 75 per cent (Threlfall 1996) or 90 per cent (Valiente 1995) of its budget has been

spent on the IM's own staffing and running costs, rather than on supporting extra-institutional groups, has been a source of contention. Support funding has tended to take the form of larger sums for a smaller number of entities: from a high point of 366 projects in 1986, 1993 saw a fall to 75, although the total sum disbursed was almost three times larger. This may mean a more effective targeting of support, but it also means more disappointed applicants. Significantly, the number of applications has plummeted from a high of 962 in 1987 to 160 in 1993 (IM 1994).

5 For a detailed discussion of the articulation of equality and difference in the work of the Institute for Women see Gil Ruiz (1996).

6 The first section of Article 32 reads 'El hombre y la mujer tienen derecho a contraer matrimonio con plena igualdad jurídica' (Men and women have the right to marry in full legal equality). The first section of Article 35. reads: 'Todos los españoles tienen el deber de trabajar y el derecho al trabajo, a la libre elección de profesión u oficio, a la promoción a través del trabajo y a una remuneración suficiente para satisfacer sus necesidades y las de su familia, sin que en ningún caso pueda hacerse discriminación por razón de sexo' (All Spaniards have the duty and the right to work, to the free choice of profession or post, to promotion through work, and to a remuneration sufficient to meet their needs and those of their family, without discrimination on grounds of sex.) For remaining sections and commentary see Tamames (1992).

7 Although many of women's most significant legal advances came under PSOE, it was UCD that proposed the divorce law, and PCE that took the initiative in proposing the abortion law (Paz Benito 1993; Durán and Gallego 1986). Partly as a result of the complex bargaining processes involved in the drafting of the Constitution and its subsequent enshrining in law, parties on the right agreed to the change to equality in marriage, while the centre supported a more liberal divorce law.

8 As usual these figures vary with geography, income and other factors. In Castilla and León, for example, women's life expectancy is over 82, while in Ceuta-Melilla it is under 79 (IM 1995e).

9 This has contributed to the growth of self-help publications on women's health. An influential example is Castaño and Palacios (1996), in which leading academics and professionals offer women advice on general health issues as well as sex, love and employment.

10 This was done first by the 1983 Ley de Reforma Universitaria (LRU) (University Reform Law) and two years later by the Ley Orgánica del Derecho a la Educación (LODE) (Right to Education Law). The LRU gave increased autonomy to a university system which had been subject to tight central government control under Franco. The LODE was designed to stimulate the participation of all interested parties, including teachers, parents and children in decision-making processes. It also addressed fact that around 20 per cent of the education system was privately run – virtually all of it by the Catholic Church and for the wealthier middle classes – by eliminating discrimination in admissions and making all compulsory schooling free.

11 De Miguel (who cites Rodrigo without comment) goes on to note that girls were 0.8-2 per cent less likely than boys to repeat EGB than boys in 1991/92 (De Miguel 1994). In addition, consistently fewer girls received the Certificado Escolar (School Certificate) qualification for completing the EGB course but not the exam, while consistently more obtained the higher Graduado Escolar (School Diploma) qualification for completing both the course and the exam: a difference of 5-6 per cent in both cases.

12 The LOGSE provides for a 25-hour per week core secondary curriculum which includes environmental, social and cultural studies, art, PE, Spanish (and the autonomous language where appropriate), literature, foreign languages and maths (Ministerio de la Presidencia 1994). The remainder of the curriculum is determined by the Education Ministry of each autonomous government. The LGE had already introduced the possibility of sex education. Though it is still a minority subject it is being introduced – not without controversy – into all new teaching centres.

13 As recently as 1990 there were 34 universities: at the end of 1994 the figure was 51, including three private and four Catholic universities, and UNED (El País 1996). UNED offers courses for mature students who (because their education was interrupted by work, family or other commitments) do not meet the standard university matriculation requirements, as well as for people living in more isolated rural areas.

14 As usual, this statistic obscures significant variations. At UNED, which operates a policy of positive discrimination, women reportedly made up 39 per cent of staff in 1989, while at Alicante University it was 16 per cent (Fernández Villanueva 1989). Largely as a consequence, women's representation in university decision-making bodies was also low, and only around 3 per cent held chairs. Figures tend to be lower across the board in the (mostly Catholic) private universities, with an average of 22 per cent women staff in 1989 (Fernández Villanueva 1989). The number of women academics does fluctuate, however, and not always as a result of equal opportunities policies. In 1989, for example, Concepción Fernández Villanueva noted an increase in the number of women technical and scientific staff, and traced this to improved employment prospects and salaries in these areas which were tempting male academics into industry, reportedly causing women to be recruited to make up the shortfall (Fernández Villanueva 1989). While this marks the triumph of pragmatism over prejudice, if the underlying prejudice remains unchallenged it will ensure that the move is reversed as soon as industrial salaries fall back. On the other hand, provided too many ideological and other obstacles are not put in their way, giving women an opportunity to demonstrate their capabilities might help to weaken prejudice and prompt a pragmatic decision to retain women staff, as has happened in certain other sectors.

15 As in English, 'analfabetismo' (illiteracy) can signify a lack of basic education, a total inability to read, or (more usually) a reading level so low as to be effectively non-functional. Here the last of these, 'functional illiteracy', is assumed, although this too is problematic when abstracted from a functional context.

3   Between the family and the workplace

S OCIAL CHANGE is a complex affair. Although women's educational opportunities and choices have been a key factor in the much-debated transformation of their social roles, these changes and choices are inextricable from new working and family patterns. And these, in turn, reflect and contribute to a range of other factors: the foreshortening of men's working lives by longer studies and earlier retirement; demographic changes, such as the falling birthrate; the expansion of the state and the substitution of domestic by state and private production; and the national ramifications of European and international economic restructuring. Meanwhile, the progressive erosion of the moral authority of the state and the Catholic Church has encouraged women to respond more pragmatically and autonomously to these shifts. This chapter considers their responses and some of the factors that condition them in the home and the workplace.

Women who undertake domestic maintenance, cooking, caring and childrearing tasks are patently not unemployed, though – unless it is undertaken in the homes of others – few women receive cash payment for their labour. Nor is it uncommon for women to undertake additional, paid, work within the home. In Franco's time this might have been sewing or laundry work. In the 1990s, mass production has meant that dressmaking has tended to become deskilled, and homeworkers are more likely to undertake the piecework assembly of clothes, leather goods, shoes or furs, or the production of toys and craft items. In a small but increasing number of cases they may run some form of business from home on their own account. The fact that these women, like those in paid employment outside the home, are usually expected to retain all or most domestic responsibilities is widely seen as one of the most pressing inequities facing Spanish women today (Alberdi et al. 1994). To perpetuate a distinction between work in the home and work outside it is, in some sense, to compound this inequity. It also affirms the separation of the social into public and private spheres – an arrangement which from classical times has broadly assumed men's privileged place in the first and women's natural place in the second IM 1992). Many women opt (or for a variety of reasons find themselves obliged) to work within the home rather than in paid employment. However, the assumption that this is the only normal and natural course available to them has enabled modern states to disavow their dependence on the family as an institution. In Spain, the Franco regime's institutionalisation of a particularly oppressive family model has tended to heighten this ambivalence towards the family as an institution, without discouraging democratic governments from targeting women with children for specific politico-juridical and welfare support. This, in turn, has accelerated the imbrication of public and private spheres, and helped to bring the distinction between them – a distinction that was invisible when it functioned efficiently – to centre stage and, most recently, to crisis.[1]

The roots of this crisis can be traced back to the so-called economic miracle of the 1960s and early 1970s and beyond. Franco's response to the two decades of socio-economic growth lost during the Civil War, and to the international isolation occasioned after World War II by his dealings with Hitler, was a policy of national economic self-sufficiency which remained in place, virtually unchanged, until the late 1950s. Autarky relied on increasing state intervention in the economy and rapid industrial expansion, both of which proved impossible without the raw materials for domestic industry or the income to purchase them. And despite the special priority given to agriculture, the regime was unable to produce (or import) enough food to feed the population. During these years of hunger, as they became known, women played a key role in agricultural production. Some three million Spaniards, most of them men, had died in the war and in some cases widows or daughters took over their responsibilities. More often they continued to work as unpaid 'ayudas familiares' (family helpers) or as low-paid 'jornaleras' (seasonal day-labourers). But as rural decline began to bite increasing numbers sought employment in the cities. There was little to be had. Some found work in textiles and a smaller number in construction, metalwork or other industries. Many more ended up in domestic service – around half a million at the 1950 census – while some had recourse to prostitution (IM 1992). But only the poorest women tended to seek paid work during the 1940s. By 1950 the national census put their total at 16 per cent, although many more were working in the invisible economy – particularly unpaid agricultural work or domestic service (IM 1992). This was despite the regime's postwar demographic policy, which used a range of threats and incentives to enlist women's help in rebuilding the nation by making them stay in the home. Its first law to restrict which women could work and where was the 1938 Fuero de Trabajo (Labour Charter). This stated that '[e]l Estado en especial prohibirá el trabajo nocturno de las mujeres, regulará el trabajo a domicilio y libertará a la mujer casada del taller y de la fábrica' (in particular, the State will prohibit nightwork by women, regulate homeworking and liberate married women from the workshop and the factory) (cited in Roig 1989: 317). It was reinforced by a traditionalist Catholic hierarchy which promoted a model of women as only truly womanly when inside the home or the local church.

The will of Church and state in these matters was enacted through Falange's SF, particularly (but not exclusively) through its management of 'el servicio social' (social service), the female version of military service. For six months, childless widows and single women under 35 followed courses on topics including religion, the family, sewing, domestic science and economy, childcare and physical education, and did volunteer work in hospitals or offices. Initially a prerequisite for government employment, from 1945 social service became compulsory for all women seeking a passport, a driving licence, or membership of various sporting and cultural associations (Shubert 1990). Although some undoubtedly benefited from the health education and literacy training programmes SF's primary task, particularly in the postwar years, was to restrict women's ambitions to the role assigned to them by the regime (Sánchez López 1990; De Miguel 1991). Women who accepted this role could expect a range of rhetorical and, in some cases, financial forms of support. The 1938 Fuero del Trabajo had declared the family '[la] célula primaria natural y fundamento de la sociedad y al mismo tiempo [una] institución moral, dotada de derecho inalienable y superior a toda ley positiva' (the primary natural and basic unit of society, and at the same time a moral institution, invested with inalienable rights which supersede any human law (Del Campo 1991: 88)). The regime's support for large families in particular was reaffirmed in the 1945 Fuero de los Españoles (Spaniards' Charter). Postwar repopulation measures included payment of a 'subsidio familiar' (family subsidy) on a sliding scale to the husbands of women who had produced more than two children, and inducements including national and provincial prizes for the largest number remained in place until the early 1970s (Del Campo 1991). Back in 1946, however, the limits of this pronatalist policy were clear: the 'subsidio familiar' was withheld from all husbands, no matter how numerous their progeny, if the wife worked (Roig 1989).

Relations between husbands and wives were also subject to other types of state intervention. The juridical equality recognised under the Second Republic was reversed at a stroke by Franco with the introduction of Civil and Criminal Codes based on restrictive nineteenth-century law. The combined effect of this was to make gender-based distinctions sharper across almost all aspects of society. Women became subject in law to 'patria potestad', the will and authority of the male head of the family. They were deprived of virtually all personal property rights, and subject to an institution-alised double standard which meant, for example, that until 1958 a man was legally entitled to kill his wife or daughter if he caught her in the act of adultery, while his own maximum penalty was exile (IM 1992). Married women's right to work was withdrawn in 1942 and only restored in 1961, subject to the husband's agreement. Like the family, marriage acquired increased social importance in the postwar years. Dowries became more common, with levels established by law. Between 1940 and 1955, women tended to marry later than at any other time this century as (among the middle classes) the courtship period too became increasingly ritualised and monitored (Garrido 1993; Martín Gaite 1994).

By the end of the 1950s, however, Spain was about to begin a new phase, which would mark its (albeit uneven) transition from a closed traditional society to a modernising one, with major repercussions for women. The failure of autarky brought the country to the verge of economic collapse. At this point technocratic ministers were allowed to begin implementing an alternative economic policy, based on the creation of a market economy and the liberalisation of trade and foreign investment. By this time the quickening industrialisation process, the regime's attempts to adapt to the wider international context, and social transformations being stimulated by the early stages of its integration into this wider context, were all tending to encourage women's incorporation in the workforce. By 1961 half as many women worked in Spain as in the UK, but the number was growing fast and would have been significantly higher if many Spanish men (particularly civil servants) had not taken on extra jobs as the economic crisis deepened to discourage their wives from seeking extradomestic work. It was in this year that the regime finally acknowledged women's changing social role with the Ley de Derechos Políticos, Profesionales y de Trabajo de la Mujer (Women's Political, Professional and Employment Rights Law). Having attempted to keep them in the home by all means at its disposal – including an earlier attempt to introduce payment for housework – SF had come to accept that women were being pushed into paid work by national as well as individual necessity. Believing that this trend was probably irreversible, it sought through this law to ensure that work was undertaken in what were seen as the best possible conditions and least inappropriate professions. Given the tensions between modernising and traditionalist tendencies in the Cortes and within SF itself the results were unsurprisingly riddled with contradictions. The Law acknowledged women's equal political, professional and labour rights (including the right to equal pay for equal work) while excluding them from certain professions – among them the Forces and the Judiciary – on the grounds that these involved activities which might offend or brutalise women's delicate sensibilities. Moreover, a married woman needed her husband's permission to exercise these new rights, and salaries could only be paid directly 'al menor o a la mujer [...] si no consta la oposición de los padres o representantes legales' (to the minor or the woman [...] with the agreement of the parents or legal representatives) (IM 1995a: 78). But nowhere is the modernisers' desire to avoid alienating more conservative social forces clearer than in the Law's preamble, where sponsors insist that 'de modo alguno queremos hacer del hombre y la mujer dos seres iguales' (the last thing we are proposing is to make men and women two equal beings) (Roig 1989: 382).

Throughout the 1960s, women remained at the epicentre of tensions between the competing demands of their official domestic role and the regime's growing need for an enlarged workforce. Women who had been too young to experience the restrictions of the 1940s and 1950s were among the first to seek salaried employment in large numbers, and by 1964 women between 15 and 24 were more than twice as likely to be in paid work as all other age groups (Garrido 1993). Henceforward, women would participate increasingly in the industrialisation process and in the production of the goods and services that would in turn make their domestic responsibilities less arduous. In the process these women contributed to the growth of consumer society, the associated social and demographic changes, and the expanding urban culture, all of which helped to hasten the modification and (in some cases) displacement of traditionalist values.

But women's incorporation into the labour force was not a sudden or homogeneous process. As Luis Garrido has noted, the key years of developmentalism (from the mid-1960s to the mid-1970s) fell into two distinct phases. The years to 1969 were relatively stable, with around 2.8m women working in 1964 and 3m in 1969; meanwhile, men's work increased almost twice as fast, from around 8.8m to around 9.2m (Garrido 1993). From 1969 to 1974, however, the situation reversed: the sectors in which women worked expanded, generating over 870,000 new jobs, while men's actually contracted by 148,000 (Garrido 1993). This growth encouraged more women to seek work, particularly in the service industries – and most notably tourism – which were seen as appropriate to women's social role and were segmented enough to fit around their often extensive domestic commitments. But at the same time expanding industrialisation and demand for consumer durables saw the numbers of women in (largely unskilled) factory work increase, especially in textiles and garment making, chemicals, footwear and hides. Here they tended to be given the most tedious, routine and poorly paid work – work which would later be among the first to be mechanised.

Despite this accelerated growth, Spain's official female labour force was (and remains) one of the lowest in Europe. By 1974 it totalled 3.7m, compared with 9.3m men (Garrido 1993). But a combination of the oil crisis, the technologisation process and Spain's sociopolitical uncertainty was plunging the economy into a crisis that would last for almost a decade. Women's response was to turn progressively to the expanding service sector – less vulnerable than traditionally male sectors like heavy industry or construction – where they soon made up the majority of education and healthcare employees and a significant proportion of staff in public administration. In 1993, over three-quarters of working women remained in the service sector (especially finance and insurance, hotel and catering and public administration), while under 4 per cent were in construction, 13.5 per cent in industry and 8 per cent in agriculture – although their representation in the last two, shrinking, sectors has halved since 1980 (IM 1995e). Because of educational commitments and high youth unemployment, the greatest concentration of women workers is in the 25-29 age group, where in 1992 there were 105 employed women for every 100 men (Garrido 1993). By contrast, rates for women over 50 remained close to 1976 levels.

Women are increasingly represented in areas once officially or unofficially closed to them. Particularly striking has been the rapid increase – 70 per cent between 1989 and 1992 – in the number of women describing their work as professional or technical (IM 1994d). But while women now make up around 48 per cent of the total workforce in these areas they remain over-represented at junior levels. In the Judiciary, for example, women have advanced from a single public prosecutor in 1973 to form a quarter of all Spain's judges, largely as a result of their success in 'oposiciones' (competitive entrance examinations) (Rollin 1995). Yet they remain significantly under-represented in the most senior judicial bodies, where individuals are appointed rather than examined, and where opportunities for discrimination abound (EV [sic] 1994a). In the public sector, too, women made up 42 per cent of public service employees (and over 60 per cent in some departments) in 1992, but only 14 per cent of senior managers in the following year – despite a tendency to be academically better qualified than male counterparts (IM 1993c; El País, 27 February 1994). They are also less likely to be invited to participate in interview panels. The effects of measures by the IM to address this imbalance – including censuses on women in the different areas, and educational and consciousness-raising programmes within central and local administrations – and the new government's proposed rationalisation of Spain's public administration remain to be seen (IM 1993a).

Gender imbalances, especially at senior level, are particularly intractable in the private sector. Women make up under 5 per cent of company directors, and some of these have an exclusively public relations role (El País, 27 February 1994). A proportion of the remainder are at the head of their own companies. In the early 1990s European women reportedly generated 30 per cent of employment growth in the form of self-employment, co-operatives and small businesses, encouraged by a range of national, local and EU initiatives – in particular the New Opportunities for Women and Community Action programmes (IM 1992; Pérez Oliva 1994). A quarter of Spain's half a million self-employed women are based in the shrinking agricultural

sector which has borne much of the brunt of economic restructuring
since the mid-1980s. Around half are in the commercial sector and a
further 18 per cent in the service industries, both of which continue
to expand (Romero López 1996). There has also been a growth in
subcontracted homeworking, often characterised by long hours,
financial risk, low returns and additional domestic responsibilities.
Similarly buoyant is the number of women with small businesses. In
1992 this stood at 92,000 (Romero López 1996). Most of these
businesses offered services to industry or were based in the traditionally feminised areas of retailing, dressmaking, hairdressing and
footwear, and over two-thirds had under five staff. A small business-
woman can, in theory, expect levels of social recognition, autonomy
and timetable flexibility which are unavailable in paid employment.
As with men, however, these are often combined with high levels of
stress and anxiety. At the same time, it has been suggested that
tensions common to many working women – as they negotiate
between a persistent identification with the affective and the domestic
sphere and a new, professional identity oriented towards productivity
and the public sphere – are at their most intense in businesswomen
and can give rise to particular role conflicts within and between
women (Romero López 1996). Limited exposure to vocational and
management training may also contribute to stress and a lack of
confidence not only among middle-aged women with relatively little
formal education, but also among the more than 20 per cent of
businesswomen who have degrees.

Although some working women enjoy stability, job satisfaction,
and working conditions comparable with those of their male counterparts, many do not (IM 1994b). Most commentators agree that legal
workplace discrimination has been virtually eradicated in Spain: first,
by the 1980 Workers' Charter (which established the right not to be
discriminated against when seeking or in employment); later, by a
series of laws promoted by the IM, including the groundbreaking
April 1989 labour law which (among other things) shifted the
burden of proof in sex discrimination cases from the accuser to the
accused.[2] In practice, however, many women – and particularly
casual workers in the black or informal economy and other officially
invisible areas – are extremely vulnerable to discriminatory treatment
and enjoy minimal rights. They are also beyond the reach of trade
unions which, in any event, have relatively few women members
(partly because they are active at levels and in sectors where women

tend to be less represented) and a poor record on fighting sex discrimination. At the other end of the spectrum, many professional women continue to endure working conditions evolved by and for men who could count on the total domestic support and career servicing of wives. The combination of unsocial hours and a 'second shift' of domestic responsibilities when they get home, exposure to forms of sexual abuse and harassment, tokenism (or ghettoisation in areas of traditional over-representation), and senior staff's tendency to demand more of women than men – to treat women's absenteeism or lower productivity less leniently, for example, particularly if childcare is a factor – has been well documented (IM 1992; Paz Benito 1993; Sáez Lara 1994). But women also suffer disproportionately in the unemployment stakes, particularly if they are seeking their first job or if they have a degree. In 1982, women formed around 29 per cent of the workforce and 36 per cent of the officially unemployed; in 1993 they were 34 per cent of the workforce and 47 per cent of the unemployed (IM 1994d; Rollin 1995). Figures for young women – 54 per cent among 16-19 year olds, and 45 per cent among 20-24 year olds – are especially alarming (Rollin 1995). Yet while anxiety has been expressed that the (rather lower) unemployment rate for young men might give rise to social conflict, there is noticeably more social tolerance where young women are concerned. For reasons which include the sectors in which they work, their concentration at more junior levels, and their often non-standard and more disadvantageous contracts, women's salaries tend to be 20-30 per cent below men's, and this gap increases to 40 per cent where higher status jobs are concerned (Threlfall 1996). And because of career breaks and the effects of 'el techo de cristal' (the glass ceiling which tends to prevent women from gaining promotion and pay-rises at the same rate as men) this gap usually grows as women age (IM 1994d). This fundamental inequity has been compounded by labour market reforms and other economic restructuring measures designed to promote job flexibility, in response to EU convergence criteria and globalising economic forces. Under Franco, only permanent full-time jobs could be created; redundancies had to be government approved and attracted the highest compensation rates in Europe. By contrast the 1980s saw the introduction of new redundancy provisions, early retirement incentives and increasingly (from 1984) of so-called flexible working practices, which have encouraged a proliferation of part-time and other non-standard contracts. While these flexible practices chiefly affected women, they were largely seen as uncontentious, since part-time work in particular has traditionally been attractive to women seeking to combine employment with domestic, educational and other commitments. However, their extension to many traditionally male areas has been widely contested, chiefly because they have tended to erode pay and conditions and make full- as well as part-time jobs in all sectors more precarious. Yet part-time working remains a mainly female, and still fairly limited, activity. In 1993, 14 per cent of all registered employed women worked part-time – way below the 40-60 per cent recorded in Holland, the UK or Denmark – compared with 2 per cent of men, and women held 60 per cent of Spain's one million registered part-time contracts (IM 1994d). The EU's broad support for enhanced part-time workers' rights acknowledges both the advantages for women of this mode of working and the need to guard against exploitation. In practice, increased rights may tend to discourage the issuing of part-time contracts in larger firms (which are usually more generous than smaller ones can afford to be) without signficantly improving the situation in smaller ones, not all of which observed the more limited rights. Temporary contracts invariably confer less protection than part-time ones – for example, against unfair dismissal – and are increasingly common, particularly in the 16-19 and (to a lesser extent) 25+ age groups (Pont Chafer 1994). Between 1987 and 1992 the number of women covered by them rose by three-quarters of a million, to 1,142,000 (Rollin 1995). More recently, government policy has actively encouraged growth in this area, with the introduction in 1993 of a range of job creation measures: among them, apprenticeship and other forms of part-time and non-standard contracts to be paid at 60-75 per cent of the 'salario mínimo interprofesional' (SMI) (national minimum wage), with reduced social security payments for employers and reduced protection for employees. Unlike their counterparts in the development period, however, many Spanish women no longer see the home as their natural base or retreat. When their temporary contract comes to an end and they are expelled from the formal economy they are more likely than ever before to register as unemployed, while a significant proportion of (usually poorer) women enters the black economy until something better comes up. Employed chiefly in homeworking, sweatshops, seasonal agricultural work, subcontracting in various forms, domestic service, or prostitution, women in the 'informal' economy can expect high levels of job instability, little chance of career development or status, poor pay and working conditions, and (except in rare cases) no contractual basis for improving their situation. Despite this shift in their response to unemployment, however, women continue to be represented in some quarters as a reserve labour force and are subjected to increasing pressure to remain at home while jobs for men are scarce – and the refusal (or inability) of most to comply is attracting criticism even in some supposedly more liberal quarters (Rubery 1993; El País, 15 January 1995).

The current instability in the job market has been represented as a key factor in the reported loss of self-confidence among some younger men (Santos 1994a). By contrast, a history of unstable employment and conflicting domestic commitments has helped to preadapt women to the complex uncertainties of today's job market. In ways early feminists could not have predicted, the playing field is gradually becoming more even, as the traditional precariousness of women's work is extended increasingly to men's. But particularly among women most exposed to the competing demands of the home and the workplace, these rapidly shifting relations are producing often conflictual changes of consciousness. And in the process, the referent of the term 'woman' is becoming increasingly uncertain. In the 1960s women with children tended to work only if they needed money and were doubly burdened, since work tended to be seen as a distraction from the real business of motherhood, socially acceptable only as long as it did not interfere with domestic and reproductive responsibilities. But by the early 1980s, women were progressively less defined by their reproductive capacity, the proportion of working women was larger and (particularly among the middle classes) it was increasingly accepted that those with older children might want to work for their personal satisfaction and autonomy, whether or not they were economically obliged to do so (Paz Benito 1993). In the 1990s, however, the fluctuating cycle of entry into and departure from the workforce is, once again, increasingly determined by economic rather than personal factors. Meanwhile, tensions between and within what may broadly be characterised as 'traditional' and 'modern' values (for example, between Catholic, family-centred worldviews and feminist, career-minded, liberal-individualist ones) continue to vibrate in the workplace and the home. While formal education remains largely a function of the state, the broader

socialisation of the young (for conditions which can no longer be
predicted with any certainty) is increasingly the responsibility not of
the school or the Church but of parents. But these parents may be
divorced, separated or unmarried, they may have major extradomestic commitments, they may be struggling to find work and/or
a sense of their own social role. Their age, educational level, location,
ethnicity, personal biography and associated values and priorities will
help to determine their responses. But the complexity of these
determinations makes it difficult to estimate to what extent women's
changing consciousness is a cause and to what extent a consequence
of increased integration in the workplace, for example, or the
universities. In the meantime, the tensions associated with rapid
socio-economic change are played out not only in the home and the
workplace but also on the bodies of women. As noted in chapter 2
this is reflected in the state's increased involvement in women's
health training and monitoring, but it is arguably clearest in the
increased demand for and availability of contraception.

The widespread adoption of contraceptive practices has greatly
enhanced women's ability to determine their life patterns, and to
match these patterns to the changing demands of the labour market.
Although it began earlier, this process has accelerated since the late
1970s. Spain's first feminist family planning centre opened in Madrid
in 1977, and over 3,000 women attended in the first year (IM
1995a). A year later contraception was legalised with the repeal of the
Criminal Code article which, since 1941, had banned the supply and
use of contraceptives, sterilisation and abortion.[3] Although pronatalist
measures remained in place into the 1970s, within two years of
Franco's death the UCD government set up a network of 'family
orientation centres', the first institutional move in this direction.
Because it did not provide for birth control to be integrated into
women's healthcare, however, early provision was private and
beyond the means of poorer women (Threlfall 1996). Consequently,
feminists on the left sought the (initially reluctant) support of their
parties and, along with some other women's associations, helped to
persuade some of the newly democratic local authorities to offer
family planning as part of their health services provision (Parra 1986;
IM 1995a). By 1983, almost 200 reasonably priced independent
clinics were reportedly in existence, although their geographical
distribution made them unable to meet all the potential demand
(Threlfall 1996). Three years later the Ley General de Sanidad

(General Health Law) provided for state-funded family planning services. Today there are some 640 centres across Spain and the pill is available on prescription, while condoms and spermicides may be bought over the counter (IM 1995a).

Unsurprisingly, in this still largely Catholic country, precise details of contraceptive use are not easy to come by and current IM publications still use 1985 data. However, an influential study based on a 1990 government report found 88 per cent of 25-40 year olds in favour of contraception, while 51 per cent of all women (compared with 60 per cent of all men) reported having used it at some time. Support was strongest among 'modern' groups: the young, those who worked, who were on the left of the political spectrum, or those with higher educational levels (Alberdi et al. 1994). Even among Catholic respondents support stood at 74 per cent overall, compared with 59 per cent on the (less pragmatic) political right. The condom was the preferred contraceptive method of almost half of the under 40 year olds surveyed, partly as a result of AIDS awareness campaigns. Next in popularity was the pill, used by over 47 per cent of 26-40 year olds and particularly married, middle- or upper middle-class respondents with a more modern profile. Under 18 per cent of respondents reported using the withdrawal method, while other contraceptive forms – including, in descending order, the rhythm method, IUDs, diaphragms, and contraceptive injections – were used by between 8 and 1.2 per cent of the sample (Alberdi et al. 1994).

Much more controversial than birth control has been the issue of abortion rights. Despite the 1941 ban on abortion it remained a fairly common method of birth control throughout the Franco years. In 1941 the official abortion total was 16,605 (3.3 per 100 live births) and this rose fairly steadily to 24,140 (3.7 per cent) in 1960, before falling back in 1970 (to 16,810, or 2.6 per cent) as alternatives became more readily available (Del Campo 1991). However, actual figures – including abortions resulting from extramarital relations, prostitution and, perhaps most commonly of all, among married women – were no doubt much higher. Under-reporting was encouraged by the fact that, until 1985, anyone deliberately inducing an abortion was liable to between 6 months and 12 years imprisonment. Health professionals carrying out an abortion were automatically given the maximum sentence, as well as being fined and struck off. And a woman who procured or consented to the abortion of her foetus was liable to between 6 months and 6 years imprisonment, regardless of any risks to herself or her foetus, or of whether she had been a victim of rape or incest. However, 'si el motivo del aborto ha sido ocultar su deshonra' (if the abortion was undertaken in order to hide her dishonour) the woman was liable to a reduced term of between one and six months (Pérez and Trallero 1983). From the early 1970s, however, women's activism did much to change the climate of opinion around abortion and, with the legalisation of abortion in Britain, Spanish women of means began to head for London at an estimated rate of 50,000 per year (IM 1995a). Meanwhile, those without means continued to risk imprisonment at home. In 1979, for example, 11 Bilbao women were prosecuted for abortions carried out between 1966 and 1976, although after mass protests 9 had their cases dismissed.

This situation changed in 1985, with the revision of Article 417 of the Criminal Code to allow abortion by or under the direction of a doctor, in a healthcare centre or establishment, and with the woman's consent, in the following circumstances:

- when necessary to avoid grave danger to the life or physical or mental health of the pregnant woman, with a supporting medical report from a specialist other than the one who will perform the abortion. (In 1992 this was extended to include women medically certified as suffering from clinical anxiety, in the first three months of pregnancy.) And in cases where the woman's life is at stake the medical report and consent may be dispensed with.
- when the pregnancy is the result of rape as defined under Article 429 of the Criminal Code, providing the abortion is carried out within the first 12 weeks of pregnancy and the crime is reported.
- when the foetus is presumed likely to be born with serious physical or mental defects, in which case the abortion is to be carried out within the first 22 weeks of gestation and a medical report is to be provided in advance of the abortion by two specialists (other than the one carrying out or overseeing the abortion), from an accredited healthcare centre or establishment. The pregnant woman is not liable to prosecution, however, even if the abortion is not carried out in an accredited healthcare centre or establishment or if the required medical reports have not been completed.

Limited and (at least initially) unsupported by increased facilities, the 1985 law did not stem the flow of women to London and other

European capitals. And while over 152,500 legal abortions were recorded between 1987 and 1991, public centres remain unable to meet escalating demand, with a reported 95 per cent of Madrid's abortions being arranged through private centres in 1992 (IM 1995a; Dirección General de la Mujer 1992). This growth reflects a certain softening of attitudes towards abortion – especially where the health of the mother is at risk – despite some polarisation each time Parliament considers broadening the existing law. Despite this, support for abortion on a 'women's right to choose' basis remains low and, partly for this reason, Spain retains one of the most restrictive abortion laws in the EU. The 1985 law was drafted in terms that made its operation dependent on the interpretations of medical staff – with the definition of grave danger proving particularly contentious – and its provisions alienated the Catholic hierarchy, most Spaniards on the right and a large section of the medical profession,[4] without satisfying feminists and other women's groups who demanded much broader rights (Threlfall 1996). It was with these broader rights in mind that, in June 1994, a bill was put before Congress which sought to establish a fourth category, making abortion available within twelve weeks of conception in cases where serious personal, family or social conflict was likely to result from the birth of the child, and subject to the pregnant woman being given counselling and information on the financial and other state assistance available to her were she to decide to go ahead with the birth. The bill failed (as it would in 1995 and, albeit more ambivalently, in 1996) because Catalan nationalists refused to support the PSOE government. It is likely to be some time before a further opportunity presents itself. And in the interim, the new political climate has reportedly been encouraging some judges to take a less sympathetic, if not openly hostile, attitude to the work of abortion centres (El País, 28 April 1996).

Changing attitudes to contraception and abortion are inextricable from the wider evolution of the family since the 1960s. Although there has never been a single, uniform Spanish family model, the extended household predominated throughout the Franco years and persists particularly in northern rural areas, largely as a result of the prevailing inheritance system (Centre d'Estudis Demogràfics 1990). This arrangement offers women more opportunities to share domestic responsibilities, while ensuring there are more to share. Throughout the development years, however, more women began to embark on paid extradomestic work producing and, in time, buying the new consumer durables. With more money and labour-saving appliances, but less time, these women helped precipitate the displacement of the extended (productive/reproductive) family in favour of forms of nuclear consumer unit (Folguera 1993a). This process was particularly marked in more economically and demographically dynamic urban areas. Today both family models persist – although forms of nuclear family predominate – alongside a range of non-institutionalised households. In 1991, for example, although 64 per cent of families were of the two-generation nuclear type (parents plus one or more children), 16 per cent were couples without children (Durán 1993). The number of lone parent households headed by women is also rising: in 1989 it stood at around 237,500; three years later it was 243,100 (Durán 1993; IM 1995e). Over 40 per cent of these women are widows, most of whom live with adult children (IM 1995e; Alberdi 1996). A similar but growing proportion is separated or divorced. Usually with the assistance of domestic help, some of these women are able to combine parenthood with satisfying well-paid work and a measure of autonomy. But the majority are more likely to be trapped in precarious and poorly-paid jobs by their need for paid employment to meet outgoings, by the difficulties of finding it in a contracting labour market and in the face of employer prejudice and, once found, by the stress of trying to reconcile it with childcare. Childcare in such cases usually consists of *ad hoc* arrangements with family and neighbours, some of whom will have their own work commitments to negotiate. A few women respond to these conflicting demands by working from home, a mode of working effectively unregulated by law, which usually involves piecework and (combined with domestic responsibilities) ensures that women are never off duty. Many more fall back on their family, however, while an estimated one-third rely mainly on state welfare payments – and in a culture without a strong welfare tradition, this can compound their problems by making them the target of local resentment.

The growth of one-parent families is a Europe-wide phenomenon. Rather less common is the tendency of young Spaniards to live in the family home to a relatively late age. Despite a move towards earlier marriage in the development years, this pattern was reasserting itself by the late 1970s (De Miguel 1993). Encouraged by a combination of longer studies, the unavailability and high cost of housing, and high unemployment a reported 71 per cent of men and 50 per cent of women in the 25-29 age group are currently living with their parents or other relatives (Iglesias de Ussel 1994; Delgado 1996). Under these circumstances high levels of domestic tension and dissatisfaction might seem inevitable. In practice, however, these more concentrated family units have helped to promote high levels of tolerance and closer affective and support links between many young people and their parents, particularly among the middle and upper classes (Iglesias de Ussel 1994). Thus, while intergenerational conflict persists (particularly where compounded by economic and other material problems), surveys consistently indicate that 'la aplastante mayoría [...] identifican vida familiar con satisfacción' (the overwhelming majority [...] find satisfaction in family life) (Durán 1993: 29). And in this respect the family rates way above all other social or political instititutions. The fact that satisfaction levels are particularly high where mothers are concerned highlights their often more compatible values, and the extent to which tensions between the discourse of women's subordination and the wider social acceptance of sexual equality are more easily negotiated by the young.

During the 1960s and early 1970s married women had tended to begin work after having children. Today northern Spanish and urban women in particular are more likely to delay childbearing until their 30s, as they seek to establish themselves in their profession or support partners who are finishing studies (Alberdi 1996). And when they do have children, they are more likely to continue working. This is eased by a relatively generous 16 weeks of maternity leave (18 weeks in the case of multiple births), some of which can, if desired, be taken as paternity leave. The leave-taker is entitled to three years of job protection, with the original post being kept open for one year, and an equivalent offered thereafter. Women in the informal sector do not enjoy these rights, however, while women in formal but precarious work are unlikely to exercise them. Partly because of the persistence of traditional extended family networks, and partly for reasons of cost, state-funded childcare has been given low priority in Spain. As Monica Threlfall notes, this is despite the fact that traditional school-hours (9-12, 3-5) do not fit easily around Spanish family patterns and are difficult to combine with even part-time work (Threlfall 1996). In all but the best-paid jobs, the cost of private childcare means that returning to work is linked less to economic necessity than to a desire for the relative independence, social contacts and acceptance that work – when it is supported by the family – can bring. Part-time jobs tend to be rare at senior levels (which is precisely where more women might want to retain jobs) and job-share arrangements are virtually unknown in Spain. A speech by Felipe González in January 1996 advocating job-sharing as a way of tackling unemployment was greeted with scepticism by both employer and worker representatives.

Women who manage to overcome all of these obstacles in order to combine paid employment and motherhood are liable to find themselves caught up in conflicting time patterns. Extradomestic work tends to generate fast and more immediate demands for shorter periods, while motherhood has a slower, more rhythmic but more unrelenting pace. Like the need to retrain or update skills, this conflict increases the stress levels of many working women. In some cases, the experience of negotiating competing demands enables women to outperform their male counterparts. In other cases, stresses associated with childcare and other domestic commitments can affect the concentration, performance and availability of the women involved and help to fuel employer prejudice (Paz Benito 1993). Small wonder in these circumstances that more women are going as far as they can in their chosen career before having children.

Among the predominantly urban and middle-class groups where childrearing is tending to be deferred, marriage too has come to seem less pressing. In 1980 women's average age on marrying began to rise, and by 1991 it stood at 25.99, while (at 5.5 per cent of the population per annum) Spain's marriage rate is currently one of the lowest in Europe (Alberdi 1996; Threlfall 1996). At the same time the move away from a predominantly traditional model to a 'legal-rational' family unit has opened the way for greater diversity in family models and values (Alberdi 1996). And along with increasing secularisation, the general availability of contraception and increased state welfare and educational provision, this has made young people more likely than ever before to form (relatively) stable unmarried couples ('parejas de hecho') when they eventually leave home. In addition, a small but increasing number are adopting what has been called 'la versión hispánica de los LAT' (the Hispanic version of LATs) (Alberdi et al. 1994: 148). 'LATs' is a US term for individuals who 'live apart together', in the sense that they maintain a stable relationship with a partner without setting up a shared home. Although US-style LATs do exist, Spaniards' disinclination to live alone – under 10 per cent of the population were doing so in 1994 (Ministerio de la Presidencia 1995) – and greater tolerance within the family have led to a more common 'Hispanic' version, in which one or both partners continue to live in the parental home. This is particularly common where the mother does not work and is prepared to attend to the needs of her (usually male) adult offspring.[5] The marked trend towards cohabitation and widespread acceptance of premarital sex, especially among the young and the more educated, underline the growing separation of sex from procreation. Since most cohabiting couples marry before starting a family this trend has not contributed significantly to the recent spectacular increase in Spain's extramarital birth-rate – which at around 11 per cent is still less than half that of the UK. The fact that much of this increase has been among adolescents has given rise to some concern, however, prompting official research into its causes, awareness training programmes for health professionals, and sex education and pregnancy prevention measures in schools (Martín Barroso 1992; IM 1993a).

Today, Spaniards who do marry are increasingly likely to divorce. Legalised in 1932 under the Second Republic, divorce was effectively banned when marriage became subject to canon law (and thus indissoluble) under Franco in 1938. Although the 1978 Constitution permitted both civil and church marriage, divorce did not finally become legal until three years later. Owing to pent-up demand over 21,000 took place in the first full year after reintroduction, and in 1995 (after some fluctuation) the figure stood at 33,000 (Ramírez 1996a). Separations consistently and increasingly exceed divorces – in 1991, for example, there were 29,000 divorces and 39,000 separations – reflecting a preference for judicial separation among the middle and upper classes, partly for financial reasons (IM 1994d). The separation is the first stage in a contested divorce; it can be applied for a year after the marriage has taken place. Provided satisfactory arrangements are made for any children and the disposal of the home and other assets, divorce can follow a year later.[6] Judges have tended to award custody of children – and often the family home with it – to mothers, but this is increasingly being contested by husbands with the support of some less progressive judges (Ramírez 1996a). The fact that separation is normally sought by women, in anticipation of a more independent life for themselves and their family, partly reflects the erosion of women's affective and economic dependency on men over the last 20 years, and where there is a measure of financial security, stable and independent households can result. But maintenance arrangements are difficult to enforce and state financial support is limited, so if an ex-partner defaults divorce can mean a significant drop in income and security, and increased dependence on the extended family. As Monica Threlfall has noted, particularly outside of urban areas separation and divorce are also taken to imply a fall in social status, encouraging more traditional couples (who are often older and less likely to remarry) to lead separate lives in the same house (Threlfall 1996).

Despite the gradual politico-juridical recognition in Spain of the Europe-wide trend towards non-traditional households, it can be difficult to communicate with the Spanish state except as a member of a family. This has encouraged representatives of lesbian, gay and other non-traditional couples to demand family status for legal and economic reasons (including pension and inheritance rights) as well as for reasons of affection and intimacy (Sánchez Rodríguez 1995). Although it could be argued that this reinforces the claims of family models that many of these groups would reject, their actions have already precipitated a substantive extension of asylum, habeas corpus and (particularly at local level) adoption law (Martínez 1992). At the time of writing inheritance and pension rights remain under review, although their liberalisation is unlikely to be a priority of the new government.

Most of the tensions arising from the so-called crisis of the family can be traced to the fact that the existing social contract is still in the process of adapting to these new relations, and to the enlarged sense of equality and justice (particularly among women under 40 and the young) that they tend to invoke. As recently as the early 1980s over a quarter of women felt that a woman's first duty was to tend her family: by the early 1990s the figure was negligible (De Miguel 1993). But if traditional beliefs promoted by Church and state under Franco are losing their force, new ones can claim no equivalent source of legitimation. The resulting 'value disorientation' has been linked to signs of a return to more traditional positions, especially among some young people. Those in the 18-24 age group are, reportedly, increasingly likely to express a preference for a full church wedding, for example, or to identify themselves as Catholics, albeit 'no practicantes' (non-practising) (De Miguel 1993, 1994). Among younger women, this general disorientation is compounded by the fact that education currently prepares them for paid work more efficiently than the Mediterranean tradition of sex segregation prepares men for unpaid domestic labour. While married women are generally younger and have a lower educational level than their husbands, women who cohabit are increasingly likely to have a higher educational level than their partner and to be closer in age (Alberdi *et al.* 1994). Like the decision to cohabit rather than marry, this may reflect women's desire to have a stronger negotiating position where the distribution of roles and other decisions are concerned. This may be paying off: survey data suggest growing support for a more equitable distribution of domestic responsibilities, and a gradual redefinition of domestic roles, particularly among women and more 'modern', childless couples (De Miguel 1994; Alberdi 1996). But as with all opinion surveys this support is not necessarily reflected in practice. When children arrive, for example, there is a marked tendency to revert to more traditional roles, and overall the enormous majority of routine domestic responsibilities – an estimated six and a half hours per day – continues to devolve to women (IM 1995e). Partly for this reason, the wages for housework debate continues (Montañés Serrano *et al.* 1994). Meanwhile, the IM – presumably believing that it is easier to change consciousness than to boost welfare funding – continues to press for a sustained, equitable distribution of responsibilities between the partners (IM 1993a, 1995e).

Issues like domestic parity are the concerns, primarily, of 'modern' groups. Away from the urban centres, however, many women negotiate domestic and productive responsibilities in accordance with different priorities and in very different contexts. But even in rural areas factors such as European integration and improved communications are helping to accelerate social change. For many older women in particular the effects have been largely negative. EU agricultural policies are affecting the profits (and thus the status) of what are still predominantly family farms, for example. New technology – the most valued part of the modernisation process – is largely reserved for men, while the low esteem which tends to result from their internalisation of secondary 'helper' roles discourages women from seeking opportunities to retrain for new socio-economic conditions (Principado de Asturias 1995). Their daughters, meanwhile, are looking further afield, seeking work in the subsidised light industrial and other units being established in areas of high rural unemployment, or competing with their urban counterparts for salaried posts in the professions and technology (Mazariegas *et al.* 1993). In Andalucía, for example, they are the beneficiaries of new high-technology forms of agricultural production, in particular of flowers for export. And in between they continue to substitute for men in informal seasonal labour pools, to carry out their low status and usually unpaid responsibilities on the family smallholding, in the home and, in some cases, in the greenhouses of their future partner.

These young women are negotiating rapidly changing situations with a combination of traditional and newer responses, and in the process they are modifying the context for future changes. But there are many other Spanish women who, for a variety of reasons, are at best marginal to this process. These are the focus of chapter 4.

Notes

1 The growing interest in social volunteers is a sign of this imbrication, at a time when labour-market restructuring is forcing many young people into enforced idleness and many older ones into premature retirement, and when the desire to express social solidarity (especially among the young) is increasingly in evidence. Within the Community of Madrid the use of volunteers to supplement welfare provision has been actively encouraged since the early 1980s, and most recently in its 1994 'Ley del voluntariado social' (Social volunteers law), which seeks to regulate the use and protect the rights of volunteers while discouraging their use as substitutes for paid employees or to undermine working conditions. However, critics of the strategic development of the volunteer sector are sceptical as to how the deliberate or incidental exploitation of volunteers might be prevented in practice.

2 Some of the most important of these laws related to workers with family responsibilities (1985), equality of social security provision (1986), and equal treatment – including maternity rights – for self-employed workers (1986) (IM 1995a). A number incorporated European (or wider international) rulings into Spanish law, such as the EU's Community Action Programmes for Equality of Opportunities.

3 Despite this ban contraception was practised throughout the Franco years, as reflected in the decline in family size between 1930 (when 38% of married women had more than four children) and 1970 (when this figure had fallen to 17%) (Parra 1986; Longhurst 1991). In 1963, 82% of doctors reportedly believed their patients were using some form of birth control and in only 34% of cases was this thought to be the withdrawal method (Del Campo 1991). In the late 1960s, half a million women were reportedly using the pill as a treatment for hormonal disorders; by 1979 this had risen to one million and a year later to 1.3 million, indicating rapid growth at a time when northern European women were tending to move away from chemical-hormonal contraception (Parra 1986; Longhurst 1991).

4 A significant number of doctors in the public sphere remain reluctant to perform abortions, either for reasons of conscience or because they fear recriminations among colleagues. Madrid's biggest hospital actually ceased to carry out abortions in 1989, and a second followed suit two years later (Dirección General de la Mujer 1992).

5 The more traditional worldview of many women in their late 40s or above means that daughters of older mothers can expect sometimes onerous domestic responsibilities – possibly including the servicing of brothers – and are thus better equipped, and often more inclined, to leave home earlier.

6 Practising Catholics are obliged to sign a confession in order to finalise their divorce, and to seek an annulment before remarrying (Pujol Algans 1992).

4 Towards the margins

D ESCRIBING A PROSTITUTE or an illegal immigrant as marginal implies no stable or essential relation to other, supposedly more 'central', women. The meaning of the term 'marginal', like that of 'modern' or 'traditional', varies with context. Despite a disturbing tendency in the media and elsewhere to represent advancing age in pathological terms or as parasitic on younger taxpayers, for example, a healthy 70 year old surrounded by her extended family is not in any simple sense marginal. On the other hand, some of Spain's most profoundly isolated individuals are elderly women who live alone and in poverty. This chapter focuses on women who, for a variety of reasons, experience more systematic social exclusion: abused women, gypsies, illegal immigrants, drug users and prostitutes. It concludes with a discussion of one of the least visible of all Spain's marginalised groups, lesbian women.

Cases of systematic or arbitrary violence against women raise important general questions about gender relations. In Spain, as elsewhere in the EU, cases of sexual violence have increased significantly in recent years. The number of 'delitos contra la libertad sexual' – offences against sexual liberty, which include rape, sexual assault, incest and corruption of minors, the targets of which are overwhelmingly female – has risen from 5,435 in 1990 to 6,344 in 1994, to form 0.7 per cent of all reported crime (El Mundo 1993; El País 1996). In 1994, more than 40 per cent of these involved sexual assault and over a quarter rape, despite the fact that rape is generally held to be one of the most under-reported of all crimes (El País 1996).[1] In the Franco years this under-reporting had less to do with the influence of the Catholic Church – which was more concerned with suppressing women's sexuality than men's – than with the fact that women tended to see rape as a source of humiliation and shame. Especially for girls with little education or confidence, reporting a rape to often unsupportive authorities was complicated and traumatic, obtaining sufficient proof of innocence to satisfy the authorities was difficult, and the consequences tended to be far more negative for the accuser than the accused. Despite a trend towards greater concern and support for women who have been raped – partly because rape is more likely today to be indiscriminate, to affect all social classes, and to surface more often in the public domain (Roig 1994) – these attitudes persist in certain sectors of the population, and particularly among some older, rural Spaniards.

Definitions of domestic abuse also tend to be narrower, and tolerance of it consistently higher, among these groups and among the already disadvantaged (CIS 1991; Haimovitch 1990). Like rape, domestic abuse is not a new phenomenon but it was rarely discussed before feminists began to open up the private sphere in the 1970s, and tolerance of it tends to be lowest among younger urban women exposed to feminist arguments and educated in a more egalitarian climate (Foessa 1994). This parallels, and is reinforced by, a broad reduction in the gap between the attitudes and values of younger men and women, making them less likely to disagree fundamentally (and potentially violently) on key issues than their parents. Given the speed with which attitudes to domestic violence appear to be changing, the number of women who report abuse has crept up very slowly indeed since statistics were first collected in 1984, from around 14,000 to just over 15,000 cases per year (Foessa 1994; IM 1995e). As with rape, however, there appears to be substantial under-reporting. Until a crisis occurs, neighbours and families can be completely unaware of a tyranny that has lasted for years. Among older women, reasons for this under-reporting are not hard to find: those who have never worked outside of the home, have no independent source of income, anticipate little in the way of social security and pension rights, and stand to lose family, friends and social status if their marriage breaks up are liable to place considerable stress on its survival. Few women risk publicising what they consider private problems and, except in extreme cases, public condemnation may be muted, even among friends and neighbours. To call in the police is to risk humiliating themselves and their partners, in the process losing household income on a fine, and possibly losing the partner. Moreover, some women expose themselves to all of these risks only to find the courts reluctant to apply the existing sanctions (Gutiérrez 1990).

One factor in the persistence of reported abuse, even as tolerance of it appears to decline, may be the growth of the nuclear family.

This has increased opportunities for intimacy and intensity of effect, but it has none of the shock-absorbing capacity of the extended family. Instead it can act as a sponge, absorbing and refracting tensions generated elsewhere – by job insecurity, for example, or money problems. When a man who has lost his job comes home and hits his wife, he is discharging externally-produced tension in a way that does not directly unsettle the social order. To this extent, domestic violence aids the smoother functioning of that order, but only where the presumption exists that women are available to men for this purpose. Particularly where older and less educated women are concerned, this presumption is sustained by a tradition of self-abnegation which prevents many from recognising their own needs, desires and frustrations when an opportunity arrives to express them. Younger, 'modern', men and women are reportedly less subject to this type of tension, and more likely to see a clear correlation between violence and inequality – in principle at least (Foessa 1994). But women may be on the fault-line of these changes. Caught up in new work-related stresses for which they have as yet no socially-legitimated outlet, which are often compounded by the demands of the double shift, and in return for which they are likely to receive less money and fewer promotion opportunities than male counterparts, some express their tensions in depression and a loss of self-esteem (Haimovich 1990). And in such circumstances, even random aggression may be experienced as retributive.

The work of feminist and other campaigners has been instrumental in changing (men's and women's) attitudes towards domestic and sexual violence. In addition the IM has sponsored Criminal Code reforms under which inflicting regular physical violence on a partner, child or dependent minor is punishable by between one and six months' imprisonment. No legal definition of abuse or regularity was included, however (making it difficult to apply in practice), and neither were mental or emotional cruelty. Other IM-sponsored measures have sought to standardise reporting, police investigation, and detention procedures in assault cases, and women's treatment in refuges. The unsympathetic treatment reported by some women when filing charges of abuse and sexual violence at police stations has been addressed with the introduction of specially-trained women officers in central locations. Despite the small number of women officers nationally these arrangements are now largely in place. Spain had 51 women's refuges in 1993: three-quarters of them public,

mostly run by local government; the remainder administered by
private bodies, including charities and NGOs (IM 1995e). Virtually
all are day centres, however, and where overnight accommodation is
offered it is only the minimum of time required to resolve the most
pressing social, financial and legal problems of the women concerned
(IM 1995e).

Violence associated with racism has, until recently, been quite rare
in modern Spain: because of its historic emigration patterns, its
inhabitants' much-vaunted tolerance and, especially, immigration
levels which – though rising – are still only one-sixth of the EU
average (Landaburu 1996). Since the late 1980s, however, the
opening of borders, the greater visibility of immigrants in metropolitan centres, job insecurity and record unemployment have
contributed to an increase in racist attacks, some of them by
organised skinhead and other groups (Adán Revilla 1995). Most
Spaniards, especially young people, continue to advocate the integration rather than the repatriation of immigrants, however, and at
community level pro-tolerance groups are proliferating (De Miguel
1994).[2] Nationally, and in line with EU policy, the socialist
government responded in 1994 with the Plan de Integración Social
de los Inmigrantes (Social Integration Programme for Immigrants)
which sets out a framework for all local, regional and national
government measures. Broadly, this seeks to balance tighter controls
against illegal entry with measures to combat the social exclusion of
legal immigrants. And at a time of growing national and European
regionalism its focus is on citizenship rather than nationality. In
1992, the 40,150 immigrant women with work permits made up
over 40 per cent of these legal immigrants, of whom almost half
came from Latin America, a quarter from Africa, and most of the
remainder from Asia (IM 1994d). Regardless of their educational and
employment backgrounds, many of these are employed in domestic
service. This is easier to find than the rural and construction jobs
traditionally taken by male counterparts. Consequently, where men
have traditionally come first to find work and accommodation for
their families, women are now increasingly leading the way.

Since 1992, the influx of women from the Dominican Republic
has made them one of the highest female immigrant populations in
Spain (Camacho 1995). Almost all are based in Madrid or Barcelona,
where they tend to work as live-in servants, in elderly care, cleaning,
or (particularly in the case of illegal entrants) as prostitutes. The jobs

are invariably casual and precarious, and workers have minimal support in law. Employers are often professional women unable to cope alone with a double shift, and may treat their 'asistentas' (cleaners or domestic help) with consideration. But domestic workers are often poorly paid and have low social status. In the case of sex workers – and particularly illegal immigrants forced into prostitution – there are the added risks of violence and intimidation. Separated as they are from their community, family and children Dominican women have established informal support networks that help new-comers to find employment relatively quickly while tending to steer them (at least initially) into the existing, extremely limited range of jobs. These groups are maintained through regular contact, and in the capital this has focused around the Aravaca quarter where some of Spain's first Dominican workers settled. By 1991, however, as numbers grew so too did tension with local residents. This resulted in a heavy-handed police clamp-down on women thought to have entered Spain illegally, which came to a head in 1992 with the death of a Dominican woman at the hands of a civil guard and three local youths. The ensuing media-led outcry opened the way for more concerted attempts at dialogue. But four years on, although support networks continue to grow and some Dominican women are now establishing small hairdressing or restaurant businesses, low-level tensions with neighbourhood groups persist. However, if social services proposals to grant legal status to women immigrants independent of their partners become law, future immigrants should see a significant improvement in their personal autonomy and – where desired – in opportunities for integration.

The difficulties associated with integration – adapting to unfam-iliar values and symbols, different types of work, new customs and lifestyles, and participating in new institutions – are not exclusive to women from other countries: they may affect Spanish women moving from rural to urban environments, for example (Solé 1994). But where women from different ethnic groups are concerned, the tension between a desire to maintain their existing cultural values and the need to adapt to those of the host environment can add significantly to stress levels. This is particularly true where gypsies, Spain's most significant minority group, are concerned. Although the romanticised gypsy-artist is in vogue in Spain and in Europe at present, the flesh and blood variety remains as ambiguous a figure as ever.[3] Thus, most Spaniards 'consideran racista el trato a los gitanos,

pero no los quieren cerca de sus casas' (believe gypsies are the object
of racist treatment, but do not want them as neighbours (De Miguel
1993: 480)) The recent history of this uneasy relation can be traced
back to the economic crisis of the late 1970s and early 1980s, which
saw many gypsies displaced from the labour force: first, by disadvantaged working-class 'payos' (non-gypsies), who were compelled by
necessity to take up fringe activities traditionally favoured by gypsies
– street vending, rag collecting, begging – previously seen as
unacceptable; second, by the growing number of women seeking
casual and part-time work outside of the home, particularly in the
agricultural sector in which a significant number of gypsies (women
and men) had traditionally found seasonal work. At the same time,
items traditionally hand-made by gypsy women – baskets, for
example, and floral decorations – were displaced by cheaper mass-
produced versions (Fernández 1994). The erosion of their culturally-
recognised occupations affected younger gypsies in particular and
over the next two decades this displacement would produce 'un
cambio vertiginoso' (a dizzying transformation) in poorer gypsy
communities (San Román 1986: 236). Gypsies' nomadic culture and
the weight given to transmitting their communities' own cultural
values have meant that formal education has not been prioritised,
with elders in particular tending to discourage what they see as an
induction into non-gypsy culture. In 1993, for example, only 36 per
cent had completed EGB while the figure for girls has tended to be
significantly lower, largely because mothers – who rarely have
formal education themselves and tend to see little need for it –
assume that daughters will give priority to looking after younger
siblings or doing paid work as it becomes available (Giménez 1994;
Fernández 1992). Those who do attend report feeling alienated by
the cool or hostile reception received from some teachers and
parents, the absence or marginalisation of their culture in school
textbooks, and uneasy relationships with other pupils (Fernández
1994). Irregular attendance may also be compounded by poor
health. In 1993, over 70 per cent of the gypsy population lived in
extremely poor conditions, and many continue to suffer the
malnutrition and general health problems associated with extreme
poverty (Giménez 1994). This tends to be aggravated by the fact that
few are familiar with the workings of the national healthcare system
or prioritise key preventive measures such as vaccination, birth
control and personal hygiene. And conversely, health professionals'

own unfamiliarity with gypsy lifestyles can hamper diagnosis and treatment. In 1985 a gypsy's life expectancy hovered around 50, compared with well over 70 for the population as a whole (San Román 1986; IM 1994d).

Factors like these have hardened prejudice against gypsies among some groups, making work still more difficult to come by. In this context, and analogously with alienated non-gypsy males, some young gypsies have turned to crime: to drug dealing, for example, and other crimes organised by 'payo' or gypsy gangs. One effect of rising levels of criminality has been to trigger more police interventions in gypsy communities, often leading to accusations of harassment and institutionalised racism (Fernández 1994). And these may be compounded by the inability of much of the Judiciary to acknowledge the particularities of gypsy culture (Giménez 1994). Many younger gypsies are increasingly disinclined to submit to the will of the extended patriarchal family or 'rai', reducing their investment in the distinctiveness of the community and weakening any subsequent claim on their part to its accumulated cultural capital. Partly as a result traditions are losing their hold, becoming increasingly hybridised, and can no longer claim to encapsulate or symbolise the difference of the gypsy from the non-gypsy population, or to act as a ground for gypsy identity in accordance with traditionally-sanctioned formulae.

It is in this context that some gypsy women are seeking to adapt the traditionally rigid gender roles within the community to new conditions, while preserving the cultural framework that sustains them. Although the role of women varies according to the clan – and in more conservative clans they are not allowed to leave the home – they are, traditionally, always subordinate to men. As one gypsy writer unambiguously puts it: '[d]e pequeña obedece a su padre; de jovencita obedece as su padre y a sus hermanos; una vez casada, obedece a su marido; y ya vieja, obedece a sus hijos' (when she is small she obeys her father; as a young girl, she obeys her father and her brothers; once she is married she obeys her husband; and when she grows old she obeys her sons (Mateo Maximoff, cited Asociación de Mujeres Gitanas ROMI 1994: 51)). Her traditional role is restricted almost exclusively to domestic activities, while sons are taught that a man comes into the home and sits down (Fernández 1994). As the traditional repository of a community's cultural capital and transmitter of its values, girls enjoy far less liberty than their brothers. This is linked to the investment of the 'rai' in the virginity of its female members. The honour of the clan rests on its successful verification, immediately before the marriage ceremony, in the 'prueba del pañuelo' (handkerchief test), which is traditionally administered by a group of married women (Ardèvol 1986: 102). Opportunities to lose one's virginity in advance of the test are significantly reduced by the fact that girls are deemed women from the onset of menstruation, and typically marry at 15 or 16. The wedding itself, a ritualised clan event, is seen as 'la antecámara de la maternidad' (the anteroom of maternity) (Presencia Gitana Equipo de Estudios 1990: 48). The pressure to produce children is offset to some extent by the enhanced status it confers within the 'rai'. But this status is only in relation to other women. Although a male child further enhances her status, she becomes subordinate to him when he reaches his majority. In the meantime, gypsy law entitles a man to strike his wife 'por una causa justa, o una causa grave' (with just or serious cause), including non-compliance (Fernández 1994: 29). A woman can leave her husband – subject to the approval of the community – if this licence is abused and divorce may also be possible, particularly if there are no children (Ardèvol 1986). In practice, however, many women tolerate what non-gypsies would consider high levels of abuse, either because they hold strongly to the community view that marriages are lifelong, or because a failed marriage means loss of status within the clan.

In addition to their domestic responsibilities – and depending on the openness or otherwise of the 'rai' elders – young gypsy women are increasingly likely to undertake some work outside their community. Throughout the 1970s and 1980s, their usually poor educational levels helped to ensure that very few sought or obtained salaried jobs. Despite improving qualifications – including a small number attending university – salaried workers remain a tiny minority, partly as a result of employer prejudice. At the same time, the changing labour market and the banning of most forms of street vending have removed virtually all of the opportunities traditionally available to their mothers. With old avenues closing and newer ones slow to open, gypsy girls are being forced to compete with immigrant labour for casual domestic work, and in 1994 the majority were reportedly employed as cleaners (Fernández 1994).

In the late 1970s, when feminism was at its height in Spain, a small number of gypsy women had begun to reject some of the more repressive aspects of their treatment in the community, first verbally, then by working to defer marriage – and, in a very few cases, by marrying non-gypsy men. What this group was rejecting was not the community's cultural norms so much as their abuse (Ardèvol 1986). Like 'payo' feminism this tendency had lost momentum by the mid-1980s, but by 1990 a renewal of concerns led to the establishment of the Asociación de Mujeres Gitanas ROMI (ROMI Association for Gypsy Women). This seeks to improve educational levels by raising awareness among mothers, first, of the value of sending daughters to school and, second, of preventive and other measures designed to improve general levels of health. Help in this task has come in the form of funding under the national Programa de Desarollo Gitano (Gypsy Development Programme), as well as support from gypsy and non-gypsy volunteers and other organisations (Asociación de Mujeres Gitanas ROMI 1994). In pursuit of these aims it targeted what was, in 1990, a total absence of women in gypsy decision-making bodies; four years later, most major federations reportedly had women on their executives (Fernández 1994).

ROMI is a women's organisation and not a feminist one, and describes itself as a pressure group oriented towards adapting gypsy culture from within in order to ensure its survival (Fernández 1992). It owes its continued existence to the fact that it is not perceived as a threat to gypsy culture. But threat it is, and arguably a necessary one. The group developed at least partly because there was a demand for it and, to that extent, its existence has provided a safety valve for pressure from (particularly younger) women increasingly aware of the gap between their own expectations and those of non-gypsy counterparts. Yet, if the recent 'payo' experience is any indication, the increased educational and employment opportunities ROMI demands, if secured, are likely to stimulate further demands and further changes in women's role in the gypsy community. It is difficult to see how the profoundly patriarchal structure of traditional gypsy culture could withstand such changes.

As noted, Spain's uneasy relation with its largest ethnic group has a long history. One social group that has gained a high and controversial profile over a much shorter period is hard drug users and drug dealers.[4] Despite penalties targeting suppliers, by the second half of the 1980s and early 1990s the growth in trafficking, the concentration of street dealers and customers in certain inner-city neighbourhoods, and the apparent inability of the police to prevent it, was prompting some residents to take the law into their own hands. A number of the larger cities saw demonstrations and some violent clashes, vigilante-style 'patrullas urbanas' (urban patrols) sought out dealers while, in their shadow, routine low-level aggression was turned on the more vulnerable heroin-addicts and AIDS sufferers. Since then measures introduced under the Programa Nacional de la Droga (National Drugs Programme) have reduced levels of neighbourhood conflict, by driving a proportion of hard drug users and traffickers indoors and incarcerating others. Despite this, in 1995 the number of drugs-related detentions exceeded 25,000 for the first time (El País 1996).

In 1993, over 40 per cent of Spaniards regularly drank alcohol, a third habitually smoked cigarettes, 16 per cent smoked cannabis, around 4 per cent used cocaine, 2 per cent Ecstasy and other synthetic drugs, and 0.7 per cent heroin (El País, 16 October 1994). Since then, alcohol and tobacco consumption trends among the young (and particularly among women) have given rise to increasing concern; cannabis consumption (highest among less affluent and less well-educated young people) has been boosted by a bumper 1995 harvest; the use of Ecstasy and other synthetic drugs has rocketed, especially among the young middle classes (Bayón 1996b); and although AIDS awareness campaigns have reduced intravenous heroin use, the age at which Spaniards take up the habit has continued to fall, with over half of new users reportedly starting before they are 18 (Ministerio de la Presidencia 1994; Bayón 1996a). Historically, women have been under-represented in statistics for (non-pharmaceutical) drug use, but this gap has narrowed in recent years. In particular, the growth in intravenous drug use has led to a dramatic rise in the number of women with AIDS. Spain registered its first AIDS case in 1981; by 1995 its total of 34,618 cases was the second highest in the EU (after France), and the ninth in the world (El País 1996). The enormous majority of these (over 22,250) are the result of intravenous drug use, and a further 607 cases in 1995 were of children who contracted AIDS via HIV positive mothers (El País 1996). Back in 1985 there were only 12 women registered as having AIDS (under 8 per cent of the national total): a decade later, this had rocketed to 6384 (almost a fifth of the total) (IM 1995e; El País 1996). Most at risk are young women between 20 and 29 (compared with 25-39 in men) and those in marginal situations (IM 1995e). At the end of 1994, for example, over 30 per cent of all women behind bars were reportedly addicted to drugs, 21 per cent shared syringes, and the same proportion were HIV positive (Main TVE news bulletin, 15 December 1994). But even sufferers who are not in marginal groups when they contract the illness may find themselves marginalised by social attitudes towards AIDS, including the trend among employers to demand AIDS tests of prospective employees, and by the difficulties of obtaining insurance cover in the event of a positive result.

Some of Spain's most vulnerable women fund their drugs habit with prostitution. And, as in the case of illegal immigrants, their vulnerability is linked to their ambiguous status. In theory, neither sex workers nor their clients are punishable under the Criminal Code, which focuses instead on pimps, procurers and others who profit from prostitution. In 1970, however, prostitutes became subject to the Ley de Peligrosidad y Rehabilitación Social (Social Menace and Rehabilitation Law) under which (following complaints from members of the public or the police) they could be sent to retraining centres, prohibited from living in or visiting designated areas, and placed under surveillance by the authorities. But this law is hated less for its anachronistic and authoritarian provisions – which have not been widely invoked in practice since the Transition – than for the way it has been used to justify routine harassment, and in some cases exploitation, of prostitutes by members of the police. Because of this ambiguous status, because definitions of prostitution vary, and because policy on prostitution has tended to be formulated by regional governments and implemented in town halls with little national co-ordination, there is no single authoritative estimate of the number of prostitutes in Spain – although a pioneering study in the late 1980s put the figure at around half a million (Fundación Solidaridad Democrática 1988).

In Spain, as elsewhere, governmental and non-governmental approaches to prostitution conform broadly to one or other of three overlapping tendencies: prohibitionist, abolitionist or regulatory. Generally speaking, prohibitionists seek the criminalisation of prostitutes, although they are usually much more ambivalent where clients are concerned. Supporters include many residents of neighbourhoods with large concentrations of prostitutes (although historically many such neighbourhoods were relatively conflict-free before the growth of higher-profile drugs-related prostitution) and some feminists, who advocate solidarity with women who work as prostitutes but an end to prostitution as an activity. Prohibitionists argue that entering prostitution is rarely a woman's free choice and that feminists should not attempt to dignify what is, in effect, an occupation designed to benefit 'chulos' (pimps), partners or fathers, and clients. Instead they advocate skills training, so women who want to leave prostitution have other options available to them, and health awareness training, so they can enjoy their current or their new occupation in good health. There are a number of such schemes in operation in various parts of Spain – particularly the big cities – some of which are funded by regional or local government, and others by voluntary prostitute support groups (Uribarri 1991; Roldán 1994). In practice, however, the most successful of these rehabilitation programmes tend to be supported mostly by older prostitutes, since younger women are likely to focus more on the short-term benefits of prostitution than on its uncongenial or high-risk nature. Nor are measures like training centres popular with residents. Even those who theoretically support prohibition tend to be concerned that high concentrations of (even retraining) prostitutes will alter the character of the locality and, in the case of businesses, affect trade and rents – a particularly sensitive issue for local authorities. As a result, prostitutes' ambiguous status can be compounded by political incoherence, when regional governments impose policies which local governments are unwilling to implement for fear of alienating residents.

By contrast, abolitionists reject the prohibition or regulation of prostitution, on the grounds that it is a matter of individual rights rather than public morality. This view has gained ground in recent years – as taboos around women's sexuality continue to break down and their status as autonomous moral agents is more widely recognised. It assumes, for example, that prostitution is a job like any other – not so different in nature from a loveless marriage or secretarial work (Puleo 1994) – and that selling sex is not a mark of the vendor's vice but the recognition of a common need. Although there has been little international agreement on attitudes to prostitution, some version of abolitionism is national policy in a number of Western European countries, including Spain (IM 1990b, 1992). One of its basic tenets is that the criminalisation of prostitution exposes women to harassment and risk, while their pimps are routinely tolerated, usually in return for payment (Puleo 1994). A study from the late 1980s notes that it was not uncommon for the police to demand free sex from women on their patch, while those who had been attacked by a client or whose pimps were violent or abusive could expect little or no official response (Fundación Solidaridad Democrática 1988). Meanwhile, women are made compliant not only by direct legal or physical threats but also by the fear of social rejection and of repercussions for and from family and friends should details of their activities be made public. This is particularly true for women who live and work in the same neighbourhood and can expect harassment even when they are not working.

Abolitionists are also fundamentally opposed to regulation, which they see as designed to protect clients and local residents rather than the women themselves. Some advocate equipping sex workers for other employment through job training – not, in this case, to make them give up an undesirable career, but against the time when age, health or other factors lead them to consider an alternative occupation. This is in line with their view that the negative aspects of prostitution derive from the conditions under which it is undertaken – its marginality, ambivalence and covertness – rather than the nature of the work or the workers themselves. On the positive side, they note that prostitution enables some women with little formal education and few prospects in the regular labour market access to goods and a quality of life otherwise unavailable to them. However, this is eaten into by special expenses such as private schooling so that their children do not have to be taunted by schoolfriends, for example, the cut taken by a pimp or (in the case of drug-dependent women) the charges of a supplier.

The third broad tendency advocates the regulation of prostitution. Earliest forms focused on the control of sexually-transmitted diseases, although more recently the link between the two seems more tenuous than that between prostitution and drugs (Comas 1991; Roldán 1994). The most conservative regulators seek the identification and monitoring of women working as prostitutes, with each being documented and subjected to regular health checks. But there are a significant number of feminist and other regulators who seek the normalisation of prostitutes as a way of enhancing their physical and legal protection and encouraging greater respect and tolerance. Advocates of regulation maintain that the best way to affirm solidarity with sex workers is to improve their living and working conditions, rather than leaving them unsupported and unprotected as would be the case, they argue, with prohibition or abolition. They seek a compromise between the need for at least a measure of regulation and prostitutes' own need autonomously to affirm their actions, insisting that prostitutes should decide what form of regulation they want rather than having regulations imposed on them paternalistically, maternalistically or repressively. They claim for women working as prostitutes the full rights of any other worker. At present it has some of the characteristics common to the informal sector – poor and precarious working conditions and no union or other rights – exacerbated in many cases by high personal risk. But while the deprived backgrounds of many prostitutes have made them less able and inclined to fight for improved conditions and legal rights, younger arrivals are tending to be more vocal. Their supporters note, for example, that the ban on profiting from a prostitute's earnings effectively prevents sex workers from setting up their own businesses. If their work had formal status, it is claimed, they would be able to gain a measure of independence and significantly improve their circumstances (Puleo 1994).

Most regulators see prostitution as a job like any other, and one that gives certain material advantages to women who would in many cases have otherwise had few. Unlike abolitionists, however, they tend not to celebrate or seek to dignify the work, focusing instead on factors which condition prostitutes' supposedly autonomous life choices. In particular, they point to the quasi-class system which enables some women to work in relatively congenial surroundings while others risk their lives and health nightly in inner-city backstreets. Regulation, they argue, can help to even out these inequities. In the late 1980s, the most visible and often most disadvantaged women were those who had been forced on to the streets by pimps, by family unemployment, debt or illness, by partners, by abusive relationships, or by unwanted pregnancies, and many were from rural backgrounds (Fundación Solidaridad Democrática 1988). Today, women who work the streets are more often than not from urban backgrounds, a significant proportion are drug dependent, many have run away from home, their educational level is often low, and there is an increasing number of very young prostitutes who are particularly vulnerable to exploitation (Ordaz 1996). Although some younger women prefer the relative autonomy of street work (particularly where no pimp or regular dealer is concerned) many are older; one journalist reportedly found a woman still working periodically at the age of 69 (Uribarri 1991). Some of these older women have moved on to the streets from safer work in clubs or bars which refuse to employ them after a certain age. Once on the streets, they are exposed to the elements and to the stares, ridicule and in some cases verbal abuse of passers-by. They also have minimal protection from violent, abusive or criminal clients, pimps or dealers. Socially marginal and, in some cases, functionally illiterate these women have historically been among the least accessible to AIDS information and other health campaigns. Although this has begun to change following the IM's national campaigns and specific regional and local government initiatives, their awareness and use of contraception methods often remains sketchy and haphazard (Roldán 1994). Although few are entitled to health insurance cover for themselves and their children, their marginal status entitles them to free state healthcare. However, the cavalier treatment experienced by some at the hands of public health workers has tended to encourage those who can afford it to spend their earnings on private healthcare. The cost of this care means that they have recourse to professional advice only when they need it, rather than on a preventive basis. And like all other sex workers, they are subject to a range of other, often competing, tensions: between the liberty and the perceived need to sell sex; between the role of mother and (sexual) provider; between providing sex for money to men in general and freely to a partner. Where this partner is also a pimp it tends to be either because her partner has encouraged or forced her into prostitution, or because the pimp has become her main source of non-competitive affection and protection (Comisión Antiagresiones de Madrid 1994; Puleo 1994). However, while a proportion of women steadfastly defend their pimps, the relationship can become increasingly exploitative – in some cases abusive and violent – to the point where the prostitute on whose earnings the pimp depends can come to see herself as the dependent one. But, as advocates of regulation point out, the role of the pimp is a result of prohibition, since even women who do not have pimps may need to seek protection in the face of harassment, especially if that harassment comes from police officers (Comisión Antiagresiones de Madrid 1994). At a time when younger people in particular are increasingly aware of the health risks of casual sex, the clients of street prostitutes tend to be older, sometimes pensioners, and charges are accordingly low (Uribarri 1991). But the economic climate that drove some of these women on to the streets is reducing not only their clientele but also the community support services available to them. Despite this, the high visibility of street prostitution means that work is still being done with carefully targeted resources, particularly in inner-city areas (Uribarri 1991; Comas 1991; Roldán 1994). For example, Bilbao's street prostitution was radically reduced at the beginning of the decade by the rehousing of women in particular need, although many subsequently carried on business from their new home through personal ads.

The greatest cause for concern among residents and authorities where street prostitution takes place is its growing association with drug abuse. Traditional sex workers tend to see the (often younger) drug-dependent newcomers as unfair competition and lament the 'falta de profesionalidad' (lack of professionalism) of those who bring down 'market rates' by selling their services too cheaply. The most desperate and reckless of them shoot-up in full view of passers-by, deterring traditional clients and attracting unwelcome attention from residents and police. They are also more likely to indulge, at a price, in practices that more traditional prostitutes would reject. This makes it difficult for other women to refuse these demands, and is leading to the institutionalisation in some places of practices once broadly considered taboo. Attitudes to hygiene and general health among drug-dependent prostitutes also tend to be more casual than among women who make a regular living out of street work. This involves risks not only for clients but also, as they circulate, to long-term prostitutes whose own hygiene precautions may be superficial but reflect the awareness that their livelihoods depend on reasonable health. In moments of desperation, drug-dependent prostitutes also tend to be more ready to rob or cheat clients. Since many work without the (however ambivalent) protection of a pimp, or with only the casual and irregular support of their dealer, police intervention is increasingly common and drives away some of the more conventional clients. At the same time, the climate of recklessness, low- (and sometimes higher-) level criminality, and the at times conspicuous presence of dealers is encouraging drug use in a growing number of (particularly younger) prostitutes. One study, conducted between 1988 and 1990, found 20 per cent of the central Madrid sex workers surveyed to be drug addicts, of whom half had never tried drugs before working as prostitutes (Comas 1991). In some cases – for example, where immigrants have been tricked or threatened into taking up prostitution – addiction may be actively encouraged by pimps who want to increase a woman's dependency. For all of these reasons, the introduction of drugs is changing the face of prostitution in Spain. Women who coexisted with residents have, since the late 1980s, become the focus of concern about public safety, compounded in the case of immigrant women with (implicit or explicit) xenophobia and racism.

Women who advertise sexual services with massage and similar treatments via the press or telephone usually enjoy a safer existence and higher status than street workers. So too do those who work in the relative safety of topless clubs, 'whiskerías', 'barras americanas', 'clubs de alterne' and other specialised clubs and pubs, particularly (but by no means exclusively) in larger cities. Although women hostesses are employed ostensibly to serve drinks and earn a proportion of the cost of drinks bought for them, many offer sexual services either in the establishment's own private rooms or off the premises. Although the percentage taken by club managers is notoriously high, the more enterprising and industrious of these hostesses can earn relatively large sums. Many are from less deprived backgrounds than their street counterparts, though they do not necessarily have a higher level of education. But club work too has its class system: at the top end are the high-profile and fashionable venues where workers usually retain a much higher proportion of their takings; at the bottom are dives staffed mainly by undocumented immigrant workers on exploitation wages. Largely because of high youth unemployment rates, the middle and higher categories are increasingly swollen by students working their way through university. Generally speaking, the less experienced a woman is, the higher the premium. Juvenile prostitution is a fast growing and – for the pimps and, increasingly, gangs that organise it – an exceptionally lucrative business (Ordaz 1996). But the highest prestige is usually reserved for 'chicas de compañía' (escort girls). These are employed by some hotels and specialist agencies to provide company and (usually, but not always) sexual services for wealthier businessmen. They tend to be young and fairly sophisticated, better educated, smartly dressed and – since many of their clients are foreign visitors – with foreign language skills.

Like the weakening of the taboo on women's sexual needs and desires, this diversity is making attitudes to the selling of sex and definitions of prostitution increasingly uncertain. Among those who can afford them, for example, the more expensive clubs and escort services are seen as a legitimate and highly desirable leisure outlet for hard-pressed executives. And – since one fantasy commonly played

out in these value-added combinations of hostessing and sexual
services is the idea that sex is an optional extra, freely provided by a
woman who finds her client attractive – in such circumstances the
client's self-esteem discourages him from thinking of his escort as a
prostitute. Such attraction may exist, of course. Even in the case of
street prostitution, some women do have long-standing relationships
with particular clients which may involve a measure of reciprocity.
However, some of the men who can afford to visit the (usually) safer
and more socially acceptable clubs or hostesses but choose instead to
frequent street prostitutes find the idea of women's free sexual choice
less appealing. In such cases, the more reckless and debased the
encounter the more pleasure it affords. And for those whose
excitement is derived largely from cruising around inner-city streets
and watching women at work the pleasure is even more resolutely
non-reciprocal.

Another way of indulging a taste for voyeuristic and non-
reciprocal sexual gratification – and one which has its etymological
roots in the study of prostitutes – is pornography. The connection is
not lost on those radical and independent feminists who see
prostitution and pornography as the two principal means by which
women's bodies are procured and exchanged within patriarchy.[5]
Their links with the sex market are also highlighted by some equality
feminists who reject pornography as an infringement of women's
rights as the equals of men (Puleo 1994). While a small number of
anti-pornographers demand regulation of all or specific types of
pornographic material, however, for historical reasons the great
majority do not. Under Franco, sex was officially restricted to procreation and allusions to it, however oblique, were strictly controlled.
Official censors ('retocadores') were charged with touching up press
photographs – reducing the size of film stars' busts, for example, or
painting vests on the naked chests of boxers – and advertising images
were also closely monitored (Hooper 1995). And while the
compulsory dubbing of all foreign films offered ample opportunities
for censorship through mistranslation, here too images were altered:
lingering kisses were cut, for example, and the bare midriff of
Tarzan's Jane was painted over (Labanyi 1995a). With so little
information in the public domain, and given the diffidence of fathers
and the reserve of many mothers during this period, even middle-
class boys were expected to seek out for themselves what they needed
to know about sex (Martín Gaite 1994). Those who could afford it

paid for initiation in the regime's 'casas de tolerancia' (quasi-legal brothels) or with clandestine street prostitutes who (since the private sphere was deemed the proper place for women) could expect considerably less tolerance than their brothel-based equivalents. Boys without money sought the favours of any working-class girl who could be prevailed upon, easing some of the most vulnerable into street prostitution alongside the many rural girls who had come to the city hoping to make their fortune, to rescue their family from debt, or to escape scandal. By contrast no thought of sex was allowed to sully the minds of middle-class girls. The chastest physical contact was discouraged; as late as 1959 the Bishops' Norms of Christian Decency counselled boy- and girlfriends of however long standing against walking arm in arm (Hooper 1995). In a way reminiscent of the official and unofficial surveillance that 'public' women could expect, respectable young ladies were monitored around the clock, brought to view their already narrow world from within a protective bubble so infrequently and imperfectly penetrated by concerns of the flesh that glimpses, when they came, provoked incomprehension or obscure anxieties. And no parental – and in particular maternal – effort was spared to maintain them in this state until responsibility for their moral well-being passed, on marriage, to their husbands.

But the bishops and the regime were unable to hold back social changes associated with the onset of rapid urbanisation, and growing contact with more liberal attitudes via films, television and tourism. By the early 1960s, holding hands and even chaste public kisses were tolerated in more advanced (usually urban) circles. A decade later hardcore pornography, mostly from Scandinavia, was fairly freely available. Around the same time a survey for current affairs magazine *Blanco y Negro* reported that 42 per cent of Spanish girls had lost their virginity by the age of 20 (Hooper 1995). Even allowing for substantial exaggeration this marks a signficant shift in attitudes, since these girls were giving what they thought was an appropriately modern response. The Franco years were not the period of suspended sexual animation that officially-tolerated discourses suggested, but there is no doubt that when they ended the pace of change accelerated dramatically in larger cities and, to a lesser extent, elsewhere. Although bikinis had been banned until 1964 – and remained a focus of official disapproval long after that, especially if Spanish girls rather than tourists sported them – by the late 1970s topless bathing had begun to take hold. In 1978, Spain's first (albeit short-lived) sex shop opened, and within a couple of years striptease shows and topless bars were becoming commonplace in larger cities (Hooper 1995). These were the 'destape' years, in which repressed social energies were 'uncorked' and nudity and non-procreative sexual practices were pushed jubilantly centre stage.

Three years later, the diagnosis of Spain's first AIDS case marked the beginning of a new phase. The 'destape' did not end overnight, however, and certain attitudes associated with it have persisted in Spanish culture alongside post-AIDS anxieties. One study of Salamanca University students, for example, notes that between 1977 and 1987 condom use more than tripled (to almost 60 per cent of sexually active students) while pill use halved (López 1990). But by 1987 full sexual relations were starting up to two years earlier (17, on average, for boys, 19 for girls), and the number of respondents reportedly experiencing them each week had risen from 7 per cent to over 19 per cent of the total. More recently, the 1992 national youth survey found that almost three-quarters of 15 to 19-year-old women respondents had reportedly never had full sexual relations, compared with half of men, and this fell to 22 per cent and 15 per cent respectively by the age of 29 (Instituto de la Juventud 1993). This may reflect a trend away from penetrative sex or towards abstinence in the post-AIDS era, or simply a larger and more varied sample than in the Salamanca University study. Particularly significant was the fact that fewer than 60 per cent of the sexually active used contraceptives, and of these almost three-quarters used the condom and a quarter the pill. Older respondents were more likely to use the pill, perhaps reflecting their more regular sexual activity. Of the 15-29 age group, almost 4 per cent admitted to having had an abortion, while over 60 per cent declared they had not. However, more than a third of the sample declined to reply.

In the late 1980s and early 1990s, some commentators voiced concern that young women's sexual liberation was outstripping their personal liberation, opening the way for an increased dependence on and exploitation by young men (Gil Calvo 1990). In particular María Jesús Miranda questioned whether, having abandoned the search for what she calls sex-love, women should simply adopt the sex-pleasure model with which most men identify – however much some men might desire it (Miranda 1987). More recently, however, the source of these concerns – the persistence of certain hedonistic 'destape'-type attitudes alongside more traditional machistic ones – has seen much of its force displaced by socio-economic, cultural and generational change. The youth survey mentioned earlier, for example, suggests that fidelity in a relationship now comes before sexual satisfaction for both women and men, while other values referred to also indicate a striking degree of consensus. Another indication, perhaps, that among young people – at least for the moment – some persistent asymmetries may be evening out.

The 'destape' period had been a heady time for many younger (and some older) Spaniards, but an uncomfortable one for those whose worldview had been formed during the postwar period, and the new Constitution sought to bridge this gap. Article 20 secured the right to free expression of ideas, thoughts and opinions denied to Spaniards under the regime. In particular, its declaration that 'el ejercicio de estos derechos no puede restringirse mediante ningún tipo de censura previa' (the exercise of these rights shall not be restricted through any form of prior censorship) provided the institutional basis for today's strongly anti-censorship culture (Tamames 1992). But at the same time the Constitution recognised the subordination of these rights to the rule of law and especially the rights of all individuals 'al honor, a la intimidad, [y] a la propia imagen' (to honour, privacy and their image) (Tamames 1992: 44). Lidia Falcón has suggested that pornography went unrestricted, despite this, because socialists and communists alike saw it as a cheap and accessible source of pleasure for the (presumably male) masses (Falcón 1990). Film censorship had been abolished a year earlier, and cinema very quickly became a key force in the 'destape' (Evans 1995). Partly because there have never been special provisions for restrictions on television, even mainstream TV channels now regularly show soft porn movies after midnight and, in the case of the commercial channel Canal Plus, hardcore ones (Jordan 1995; Hooper 1995). More visible and more insistent for those sensitised to it, however, is the unabashedly gratuitous use of scantily-dressed women in mainstream prime-time programming and advertising (Peña-Marín and Frabetti 1990). Although recent campaigns by the IM and the demands of the National Federation of Views' Associations have done something to raise awareness, however, for the majority of viewers this merges almost imperceptibly into what one commentator has called television's 'continuo sexista' (sexist continuum) (Osborne 1993: 292).

But even on a continuum there is some distance between advertising images of women with glistening cleavages on the one hand and scenes of violent rape or bestiality on the other. Some Spanish feminists tend to elide this distance by not defining their terms: 'a menudo se habla de obscenidad, erotismo, pornografía o indecencia para referirse a las mismas cosas, dependiendo de quién use estos términos' (the terms obscenity, erotism, pornography or indecency are often used to refer to the same things, depending on who is using them) (Osborne 1993: 28).[6] This is not simply because terms are yet to be refined in an ongoing feminist or broader debate, however. A progressive (though uneven) privatisation of morality in Spanish society, linked to a broad secularising tendency, has accelerated the normalisation of a range of once marginal practices over the last 20 years (Garaizábal 1990). And while some women may be concerned to maintain certain taboos – as a mother, for example, in the case of paedophilia or incest – they may be just as anxious to see those relating to certain other practices overturned. For this reason many feminists are reluctant to appeal to and thus reinforce sexual taboos by defining pornography as obscene material. Instead they tend to characterise it by its ideological set towards women and, most commonly, by its objectification or explicit sexual degradation of them (Falcón 1990; Puleo 1994). But each of these terms produces its own definitional problems. For example, any rejection of material on the grounds that it degrades women would need to address the fact that some radical and independent feminists find the missionary position itself emblematic of men's ritual domination of women, and many lesbians would say the same of heterosexual relations generally (Osborne 1993; CRECUL 1994). Women opposed to pornography commonly report feeling that they are being invoked by its images, and integrated through them into a patriarchal worldview (Puleo 1994). One independent feminist pamphlet refers particularly to narratives from the 1980s in which the more independent women that feminists helped to make possible have to be coerced, often brutally, into accepting patriarchal authority (Feministas Autónomas de Madrid 1990). It notes that something similar happens with sex between women, which is invariably a prelude to the decisive intervention of the voyeuristic male. These representations actively reinforce the largely heterosexual contexts in which they are produced and disseminated, it is argued, by reducing the possibilities of sexuality to one or two dominant myths: in particular, through the triumph of coitus-centred genital sexuality, and in roles which (however ambiguously they begin) invariably end with the restoration of patriarchally-validated relations (Garaizábal 1990). Arguably more persuasive than this account – which radically underestimates the complexity of the social sphere and the diversity of today's market-led pornography – is the definition of pornography as tending to intensify and distort subject/object relations between women and men, converting both to objects (Puleo 1994).

Cutting across this definitional indistinctness, however, and crucial to arguments about the ideological effects of material defined as pornographic, is the question of how far audiences identify with or are alienated by it. Few feminist commentators defend material which encourages readers to identify with images of the often brutal humiliation of women. On the other hand, some see the regressive images of soft porn or 'novelas rosa' (romantic novels) as even more pernicious, on the grounds that they arouse less ideological resistance (Osborne 1993; Puleo 1994). Teresa del Valle is not alone in underlining the constructive dimension of what she terms obscenity: 'es creativa y repulsiva a la vez y a menos que se contempla como producción cultural sería difícil ver la parte creativa y su capacidad constructora para el cambio social' (it is at once creative and repulsive, and unless it is approached as cultural production its creative aspect and constructive potential for social change remain difficult to detect (Del Valle 1993: 141). Osborne agrees: to reject the non-tolerated elements of sex (on which most pornography is based) and permit only more bland and romanticised versions can distort the significance of certain elements of male sexuality while encouraging the development of a pseudo-romantic female version 'más teñida de los valores de dependencia y sumisión, característicos de la mujer tradicional' (more tainted with the values of dependency and submission, which are typical of the traditional woman) (Osborne 1993: 30).

But while some women take pleasure precisely in the transgressive dimension of pornography others reserve the term for ideologically incorrect (and, by implication, unenjoyable) material, referring to the rest as 'erotica'. The distinction usually turns on pornography's exclusive and mechanistic focus on arousing the reader sexually and its absence of any literary or other pretensions. Erotica, meanwhile, is deemed to place sex in a broader human context (Falcón 1990; Delgado 1990; Osborne 1993). For Juana Delgado it is 'todo material que de modo más o menos explícito muestra una actitud sexual sobre bases igualitarias' (any material which displays an approach to sex that is more or less explicitly egalitarian) (Delgado 1990: 29). This does not resolve the question of what egalitarian sexual practices might be and, in particular, how they might be represented. Nor can it account for the fact that pleasure and desire are by no means limited to politically acceptable situations. They are just as likely to reside in the infringement of social norms since desire is cultured in fantasy, a dimension in which shock and pain, however extreme, never exceed what is pleasurable (Puleo 1994). This fantasy has its limits, however. Somewhere between what are perceived as normalised and alienatingly transgressive practices are each individual's 'acceptably transgressive' ones, not yet stabilised by custom or dulled by habit, still able to shock and excite (Valcárcel 1993). Among those more open to the pleasures of pornography, several of Alicia Puleo's collaborators agree that pornography can orient young women by introducing them to certain otherwise hidden sexual practices (Puleo 1994). But while women can only become emancipated sexual subjects if they are adequately informed, the interpretative and evaluative contexts in which these practices tend to be placed make this a contentious claim, and one which the fading of the Franco years and the recent introduction of sex education in many Spanish schools may help to undermine.

The sternest critics of pornography's educational potential accept the need to explore women's sexuality more fully, however, and some of the most active contributors to this process are radical lesbians. Broadly speaking, lesbians and lesbian feminists have had a low profile in Spain, and until recently have tended to be active chiefly in mixed groups – a fact which has conditioned the development of lesbian relations and politics.[7] While relations are generally good, and some gay men are aware and fully supportive of specifically lesbian issues, others may be as sexist as any heterosexual man. This, and the fact that lesbians were often later additions to established gay groups, has meant that they have tended to figure as junior partners – a fact underlined by members of the growing number of lesbian-only groups (CRECUL 1994). One historical reason for this low profile has been the tendency (particularly in the postwar period when both husbands and housing were in short supply) of unmarried women to live with female relatives in the same position. As two members of Madrid's Feministas Lesbianas (Lesbian Feminists) note, this – and ignorance about lesbian sexuality – has meant that while two men living together have routinely been described as 'maricones' ('queers') by straight neighbours, two women in the same position have tended to be thought of as simply 'primas' (cousins) (Pineda 1994: 40; Patricia Ojeda cited in Moreno 1993: 100).

Some radical groups are working to make up for the later development of lesbian awareness by adopting a high campaigning profile and an international frame of reference (Lesbianas sin Duda 1994). Other women have opted for a lower profile in more introverted social and self-help groups preferring, in some cases, to keep their lesbian identity a secret (CRECUL 1994). Partly because they have developed in mixed groups, some of the politico-juridical issues that concern lesbian women are common to gay men: the recognition of *de facto* couples, for example, same-sex marriage and adoption, the extension of key pension and other financial entitlements to gay or lesbian partners. There are significant differences, however, and attitudes to sexuality is one of them. In the least voyeuristic of recent media attempts to bring lesbians to visibility – written in collaboration with Madrid's Lesbian Feminist Collective – Rosa Montero notes that 'lesbian' is not an ontological definition: there are many kinds of lesbian, of whom an estimated 90 per cent have had sex with a man and 20 per cent are married (Montero 1993). And in particular while some radical groups see sexuality as a defining characteristic and key campaigning issue, others do not. Some take an essentialist line, asserting that lesbians are by their nature less interested in sex than are gay men: others are more constructionist, believing that lesbian sexuality is less insistent because it has been more thoroughly repressed, and will need time to develop its own independent momentum (Montero 1993).[8] But there is another body of opinion which maintains that sex is not central to lesbian existence, because once it is disengaged from penetration it ceases to be a *raison d'être*, and becomes a part of everyday life, inextricable from affection (CRECUL 1994). In the words of lesbian feminist Patricia Ojeda 'se trata de asumir una actitud sexual natural, vivir el lesbianismo como una opción de libertad personal. No se trata de hacer campaña de nada' (it's about taking a natural approach to sex, living lesbianism as a free personal choice. It's not about campaigning) (cited Moreno 1993: 100). These differences underline the view that a woman entering a lesbian relationhip cannot simply predict what sex will be like, how roles will be distributed, where pleasures will lie. Positive though it may be, the ongoing negotiation this requires may also be a factor in the relatively short life of many lesbian relationships; so too may a certain absence of 'otherness' which can reportedly lead to a confusion of desires and overdependence (Montero 1993; Lesbianas sin Duda 1994; CRECUL 1994). Because Spanish lesbians have tended (by omission or more explicitly) not to theorise their positions, these tensions remain to be teased out.

The changing relations of heterosexual women and men – with which lesbian women's rising profile is associated – are producing their own tensions as social roles adapt to new circumstances. The increasing diversity of pornography – like that of prostitution – is in part a response to these changes. Few of the so-called adult magazines, for example, currently circulating in Spain are produced there; some are edited by women; some are designed for women; all would modify their approaches if market share began to fall.[9] To the extent that they articulate a particular worldview, it is one geared less to perpetuating patriarchy than to maximising profits for producers and distributors (Osborne 1993). Sometimes these aims coincide; sometimes they do not. The often contradictory consequences of this pragmatism are evident in other types of magazine and other media, and some of their implications for women are discussed in chapter 5.

Notes

1 These figures are calculated from National Police and Civil Guard statistics (El País 1996). Since 1989 rape – which under the Criminal Code may be vaginal, anal or oral – has been punishable by 12 to 20 years' imprisonment (Pujol Algans 1992). Rape is always difficult to prove, particularly to the satisfaction of less progressive judges, and this wider definition can make it harder. In cases of sexual assault a fine of between 100,000 and 1,000,000 pesetas is specified. This excludes cases which involve 'the introduction of objects or where brutal, degrading or offensive methods, manners or instruments are used', however, for which the penalty is between 6 and 12 years' imprisonment (IM 1995e). Under the May 1996 Criminal Code reforms, the maximum penalty for sexual violence will changed from 20 to 15 years. This apparent reduction reflects the fact that remission invariably reduces the maximum 20 years to around 14, whereas under the new arrangements the penalty awarded will represent the actual sentence served (El País 1996). The 1996 reforms also introduced a new crime of sexual harassment, punishable with up to 24 weekend detentions (El País 1996).

2 In Madrid alone there were nine NGOs active in this area in 1995, and around 20 immigrant support and refugee groups – almost all focusing on Latin America and North Africa – several with separate women's groups (Comunidad de Madrid/Médicos del Mundo 1995).

3 Since gypsies do not tend to register in national censuses, estimates of their numbers vary between 300,000 and 850,000. The figure of 500,000 is the most widely cited, although government statistics (and thus funding and other policy) assume a total of 350,000

(Ministerio de la Presidencia 1994). The difficulty of collecting data on the gypsy community was underlined in a personal communication from the resource centre for the Asociación Secretariado General Gitano (General Secretariat of the Gypsy Association) in June 1996, which notes that their most recent nationwide study was published in 1978.

4 In 1983 the socialist government withdrew drug use and possession from the Criminal Code. Penalties were restricted to the drug suppliers and varied according to whether the drug was considered soft (cannabis) or hard (others). Under Criminal Code reforms introduced in May 1996, this differential treatment became more marked, with the maximum sentence for small or larger traffickers in hard drugs rising from 8 and 10 to 9 and 13½ years respectively, while the equivalent for small and larger traffickers in soft drugs fell from 4 and 6 to 3 and 4½ (El País 1996).

5 This view is indebted to the work of US anti-pornography campaigners Kathleen Barry and Catherine McKinnon – whose (separate) visits to Madrid in 1992 helped to shape the still emergent pornography debate in Spain. The ambivalence of many men on the left may have held back the development of the pornography debate among party feminists. Particularly in the late 1970s and early 1980s, however, left feminist priorities certainly lay elsewhere. It is partly because research into Spanish pornography has not been promoted by the IM that there are no sustained empirical studies on the subject. Meanwhile, there have been some anti-pornography pronouncements by conservative women opposed more to its sex than its violence, and who maintain that pornography would disappear if women were to return to family-centred values (Osborne 1993).

6 Spain's authoritative Diccionario de la Real Academia defines pornography with reference to obscenity – 'carácter obsceno de obras literarias o artísticas' (obscene character of literary or artistic works) – while ignoring its existence elsewhere. As feminist philosopher Amelia Varcárcel has observed, the obscene is etymologically linked to what is private, not included in the scene, and is thus only realised when it is made public (Valcárcel 1993).

7 In 1993 there were around 20 associations for gay men and women in Spain. Most of them were mixed, including three of the four national bodies: Federación Gay y Lesbiana Estatal; Coordinadora de Frentes de Liberación Homosexual del Estado Español; Plataforma Gay-Lesbiana; Coordinadora de Feministas Lesbianas. The last of these has member groups in large cities in the norther half of Spain, including Madrid, Bilbao, Barcelona and Santiago de Compostela.

8 Gay men's attitudes to their sexuality are, of course, more heterogeneous than this suggests. Like many assertions of identity, these views rest on homogenisation of an 'other'.

9 A comparison of the Spanish editions of Penthouse and home-produced material like Clima, Private or Gente libre suggests why foreign magazines massively outsell their national equivalents. The latters' often black and white, amateurish and crude illustrations have none of the glossy soft-focus fantasy of Penthouse and appear to cater for a less affluent, possible older and less middle-class readership. They evoke not the bland international escapism of Penthouse but evidently home-made fantasies, often centring on middle-aged readers' photographs of themselves and/or their partners. The pages of contact addresses obliquely insist on the specific location of these fantasies – a rootedness which contrasts strikingly with the anonymity of the international magazine – while suggesting at least the possibility of following them through.

5   In the media

ONE CONTRADICTION above all exercises commentators writing on women in the Spanish media. More than any other area of Spanish society, women's high profile here seems beyond dispute. Switch on television news, for example, and at least one presenter will usually be a woman along with many, if not most, of the correspondents. So too will the afternoon magazine presenter, and many of her guests. And strong women characters are invariably at the heart of the daily 'culebrón' (serial narrative or soap). And yet, it is claimed, the media are a male stronghold that persistently fails to acknowledge women's wider social advances.

The resonance of this claim derives from the influence that many theorists attribute to the media. Setting aside for a moment the precise nature of that influence, the importance of the media in Spain seems unquestionable. Spanish radio is of high quality and very popular – particularly among older women – with an estimated 17 million over-18s listening every day in 1990 (Foessa 1994; Gil Calvo 1993). But Spain is primarily a nation of television addicts. In 1990, over 25.5 million adults watched TV every day and the more disadvantaged the viewer, the more she or he was likely to watch (Foessa 1994). By 1993, over 98 per cent of the nation's 11,300,000 homes had a set (Varela 1994). At the time of writing, viewers can choose from two national state television channels (TV1 and TV2), and six regional ones (of which the Basques and Catalans have two channels each). There are also three national commercial channels (Antena 3, Tele 5 and Canal +) and hundreds of cable or satellite-operated local ones – over 100 of them in Catalonia alone (Foessa 1994).

Since the introduction of the new Constitution, television and radio have been the object of a range of national norms, guidelines and recommendations designed to protect the rights of minorities, and to encourage democratic pluralism, respect for privacy, impartiality, and the development of regional identities and civic values (Jordan 1995). Few of these have the status of law, however, and like

EU recommendations and content quotas they are regularly flouted in practice. Being more easily verifiable, regulations relating to advertising are more often observed. As noted in chapter 4, apart from measures to protect standards of good taste, and restrictions on associating alcohol consumption with sexual success, there is little or no regulation of sex on TV, and this fact has had significant repercussions for the representation of women. Successive governments' hands-off approach to media policy has also affected the development of radio which, like television, has proliferated during the democratic period. The state radio network, RNE, has five stations, while some 500 local radio stations are run by the local authorities (Foessa 1994; Hooper 1995). As with television, proliferation in the commercial sector has been accompanied by a concentration of ownership. Of Spain's 800-plus commercial stations, more than half are owned by two national networks, Cadena SER and Antena 3. Along with Opus Dei-controlled COPE and Onda Cero (run by ONCE, Spain's National Organisation for the Blind) these powerful networks account for 80 per cent of the total audience (Bustamante 1995).

The growth of media opportunities as a result of this proliferation, and the fact that women currently make up more than half of journalism graduates, are both factors in the increasing number of women in TV and radio production and, to a much lesser extent, management. But their representation has grown most strongly in the press. An estimated nine million adults read a daily newspaper (Foessa 1994). Not all of them necessarily buy one, but those who do are likely to be swelling the coffers of one of the five media groups which between them control almost a third of Spanish dailies (including best-selling El País and Diario 16) and more than half of registered sales (Hooper 1995; Bustamante 1995). Once these and wide-circulation independents El Mundo and ABC have been removed from the calculations, the total circulation of Spain's remaining 75 dailies amounts to barely half a million (Bustamante 1995). Although they are slightly more likely than men to watch television or listen to the radio, women have traditionally not made up a large proportion of newspaper readers (Gil Calvo 1993). This gender gap has been closing in recent years, however. Implicated in this shift are the targeting of potential women readers by the self-styled general interest press, since La Vanguardia's pioneering introduction (in 1984) of Spain's first women's supplement in a national daily (Gallego 1990); the desire and (in certain cases) professional need of some working women to be more aware of so-called hard news; and, arguably most importantly, the stimulus provided by the magazine sector to read more widely.

The most dynamic publications in this sector, including five of Spain's ten best-selling magazines, belong to that quintessentially Spanish genre 'la prensa del corazón' (gossip press). Its most venerable example is ¡Hola!, introduced in 1944 but displaced in recent years by Pronto, which is currently Spain's best-selling magazine. These two, along with Semana, Diez Minutos, and Lecturas, sell around two and a half million copies per week (Hooper 1995). The gossip press uses photographs (virtually unsupported by text) to give supposedly intimate, and profoundly uncritical, glimpses into 'los aconteci-mientos privados de gente conocida' (the private lives of public figures or 'personalities') (Abril 1995). Its early popularity was based largely on the fact that it marked the eruption of the private sphere – which the so-called general information press had tended to include almost exclusively under the sign of pathology or 'social problem' – into the public sphere. When 75 per cent of readers of a magazine are female, Juana Gallego notes, it is usually characterised as a women's magazine: when 75 per cent of readers are men it is described as a general interest publication (Gallego 1990). But despite its mostly female readers, its intimate tone and its recourse to the familiar home-love-beauty sections and women-oriented advert-ising, for Gallego and others the gossip press is in a class of its own. This is because, unlike the women's press, it does not function as 'la prensa de información general del ámbito de lo privado' (the general interest press of the private sphere) (Abril 1995: 154).

But if this hybrid quality has helped to make gossip magazines best-sellers, women's magazines are closing the gap. In 1994, for example, Spain's most authoritative current affairs magazine, Cambio 16, had a circulation of under half a million, while Cosmopolitan's was reportedly approaching three-quarters of a million (Glattstein Franco 1995). Cosmopolitan is an example of what Gallego characterises as general interest women's press, the less-than-general focus of which tends to fall on home, love/sex, beauty/health, and fashion. Its leading competitors include Dunia, Elle, Marie Claire and Vogue. These Gallego distinguishes from magazines such as Ser Madre and Revista de la Salud, with their more specific focuses (on mothering and health respectively) and from single-issue publications like Labores del Hogar and Burda (housework and dressmaking respectively) (Gallego 1990).

But this distinction is increasingly difficult to maintain in practice, especially given the tendency of publications to subdivide the topics they cover for the sake of variety and greater advertising and editorial focus. Regardless of their subject, however, the enormous majority of these magazines (24 out of 30 in 1992) are headed by women (Institut Català de la Dona 1994). Like radio and television, magazine ownership has become increasingly concentrated in recent years: *Dunia* and *Mía* are controlled by a German multinational, for example, *Cosmopolitan* by a US one, *Ser Padres*, *Marie Claire*, *Vogue* and *Elle* by French ones. This international backing can give magazines considerable financial stability and, in some cases, journalistic clout. In particular, their mobilisation of a potentially lucrative new audience has encouraged certain other areas of the press to compete for women readers. In some cases this has involved adopting the more informal tone and some of the layout characteristics of women's magazines, or selecting what are perceived as more women-friendly topics. Above all, women's magazines have helped to present reading as pleasure rather than a responsibility (Fernández de Angulo 1995). Something will be said shortly about the implications of this strategy for Spain's media theorists.

As with many other areas of women's studies, the development of media research relating to women has been conditioned by the policy-making imperatives of the IM. Its sponsorship of many of the key studies of women and the media since the early 1980s has meant that the role of women as media practitioners, consumers and representations, and the importance of the media in social transformation, have tended to be studied from the perspective of ideological influence. As the best of these studies indicate, this does not rule out the elaboration of appropriate theoretical frameworks in principle, but in practice the precise nature of the media's supposed ideological influence has tended to remain implicit or under-theorised. It is widely assumed, for example, that the media reproduce or reflect the social order inaccurately by persistently failing to acknowledge women's advances, and that these distortions must be eradicated (Fagoaga 1996; Radl Philipp 1996)). For some critics, however, the media prejudice women by transmitting all too faithfully the cultural constructions of patriarchy. This state of affairs is unlikely to change, they maintain, until key feminist ideological assumptions have made significant inroads into patriarchal strongholds (Abril 1995). At issue in these debates is both the justice or injustice of media representations and the extent to which they can be said to produce, shape or more indirectly condition their audiences. The most positive gloss on this comes from media professionals like Sarah Glattstein Franco, for whom the media educate their readers in what it is to be a woman (Glattstein Franco 1995).[1] But, as with pornography, some media theorists question the educational role of representations which tend to perpetuate widely-discredited social stereotypes (Gallego 1990; Sebastián 1995). For Concha Fagoaga, Spain's leading feminist media theorist, these stereotypes are reinforced by the media's powerful combination of globalising and intimate moments, and by their ability to unite audiences once dispersed among theatres, bullrings, cinemas or town squares, making themselves a part of the everyday environment (Fagoaga 1995). Above all, it is argued, media techno-logy enables representations to figure as what is real and what is absent to figure as non-existent (Martín Serrano 1995; Radl Philipp 1996). Meanwhile, the growing popularity of hybrid forms like 'advertorial', 'faction' and 'docudrama' are blurring even further the distinction between representations of reality and fiction (Fernández de Angulo 1995).

As women's studies centres developed through the 1980s, feminist academics began to look more closely at the precise nature of media influence and its role in configuring, rather than simply reflecting, social reality (Baca Lagos 1995). The strongest claim of all for the media's configuring potential comes from Fagoaga, who (following Stuart Hall) states that television probably contributes more to the ideological shaping of the individual than either formal education or the family (Fagoaga 1996). From this perspective it is not enough for media representations of women to be fair or accurate: they must be progressive. And by analysing the conditions in which these representations are produced and disseminated, Fagoaga claims, academics can actively contribute to this process. A cornerstone of her analysis is Stuart Hall's account of the ideological encoding of a message within the media institution and its decoding by the audience. Spanish media studies have traditionally focused on content analysis, much of it informed by 'hypodermic' approaches which assume that the patriarchal or other ideological assumptions of media producers are 'injected' directly into a passive audience. But the notion of encoding is more flexible. It recognises that media messages (and their reception) are conditioned by a range of inter-related external and internal structures, conventions and procedures:

industrial or institutional norms and interests, for example, technological capabilities and conventions, departmental values, interpersonal dynamics, and questions of genre and style. Fagoaga approaches this complexity through a critical news analysis model, which tends to highlight the interaction of producers and providers in the construction of media messages, and focuses chiefly on their ideological formulation. But this tends to overlook the progressive influence exerted over the last decade by international and national policy-making bodies. UNESCO, for example, has worked since 1985 on strategies to change women's relations to public communcation (Romano García 1994). In 1986 the EC identified the media as a key sector for the development of public opinion, and in its Third Action Programme (1991-95) undertook to promote women's positive and non-stereotypical representation in media institutions and content. At national level, the IM has encouraged research into women and the media since the early 1980s. The first of its two *Plans* sets out proposals to promote a non-discriminatory image of women in the media in collaboration with the state TV and radio network, RTVE. It also sought to promote non-sexist advertising by bringing publicity into line with Article 5 of the UN Convention (designed to eliminate sex discrimin-ation) and the 1988 Ley General de Publicidad (General Law on Publicity) which outlaws advertisements which affront an individual's dignity or otherwise offend against rights and values enshrined in the Constitution (IM 1990b). *Plan* II focuses on women's representation as media professionals and as subject matter, with a list of measures designed to secure media co-operation in the replacement of regressive cultural stereotypes (IM 1993a). These include a framework agree-ment with RTVE, and broad collaboration with commercial radio and TV channels to bring representations of women into line with social reality; to encourage more peak time programmes on women's issues, and more information and educational programmes targeting women; and to ensure women's wider representation on general interest programmes. To counter claims that no women experts are available in the appropriate area it proposes the establishment of a database of women across the professions. These measures are matched with a range of checks and balances including: campaigns to sensitise public opinion to sexist or regressive media images; the creation of a register of women's appearance in advertising and the media generally; and action against advertisements which offend against women's dignity or transmit discriminatory images.

But alongside these progressive media policy forces – and with no particular interest in changing cultural stereotypes – are the economic and politial interests of a range of national and transnational bodies. There are the organisations that control most of Spain's media: major national groups like PRISA, ZETA and Banesto, and multinationals like Hachette, Bertelsmann, News International and Hearst. There are the advertising groups from which they derive most of their revenue, of which only three of the top 40 are indigenous (Foessa 1994). Within Spain there are also the powerful media individuals and families (ABC's Luca de Tena, for example, and ¡Hola!'s Sánchez Junco) with their own idiosyncracies and priorities. And in each case interests and priorities shift in response to larger economic and socio-political factors. They also interact with the norms of TV, radio and the press as industries – norms[23] which are themselves the product of interactions between the various players as institutions, as structures, as deployers of technology, and as networks of individuals. Norms and values may be enshrined in mission statements or other top-down policy documents, thrashed out in daily editorial meetings (with their attendant gender-based and other power asymmetries) or at the photocopier, perpetuated in procedures, conventions or habits, and transgressed or affirmed by individuals who increasingly bring to their work 'professional' knowledge frameworks and values acquired on journalism degrees. Lastly, but arguably most visibly all of these factors help to determine the selection and the views of the media's expert sources, authoritative commentators and analysts. All of which suggests that, if media representations help to condition social change, they are themselves complexly conditioned by it.

The under- and misrepresentation of women in media content (and its supposed effects of the formation of public opinion) has been widely linked to the under-representation of women, at virtually all of these levels, among media professionals. And this has led to many calls for their more equitable incorporation (EEC 1991; Fagoaga 1993, 1995, 1996; Varela 1994; Vera Balanza 1995). So far, the greatest numerical advances have been in the press – a medium which has seen its influence decline significantly with the rise of television. But, as noted, there are also some high-profile women in Spanish broadcasting – including the new head of RTVE, Mónica Ridruejo – and their numbers have risen in recent years.[2] A 1995 article for *Cambio 16* goes so far as to suggest that women have taken over

Spanish TV, particularly where news programmes are concerned (Ramírez 1995). As well as high-profile regional presenters such as Teresa Castañedo (Telemadrid) and Esther Martín (Canal Sur), for example, there are a range of national presenters like Rosa María Mateo (Antena 3) or María Escario (TVE) whose faces are familiar across Spain. Among correspondents and lower-level news staff women are even more prominent. TVE's Director of News Services, María Antonia Iglesias, has boasted that some 40 per cent of her editorial staff, six of the 14 foreign correspondents, and 98 per cent of national news staff are women (cited Ramírez 1995). And away from the newsroom, in magazine and general discussion programmes, women presenters enjoy a particularly high profile: Isabel Gremio, Concha Velasco, Marta Robles, Elena Ochoa and Míriam Díaz Aroca figure regularly in the gossip press. But the high profile of a relatively small group does not mean that women have taken over television. When TVE newscasters Ana Blanco and Elena Sánchez are teamed with male colleagues, for example, there is little sense that the women are in charge. And despite the IM's best efforts, the number of women who appear in the more authoritative and 'opinion-forming' role of news analyst remains negligible.[3] With notable exceptions like Pilar Cernuda and Victoria Prego, women TV producers and directors are also a tiny minority.

Any discussion of these ambiguous advances needs to consider precisely where, when, how and why women figure in the media, and a useful starting-point is the influential 1994 study for the Catalan Institute for Women of some 900 of the region's press, TV and radio journalists (Institut Català de la Dona 1994). Among other things, this found that that smaller and more local newspapers or radio stations tended to have more women (including senior women) journalists. Only 13 per cent of the Catalan staff of national daily El País were women, for example, while local papers El Diario de Terrassa and Diario de Lérida had 29 per cent and 37 per cent of women staff respectively. And while under 8 per cent of El País's total held senior positions, this rose to almost 38 per cent in the two local papers. Where Catalan radio was concerned, women journalists were again more numerous in smaller stations like Catalunya Ràdio-RAC (where they made up 44 per cent of staff) than in regional branches of national networks like RNE, SER, Onda Cero, COPE or Antena-3 (20-27.5 per cent). And among the 176 municipally-run radio stations – over 14 per cent of which were headed by women – this pattern was even clearer. In Catalonia as elsewhere, it seems, the greater the supposed public weight and influence the smaller the proportion of women. Conversely, women made up the majority — and in the case of *Labores del hogar* and *Patrones* the totality — of staff on all but one of Barcelona-based women's and gossip magazines.

The Catalan study suggests that many of the women surveyed share some significant characteristics. First, although many leading professionals — Rosa Montero, for example, Carmen Rico-Godoy and Pilar Varela — joined the profession in the 1970s or early 1980s, women journalists as a whole tend to be younger than their male counterparts. Almost a fifth of the women journalists surveyed were under 26 (compared with 7 per cent of men), and almost three-quarters of them had degrees (compared with only half of men). This supports the view that higher education is helping young women to take up the majority of new places, despite the reservations that many practitioners express about the professional value of journalism courses. Particularly significant for any discussion of ideological influences is the fact that almost 60 per cent of the women in the sample described themselves as to the left of the Socialist government of the time. Although (as noted) almost a fifth were younger, the majority of the women in the study were in the 26-35 group (some 60 per cent, compared with 40 per cent of men). Of these more than half were unmarried, around 5 per cent separated or divorced, and two-thirds had no children (compared with under half of men).

These findings will have been distorted to some extent by the relative youth of most of the women surveyed and by the tendency among working women to delay starting a family. They nevertheless seem to bear out reports of the pressure and long hours endured by women wanting a media career. As one of Spain's leading journalists and one-time Assistant Director of El *País* Soledad Gallego puts it, this 'terriblemente absorbente' (terribly absorbing) work takes over an individual's life (Gallego 1995: 87). Other women highlight the intense competition, the individualism, the absolute commitment demanded of staff, and the pressure on women to justify their presence by achieving more than male counterparts (Vera Balanza 1995; Méndez 1995). Women who try to combine a media career with a family are subject to particular pressures (Gallego 1995). As journalist Lucía Méndez notes, the two are widely viewed as incompatible by employers (at least where women are concerned), encouraging some to conceal the fact that they are married (Méndez 1995). If they become pregnant it can mean the end of a career, since even liberal employers are likely to be alienated if a woman insists on her legal right to breastfeeding breaks, or expects to find the same job waiting for her on her return from maternity leave. In such circumstances, Méndez observes, a temporary contract may not be renewed and the chances of a woman with a young child finding an alternative post are slim. Although the fact that she is employed by El Mundo – a consistent supporter of the Conservative government – may colour Méndez's view, her observations are not out of line with those of many other media women. However, most concede that the media offer a more liberal working environment than many other careers, while some suggest that they are more woman-friendly in Spain than in many other European countries (Varela 1995). But despite legal prohibitions on direct sexual discrimination in the workplace indirect forms of discrimination clearly persist, and women trying tactfully to deflect innuendo, sexual flattery and paternalism face additional psychological tensions. Almost 70 per cent of women in the Catalan study reported experiencing some degree of gender-based discrimination. Although this too may reflect a greater awareness of equality issues through education, the proportion was highest of all among the 36-45 age group, whose members are more likely to have been sensitised in the feminist mobilisations of the 1970s, or while trying to combine a career with a family. While almost 40 per cent of men acknowledged that women colleagues experienced a degree of discrimination, a significant proportion of younger men felt women enjoyed certain professional advantages. This suggests that, while younger men tend to be less sexist in their attitudes than their fathers, some clearly feel the tide has turned to the point where it may prejudice their own careers (Llorach Boladeras 1995). In this they are indirectly supported by Méndez, who cites the view of certain male colleagues that some younger women in particular use their gender and their sexuality to advance their careers (Méndez 1995). To the extent that this is true, it might reflect greater self-confidence among women who no longer see themselves as an embattled minority and, in particular, an easier attitude to their sexuality among younger women with less direct experience of being penalised for their gender.

Although they are legally entitled to equal pay for work of equal value, the fact that women journalists are concentrated at more junior levels means that their pay is on average lower than men's. This predominantly junior status also affects their job security. According to the Catalan study, only 36 per cent of women were on permanent contracts. They were also significantly more likely than men to be on less secure and poorly paid training contracts; and they were almost half as likely again to work on a permanent freelance (6 per cent to 4.4 per cent) or non-contracted (6.6 per cent to 4.4 per cent) basis. Once again, these differences reflect the high proportion of women among new entrant and younger staff, who are invariably employed on less favourable terms regardless of gender. But some media professionals observe that women are more likely to continue on this basis, and advocate positive discrimination to ensure greater equality of opportunities not only in the allocation of contracts but also where promotion is concerned (EEC 1991; Vera Balanza 1995). The title of the Catalan study – 'el sostre de vidre' (the glass ceiling) – highlights its finding that while 53 per cent of women worked as editors, less than 30 per cent had reached Director or Head of Section level, compared with almost half of men.[4] One study of the major dailies since 1983 finds a correlation between the politics and promotional policy of the newspapers concerned: the proportion of senior women staff on El País, for example, grew from around 3 per cent to a more respectable 13.5 per cent between 1983 and 1994, while on Diario 16 it crept from under 8 per cent to just over 9 per cent, and on La Vanguardia it actually fell by half to under 5 per cent (Fagoaga 1996).[5] By and large, the responsibilities assigned to these women have proved equally resistant to change. Soledad Gallego has observed that women journalists tend to avoid writing about what are usually characterised as women's issues for fear either of drawing attention to their gender or of being ghettoised (Gallego 1995). Yet those given Section Head responsibilities are far more likely to be associated with supposedly soft topics like culture, society, and local affairs than with politics or economy.

One explanation for this under-representation at senior levels and in certain areas may be that some women simply do not want promotion – they may prefer to focus more on life outside the office, for example, or may find the double shift intolerable – or that they tend to find certain topics or activities more attractive than others. But the concerns expressed by many European media professionals, and the view that women should have more equal access to promotion across all areas of the media whether or not they decide to take advantage of it, led to the production in 1991 of the *Igualdad de Oportunidades en la radio televisión: guía práctica de la CEE* (the EEC's Practical Guide to Equal Opportunities in Radio and TV). This observed, for example, that senior media staff were often appointed without advertisement, and that men were 15 times more likely to be appointed in this way (EEC 1991). With this in mind, it encouraged formal selection procedures and set out a range of recommendations to ensure their fairness and transparency. These included: gender-neutral job advertisements, job specifications and job titles; publication of advertisements in places where women are more likely to see them; the omission wherever possible of age limits that might discriminate against women returning to work after having a family; reasonably gender-balanced interview panels; positive action measures in areas where women are under-represented; flexitime and job-share options, and crèche facilities to enable work to be combined with families (EEC 1991). And in order to facilitate their promotion opportunities once in post, it also advocated management and other forms of training for women to increase their confidence.

These recommendations – some of which are being adopted in more liberal organisations – are informed by the widely-held assumption that more women practitioners in the media would help to modify the ideological climate. Fagoaga, for example, speculates that they might help to change news values – for example, by breaking down the distinction between 'soft' and 'hard' news and 'women's topics' – especially if the number of invited women experts and analysts increased proportionately (Fagoaga 1996). In particular, she suggests, a journalistic elite in which women did not have a merely token presence 'rechazarían tópicos de género' (would reject gender stereotypes) (Fagoaga 1996: 360). But it is here that her empirically-grounded social policy concerns and her theoretical frame clash in a way that she has yet to resolve. As she herself notes, gender categories are not simply an expression of the individual's biological sex, and women are not the exclusive possessors of gender characteristics associated with the female. The claims of many practitioners that women can only advance in the media by not having children, avoiding 'women's topics' and generally becoming more like men radically undermines the assumption that this enlarged cohort of women will then 'feminise' dominant media norms and values. A small number of women may not have the power to revalue and promote supposedly female values within the media but, as Fagoaga herself obliquely acknowledges, a large cohort of women who have adopted sometimes regressive professional and institutional norms in order to advance their careers would presumably be less able or inclined to try. This does not mean that these norms, values and stereotypes cannot change and are not changing in response to contextual factors such as the greater presence of women. However, it does suggest that, while the need for more women in key decision-making posts seems unquestionable, claims about their transformative potential need to be less sweeping.

Because technological, symbolic, institutional and other inter-related factors bear on the production and reception of media messages, they cannot be reduced to a single statement about gender. And this is true even when the need to evoke a rapid response, the pressure of deadlines or prejudice encourages gender stereotyping or oversights. In accordance with *Plan II*, the IM has made such oversights less defensible by publishing its first directory of women consultants in the professions for use by the media and other bodies (IM 1995c). Feminist academics have tended to refer to women's exclusion from the media, however, rather than their omission (Fagoaga 1996). This raises the question – which they rarely address directly – of the agents of this supposed exclusion. Although Manuel Martín Serrano professes to find the notion of a patriarchal conspiracy unhelpful, his own practice is more ambiguous. He observes, for example, that particularly on TV the socio-political figures as men's world, which is linked to institutions and characterised by conflict and consensus. By contrast, women figure as oriented toward primary needs rather than more abstract concerns, confined to the sphere of the everyday where conflict is ritualised in a private world marked out for them, he states, by men (Martín Serrano 1995). For Fagoaga (following Gerbner) this 'aniquilación simbólica' (symbolic annihilation) is linked to 'la expulsión de la realidad en los procesos mediáticos' (the expulsion from reality in media processes) of certain questions and groups (Fagoaga 1996: 353). At the micro-level, for example, style manuals' insistence on conciseness perpetuates the use of masculine plurals for mixed sex groups, despite the efforts of the IM to outlaw the practice (Vargas 1995). More far-reaching are technology- or convention-led practices which (by encouraging the division of media broadcasting into programmes representing different aspects of reality) lead to fragmentation and 'rolificación' (the reduction of individuals to roles) – so that women usually figure as mothers, for example, housewives or artistes (Martín Serrano 1995). A woman minister is expected to speak exclusively as a gender-neutral politician on political debate programmes, and as a mother or housewife only on programmes where that speaking position has legitimacy. In both cases (and particularly the first) they are likely to be isolated from any elucidatory context by the 'topocentrismo' and 'presentismo' ('hereness and nowness' effects) produced by media framing (Martín Serrano 1995). Meanwhile, the fact that men are authorised to speak on general issues means that although they, too, are reduced to roles, they have a wider range available to them. As Pilar Varela notes, the overall effect is that women tend to figure as 'menos capacitada[s], más débil[es y] con intereses más reducidos' (less able, weaker, and with more limited interests) than men (Varela 1994: 69). By exploiting residual and outdated social stereotypes – by ensuring, for example, that women continue to figure on mainstream TV programming chiefly as minimally-clad hostesses, assistants or audience participants in game and 'reality' shows – she insists, the media tend to reinforce and perpetuate them. And in the process, they lower the horizons and narrow the options not only of women, but also of children and men (Varela 1994).

Martín Serrano's major study of women on Spanish television highlights the persistence of some of these stereotypes, but unlike many other commentators he also gives due weight to the gradual transformation and displacement of certain others (Martín Serrano 1995). He suggests, for example, that women tend to have a wider range of roles available to them in advertising than in general programming, while supporting the widely-held view that a much smaller number tend to predominate (Peña-Marín and Frabetti 1990; De la Peña Herrero 1995; Sebastián 1995). In 1993, when the then head of the IM suggested that advertising images of women had not changed in 20 years it was chiefly representations of housewives that she had in mind (Marina Subirats, cited Del Arco 1993). A year later she was echoed by the co-author of a key IM-sponsored study of women in advertising (Cristina Peña-Marín, cited Cristóbal 1994b). In Peña-Marín's opinion, housewives should not be presented as happy or satisfied in their work, because it involves long hours and is rewarded with little social esteem and no wages. Instead, she maintained, advertisements should reflect the tedium and desperation that many housewives experience. Unlike Subirats, she conceded that some advertisers were beginning to do this. Before addressing the assumptions underlying her observations, a word on one IM response to what it represents as the regressive character of much media advertising.

In January of 1994 the Institute introduced its Observatorio de la Publicidad (Advertising Monitoring Programme). It was designed to observe and analyse sexist advertising in the media, to channel and evaluate complaints against specific examples, and to act to modify or ban them where they offended against the dignity or prejudiced the constitutional rights and values of individual women, in accordance with the IM's *Plan II* and the 1988 General Publicity Law (Tenreiro García 1995). This was, in effect, the high-profile extension of a facility which had been available for some time and had already led to the contesting of 15 advertisements in the previous year (Del Arco 1993). The programme involved a free nationwide telephone complaints line, available 24 hours a day and seven days a week, backed up by a specially-convened Consejo Asesor de la Imagen (Image Advisory Committee). This Committee collaborated with the Institute in the evaluation of offending advertisements and (with its 16 members drawn from the academy, unions, and consumer and other groups) gave weight and a measure of independence to any action taken. The enormous majority of those who used the hotline in 1994 (358 out of 385) were women and many of them called more than once (IM 1995d). The largest group (38 per cent) were in the 26-35 age bracket and almost three-quarters of them were city-dwellers. Around two-thirds of callers had secondary or tertiary education, paid employment and no children, while more than half were single. Their principal targets were advertisements for cleaning materials, which were widely seen as out of phase with social reality. There were also objections to sexism and gratuitous nudity in films (14 per cent), personal hygiene campaigns (10 per cent) and drink advertisements (almost 7 per cent). Advertisements for cars were the object of 11 per cent of complaints, on the grounds that they excluded women from the decision-making process and/or tended to include them only as embellishments. Of all the offending images, 15 became the subject of official requests for amendments or withdrawal, in response to which one was amended and two were withdrawn (IM 1995d).

By the time the complaint, evaluation and legal processes had run their course campaigns were likely to be reaching the end of their life. In some cases – most notoriously that of Membrillo El Quijote, with its rather dismal image of a lank-haired open-mouthed woman holding two quinces in front of her bare breasts – the impact of the campaign will actually have been magnified by the resulting media attention. But the deterrent effect of critical attention on some larger advertisers is underlined in the responses of advertising professionals to the Monitoring Programme. An industry journal notes that two leading advertising agency bodies had declined to send representatives to the Programme's Advisory Committee, while a third had not been invited to do so (Control 1994). The Institute's threat to boycott agencies which refused to comply with requests to modify offending advertisements was reportedly one factor in these rejections, but there were others. Some advertising professionals pronounced themselves perfectly happy for women to be used to signify desirability provided it was done tastefully – whatever that means in this context – and felt they were being made the scapegoats of consumer society: others saw the Institute's campaign as restricting their creative freedom – though it was in many cases a recourse to stereotypes that had prompted complaints (Del Arco 1993; Cristóbal 1994b). Some responses from Creative Directors were more ambivalent, however. Delvico's award-winning Tony Segarra, for example, insisted that agencies' use of sexist images reflected a deeply-rooted cultural reality, while underlining consumers' power to ensure the displacement of these images by not buying the products in question (Cristóbal 1994b). In the case of detergents (where there has been a remarkable degree of unanimity on the images used) he is clearly overplaying consumer alternatives, but Segarra is not alone in the view that agencies have no incentive to change their approach as long as consumers continue to buy the product. He suggests, quite plausibly, that creative staff are themselves bored with advertisements which are 'claramente denigratoria y ofrecen una imagen lamentable de la mujer' (clearly insulting and present a lamentable image of women), and would prefer to use more imaginative means of achieving their ends (Cristóbal 1994b: 32). Taken at face value, this highlights the dilemma in which all advertisers find themselves. To be effective, advertising must refer to what is easily recognisable in the brief seconds available, and this – along with the habits and expectations of its audience, clients' concerns for their money, and agencies' desire to retain client contracts – encourages a certain conservatism. Advertising agencies are commercial concerns, and the largest deploy a battery of audience research techniques to ensure that their message is acceptable to the majority of their target audience. Except where concerted campaigns (like the Monitoring Programme) amplify dissent, advertisers can afford to take a fairly relaxed view if a small number of women or men take exception to adverts targeting a very different group. But in tension with this conservative tendency – especially among larger agencies – is the need for an element of novelty or surprise, something that will give a sequence of images impact and memorability. This need may be intensified by commercial and professional competition, linked as they are to peer recognition via creative awards. This dynamic of conservatism and novelty – novelty which, from women's point of view, may not always be progressive – has been a key factor in the development of advertising strategies and images. Because the overall effect remains patchy, however, and some of the shifts involved are minimal, feminists like Subirats tend to insist on the undesirable continuities, while advertising professionals are more likely to highlight change (Subirats, cited Cristóbal 1994b; Unión de Consumidores de España 1995). For example, Begoña Costa, Creative Director of a leading international agency, maintains that women today are represented in a wider range of social roles and that even in domestic narratives they tend to figure as more critical and aware (cited Cristóbal 1994b). With a few honourable exceptions, this is more true where larger groups like Costa's own are concerned. But, as the Institute's campaign and the debate around it have underlined, even multinationals may try to adapt images to their conception of the local market. In one memorable instance from the early 1990s, a guitar viewed through a vodka bottle was transformed throughout Europe into Easter Island, while in Spain it became a woman's buttocks (Del Arco 1993). In the period immediately preceding the Monitoring Programme, on the other hand, a Seat car advertisement (featuring a girl with her miniskirt lifted to reveal white pants, overlaid with the title 'provocativo' or provocative) was withdrawn at the Institute's request, but circulated – allegedly without comment – elsewhere in Europe (Del Arco 1993).

Despite the incorporation of some feminist formulae in the advertising copy of certain women's magazines from the mid-1980s, the roles ascribed to women by advertisers do not tend to differ significantly from those that predominate in the so-called general interest press: housewife, sex object, seductress, or seduced (Molina Petit 1986; Unión de Consumidores de España 1995). Of these, the image of the housewife remains the most resistant to change and, in general, the most resisted by feminists, on the grounds that it perpetuates the double shift through the notion that women are naturally better-suited to the domestic sphere. But Begoña Costa is not alone in suggesting that images of housewives persist simply because the majority of Spanish women are not in paid employment. From this perspective rejection of these images is, in some sense, a rejection of housewives in general as 'marujas', dowdy and unambitious perpetuators of traditionalist stereotypes − a rejection that may have contributed to the low personal and social esteem alluded to by Peña-Marín. The noticeable shift in recent years in attitudes towards women without paid work partly reflects their changing composition, as more women take a break from careers to start a family. Advertising images of women in the domestic sphere continue to be censured for their regressive character, but this is now linked more to the lack of dignity and respect displayed towards the housewife-figure (Abril 1992; De la Peña Herrero 1995). Although this has contributed to the demise of the 'maruja' figure, advertising images of housewives remain resolutely unglamourous: the voice-over that frames their activities is invariably male, and many continue to be isolated in what one commentator has characterised as a quasi-sadistic world where products are their only route to family approval, and a source of consolation or relief rather than pleasure (De la Peña Herrero 1995).

But Martín Serrano's large-scale study suggests that some fundamental changes are in process which have implications not only for housewives. On the one hand, for example, he underlines television's tendency to under-represent women in certain roles and to present them as more superficial than men. On the other, he notes that advertising tends to balance gender roles much more than TV programmes, even where this involves placing men in unconventional domestic situations. Similarly, women in advertisements remain clearly identified with the body and are widely assumed to care more about their bodies than do men; yet men (and particularly younger men and boys) are increasingly seen dressing or perfuming themselves to please women. This is despite the fact that four out of five men reportedly continue to define themselves primarily as something other than bodies (Martín Serrano 1995). Since advertisers have a professional interest in appealing to their audiences' self-perceptions, this mismatch suggests either that they regard this information as unreliable – for example, as understating changes in younger groups – or that they are making the (increasingly questionable) assumption that women can best be interpellated as consumers through the pleasure of others. Comic glimpses of men attempting to fill washing machines, for example, do not suggest a genuine attempt to win male consumers over to a particular detergent. Impulsiveness is another quality strongly associated with women in advertisements but increasingly extended to men. Since the desire to consume (and particularly to consume less- or non-essential items) is linked closely to the relaxation of critical thought and inhibitions, this too may be an example of men being positioned as open to unplanned consumption. And it looks particularly strategic at a time when women are themselves reportedly tending to reject the notion that they are impulsive by nature (Martín Serrano 1995).

Like Martín Serrano, Vicente Verdú contends that the triviality and pleasure-seeking which characterise many media representations of women are increasingly being extended to men (cited in Gallego 1990). He associates this trend with the spread of postmodern cultural perspectives and international marketing, and claims that magazines like Hombres Dunia and Man give men access to the feminised (by which he means narcissistic) international market-place in which women take their place by becoming men. Juana Gallego is rightly suspicious of his hyperbole, which affirms the end of fixed gender relations while simply reversing them. The increased targeting of men by advertisers involves neither feminisation nor emasculation: they are, after all, not being treated as women, but as women have been treated. In the same way, power has been so closely identified with men that powerful women are too readily characterised as masculine. But the power ascribed by its editors to readers of Elle magazine, for example, is not 'masculine' power: it is the power to consume pleasurably – a power to which most women gain regular access not by becoming men but by undertaking the paid work once reserved largely for men (Fernández de Angulo 1995)). Unlike Verdú, Juan Rey declines to present what he, too, sees as a progressive feminisation of men in advertising in terms of manichean reversals (Rey 1994). Instead he traces a gradual convergence of masculine and feminine universes which is part of a broader renegotiation of identities (Rey 1994). This renegotiation, which is potentially positive for both men and women, is particularly evident in the press, where the success of women's magazines has encouraged the male-identified general information press to extend its traditional focus to the so-called private sphere (Glattstein Franco 1995). This is particularly evident in the new men's magazines cited by Verdú, where the persistence of soft porn images supports the view that what is at stake here is less feminisation than the targeting of men as understudies (and possibly, at some point, leads) in the narcissistic consumer role created for women.

As Concha Fagoaga has observed, any analysis of how messages are encoded by media producers and advertising executives is meaningless as social critique without some sense of how women decode them (Fagoaga 1996). And if the media's ideological effects tend to be more heterogeneous, contradictory and difficult to measure than is often suggested, so too do the responses of its audiences. They may indeed accept the dominant message of a media text (usually what is presented as 'natural' or 'common sense') but they may equally oppose it, reading it against the grain. More often, they negotiate with it, customising it as they overread, debate, reject, or miss certain elements, for example, or flip channels, or break from reading or viewing to answer the phone. Unlike passive audience models, a focus on this 'decoding' process places media repre-sentations of women in a more open, negotiated context. And it acknowledges the constraints on even the most regressive of them by highlighting the scope for audience autonomy, creativity and pleasure.

Feminists like Fagoaga are understandably suspicious of mass mediated pleasure, on the grounds that it neutralises or ritualises conflict and makes critical messages of any kind difficult to sustain. But Juana Gallego is one of comparatively few Spanish feminists to underline the significance of pleasure for female and male audiences (Gallego 1990). While acknowledging that the feminist press played a crucial role in feminist consciousness-raising, for example, she suggests that its often negative focus and minority political aims were incompatible with general readers' desire for entertaining and pleasurable communication. This, she claims, helped to prevent feminist magazines from significantly broadening their readership, and contributed to the demise of most of them by the end of the 1980s.[6] Feminist historian Amparo Moreno traces an equally telling incompatibility between academic media research and its object. Academic discourse, she suggests, is underpinned by Enlightenment values – rationality, coherence, the neat and orderly division of the private from the public – which are out of phase with media and other representations informed by a popular or mass cultural aesthetic. In her account, this aesthetic affirms the continuity of women's daily lives and the representations and cultural forms that weave in and out of them, the shared or individual pleasure and involvement (Moreno Sardá 1995).

An important example of this aesthetic are TV 'culebrones' (soaps) particularly, in this context, because an estimated 85 per cent of their audience worldwide is female (Cristóbal and Lechner 1996). The genre (which, like the 'telenovela', is strongly identified with Latin America) has been widely criticised as degradingly vulgar, as educating women in profoundly conservative social values and attitudes, and as sentimental pornography (Terenci Moix, cited Roura 1993; Gabriela Schneier, cited Cristóbal and Lechner 1996; Roura 1993). Yet a reported 1.6 billion women worldwide regularly watch these programmes and according to leading exponent Delia Fiallo do so because they want their solitude filled with reassuring narratives in which virtue will always triumph – eventually (O'Donnell 1996; Fiallo, cited Cristóbal and Lechner 1996). 'Culebrones' are a multi-million dollar business that has developed through the distribution and marketing skills of the networks that produced them and which (even since the genre began to decline in 1993) can still guarantee peak audiences for advertisers targeting housewives (Cristóbal and Lechner 1996; O'Donnell 1996). But this does not neutralise the pleasure that many women derive from watching them. As Moreno notes, they cannot continue to be dismissed as banal, ideologically indefensible or trivialising. If Spanish academics are to engage with media products and effects in terms that do not relentlessly misrepresent their object, she insists, a new and more open vocabulary needs to be adopted – or created – for the purpose (Moreno Sardá 1995). Valid though her general point is, however, Moreno's faith in the possibility of accurately representing mass cultural reality does not sit well with her advocacy of a critical post-Enlightenment perspective. A related tension is explored, in relation to film and writing, in chapter 6.

Notes

1 Practitioners commonly play down the notion of media influence: because they are disinclined to take responsibility for any supposed media effects; because they do not want to be accused of complicity with external authorities; or because they feel any authority they wield is more conditioned and more contested than is usually suggested (Prego 1995).

2 Unlike film and TV director Pilar Miró (who held the post from 1986 until her resignation three years later) Ridruejo has no media background, and has had little opportunity so far to demonstrate the business acumen which won her the job.

3 This is consistent with a tendency for men to appear as representatives of humankind, while women are usually expected to speak only for women (Aler Gay 1995; Vargas 1995). Some have no desire to speak authoritatively, of course, and prefer to negotiate in order to achieve their ends. Fellow-debaters, viewers and media producers accustomed to privileging authority will nevertheless tend to interpret this as a lack or incompetence on the woman's part (Radl Philipp 1996). At the same time, women who do aspire to speak authoritatively are given few opportunities to acquire the experience and confidence on which such authority largely depends. This vicious circle is not unbreakable, as some women have demonstrated, but it can make an uphill task even more forbidding.

4 The term 'senior position' should be treated with caution: 'subdirectora' (subdirector), for example, is deemed to be a senior position but it is not a managerial one. Radio journalist Isabel Marín offers a striking example of this promotion differential at the lowest organisational level, relating to a cohort of successful applicants for administrative posts with RNE (year unspecified) which included an almost identical number of men and women. Five years after they had passed their exams and taken up post, she reports, 76 per cent of the men had been promoted to the next grade, compared with 5 per cent of women (Marín 1994).

5 These figures take no account of the circumstances of individual women, which are proportionately more significant where small numbers are concerned.

6 Those that have survived have either adapted to the times, as in the case of *Poder y Libertad* (which moved from Barcelona to Madrid, where a glossy version is produced with a subsidy from the Institute for Women) or have been resurrected in a new and more 'popular' guise, as in the case of *Mujeres* (which, significantly, is also sponsored by the Institute for Women).

6   Versions of identity

WOMEN HAVE MADE major advances as writers and film-makers in the democratic period. This chapter looks at the background to these advances and some of the tensions and contradictions associated with them. Its focus, however, is on one particular tension in women's representations: between the desire to recover a more innocent past or escape to a more open future, and the sense that this desire cannot be satisfied.

In the cinema, this tension has become increasingly visible in recent years with the rising profile of younger women directors. As in so many other areas, this rise has been from a very low base. In the twenty years that Esther García (head of Pedro Almodóvar's production company) has worked in the cinema, for example, the number of women production directors has grown by 700 per cent – to a total of eight (García 1995). In the mid-1970s, she reports, the only behind-the-camera posts accessible to women were as production assistants or secretaries. Today, although their credits commonly include publicity, scriptwriting, make-up, wardrobe – and increasingly direction – they remain the exception elsewhere. This by now familiar under-representation has had two main effects. First – and with the notable exception of Pilar Miró – women film-makers have played little part in shaping the norms, values and technical development of the film industry. Second, while the industry's current crisis affects both men and women, women are more vulnerable because they are less likely to have a secure place in the technical teams of the larger, more established production companies. And as with most 'elite' women, those who do find and hold a post are often too pressured to sustain long-term relationships or to combine career and family, and this distances them from many women in their audience.

All of which, compounded in some cases by the professional and personal prejudice of male colleagues, helps to explain why many women film-makers entered the industry by indirect routes. Spain's first woman film-maker, for example, began as a dancer.[1] Its most prolific, Ana Mariscal, made her reputation as one of the regime's most popular actresses and is particularly remembered for her role in Sáenz de Heredia's *Raza* (Race) (1941), based on Franco's novel of the same name. Having starred in a dozen films and founded her own production company she turned to direction in 1952 with *Segundo López*. This used non-professional actors and a comic neo-realist style to evoke the experiences of a provincial man in Madrid and, incidentally, something of the disorientation of a woman venturing into the male-dominated world of film direction. Four years later, her second feature offered an uncompromisingly anti-Republican vision of the Civil War but, like *Segundo López*, it found little commercial success. Between 1959 and 1968 she responded with a string of more commercial efforts, most of them melodramatic in tone and folkloric in content.

Mariscal was, in a sense, the last of the old school. Her work contributed to the regime's attempts to maintain the purity of Hispanic culture and society by excluding foreign influences ('la anti-España'), and placed women at its folkloric heart. By contrast, Josefina Molina was the first of a new school, with her concern for the personal, for psychological complexity, and for questions of personal identity quite separate from the identity marked out for women by National Catholicism. Born in 1936 (only 13 years after Mariscal) she studied political science and in 1969 became the first woman to graduate as a director from the Escuela Oficial de Cinematografía (EOC) (Official Film School). This had been established by the regime six years earlier, to give new direction to Spanish film-making, as part of the strategy to modernise Spain's image abroad. It was accompanied by a (strictly limited) reduction in censorship, and increased support for new film-makers. During this period most exponents of the so-called Nuevo Cine Espanol (New Spanish Cinema) were rejecting the folkloric escapism that had characterised much Spanish film to that point, in favour of Italian-influenced neo-realism. Molina's taste for melodrama nevertheless underlines her continuity with the earlier film-making tradition. Her most recent film, for example, is a 1993 remake of Sáenz de Heredia's passionately melodramatic *La Lola se va a los puertos* (Lola goes to the docks) (1947), in which she offers a new, woman-centred, perspective on a film which she has described as an integral part of her youth (Hevia 1994). But like many other women directors Molina has also been profoundly influenced by her work in other media. In 1964 she joined the state television channel TVE, where she made more than 40 dramas, and while still at the EOC she also set up and worked with her own theatre company. Her first feature – *Vera, un cuento cruel* (Vera, a cruel tale) (1973), a theatrical psycho-drama with Gothic overtones – arose from an earlier TV project and is also clearly influenced by her theatre work. Her second feature, *Función de Noche* (Evening performance) (1981), is another psycho-logical drama, this time arising directly from the experiences of the actress-protagonist of Molina's long-running theatrical production of a novel by Delibes. In 1988 her third feature film, *Esquilache* – an adaptation of a Buero Vallejo story about the attempts of an Italian politician of the Enlightenment period to modernise his country – offered some revealing parallels with Spain's democratic moderni-sation. But two years later *Lo más natural* (The most natural thing) returned to the more personal theme of an older woman in crisis. Left by her husband for a younger woman she responds by turning from a hostile social environment to a new relationship (discussed below) with a man 17 years her junior.

This film has parallels in the work of Spain's best-known woman director, Pilar Miró. Four years younger than Molina, Miró graduated as a screenwriter from the EOC a year before her. She, too, worked with TVE – the two occasionally collaborated – working her way through the ranks from a trainee news editor in 1962 to drama production, and making over 300 programmes in all (Torres 1994). Like many of her TV dramas, her first feature film, *La petición* (The petition) (1976) was a commissioned work based on a literary text – in this case by Zola. Two years before the abolition of censorship, this powerful study of eroticised violence and sadomasochism shows its powerful central character (played by Ana Belén) being driven by desire and frustration to double murder. Given the persistence of the regime's vision of maternal, self-abnegating womanhood, the censors' outright ban was unsurprising. But Miró's refusal to negotiate sparked a public debate which finally secured the film's release. Her second film, *El crimen de Cuenca* (The Cuenca crime) (1979), has an even more troubled history, relating as it does events surrounding a real-life judicial error at the turn of the century, in which a confession was extracted under torture from two innocent men by Civil Guards. Once again scenes of violence are central to the film as Miró works through a recurring theme in her work: the dis-integration of the individual in extreme circumstances. The military authorities (who were particularly sensitive to criticism during the Transition to democracy) attempted to try her for contempt before a military court, and the film's release was delayed for almost a year and a half as, in the face of concerted public pressure, the charges were converted to civil ones and finally quashed. Despite its enormous commercial success Miró was shaken by the experience, and by an illness and open-heart surgery that followed. She chose a seemingly very different subject for her next film. Despite her denials, *Gary Cooper que estás en los cielos* (Gary Cooper, who art in heaven) (1982) is widely regarded as one of Miró's most personal films. It is an account of a successful and strong-minded TV director who takes stock of her life after a serious illness. The film avoids the comforting or eroticising fantasy of much mainstream cinema, and its focus on the central character's self-alienation and solitude, troubled relationships, strength and fragility recurs in Miró's later work (Rabalska 1996, Morgan 1994). The year 1982 saw the release of her *Hablamos esta noche* (We'll talk tonight). As if to counterbalance *Gary Cooper*, it presents an existential crisis in the life of a man who is in the process of divorcing his wife, ending one affair, and starting another with a younger woman. With its protagonist unable to come to terms with his son's sexuality, and faced with the responsibility for managing the commissioning of a nuclear plant and the depression of his best friend, the film raises a number of key social issues but is noticeably less intense than her previous work.

The film was released just before the general election that brought Miró's personal friend Felipe González to power with a landslide victory. Within a matter of weeks she became the first woman (and the first industry professional) to be offered and to accept the most important post in the Spanish film industry, that of Director General of Cinematography. In this role she sought to support high-quality film-making, to tighten up on co-productions (often simply ruses to procure lucrative dubbing permits for foreign films), created X-rated cinemas for 'pornographic' or violent films, and made subsidies for shorts discretionary, as they were for features (Torres 1994, 1995). But her spell in office is best remembered for the so-called Ley Miró (Miró Law) (1984), which was designed to strengthen and protect the Spanish cinema. Under the official film-funding formula introduced in 1965, 15 per cent of a film's box office takings reverted to its production company. Based on the French 'avance sur recette' system, the new law enabled up to 50 per cent of a film's production budget to be funded through an advance on this 15 per cent.

While it was successful in producing some high-quality films, this failed to halt the continuing decline of Spain's national film industry. Paul Julian Smith has described Miró's next film – Werther (1986), an adaptation and updating of Goethe's text and Massenet's opera of the same name, which revisits the themes of existential frustration – as an 'elegantly costumed and tastefully photographed [piece] typical of the "quality" film-making promoted by the subsidy system' (Smith 1996: 9). That the system was open to charges of patronage and cultural elitism was underlined in increasingly personal attacks on Miró and her Law by unsuccessful applicants for funding. In 1985 Miró resigned. Almost immediately after the release of Werther she was offered the post of Director General of RTVE (state radio and television), with a brief to build up state TV production. Even in 1985, TVE remained 'one of the last bastions for democracy to storm', where women were seen as distracting men from their work, and where the idea of women film directors 'was thought quite simply "a stupidity"' (Hopewell 1986: 113). Unsurprisingly, and although TVE is widely agreed to have benefited from her spell in office, her appointment was a controversial one (Torres 1994). She was quickly caught up in the crossfire between RTVE and its political masters, and in 1988 this came to a head with charges that she had fraudulently used public funds to settle personal clothing and other expenses. Convinced that a Kafkian political conspiracy rather than misogyny underlay the charges (which were later quashed) she resigned from her post and, in 1989, from the Socialist Party.

It was in the aftermath of this experience, which she represents as the bleakest period of her career, that Miró made the film which was to win her international critical acclaim and the Berlin Film Festival's Silver Bear. Beltenebros (1991) is a claustrophobic noir-type thriller with a baroquely ambiguous and labyrinthine Madrid setting, and a darkly Kafkian atmosphere that recalls the experiences from which she herself had just emerged. This was followed two years later by El pájaro de la felicidad (The bird of happiness), which returns to the earlier, more personal themes as a professional art restorer is prompted by an emotional crisis to take stock of her past. She finds a new sense of self in the isolation of an Almerían village, away from the marginalisation, alienation and aggression associated with city life (Morgan 1994). Miró's most recent film is El perro del hortelano (The gardener's dog) (1996). Its widely acclaimed screenplay retains much of the linguistic brilliance and complexity of the Lope de Vega play on which it is based. Like *Werther* before it, this lavishly costumed and sumptuously photographed period piece was not produced for mass consumption.

While Miró remains without doubt Spain's highest-profile woman director, a number of important new figures have become more active since the 1980s, despite often adverse changes in cultural and funding policy, the difficulty of learning one's skills in what is still a male-dominated profession, and of assembling a suitable technical team and producer. Miró's decision to make the funding of shorts discretionary rather than automatic, for example, instantly rendered the director's 'prentice-piece' much more difficult to finance. As a result, between 1983 and 1984, the number of shorts produced fell from 286 to 81 (Torres 1995). A collaborative agreement signed by TVE in 1980 encouraged cinema and television co-productions, but (like the subsidy system) tended to restrict the types of films made – usually to adaptations of historical or literary subjects. There was also a certain technical influence, since a significant proportion of women film-makers practised their skills chiefly within the constraints and demands of television rather than cinema production. Like Molina and Miró, Cecilia Bartolomé acquired a solid professional base at the EOC before turning to advertising, TVE film-making, and her first (and so far only) feature *Vámonos, Bárbara* (Let's go, Barbara) (1977). The narrative, which centres on a woman reassessing her life after a marriage-breakdown, offers an explicitly feminist account of women's situation in the aftermath of the Franco years. National and personal crisis drives the central character from the geographical centre to the periphery, where a new and more open life can begin in a context not structured in advance by relations with men. *Después de...* (Afterwards...) (1979-81), co-produced with her husband José Juan Bartolomé, is a documentary that engages critically with the same period, up to the 1981 coup attempt.

The closure of the EOC introduced more diversity into Spanish film-making. It meant, for example, that women wishing to learn film-making had to rely on regional film schools, smaller private schools of more variable quality, or practical experience – in television or anywhere else they could find it. Azucena Rodríguez, for example, studied at a private film school in Madrid and worked alongside leading directors like Fernando Trueba before making her debut with the critically-acclaimed short *Su primer baile* (Her first dance)

(1989). Her full-length feature *Entre rojas* (Among red women) finally came in 1994. It revolves around a young middle-class woman imprisoned (as Rodríguez herself had been) in the last years of the regime for inadvertently associating with opposition activists. Despite initial class-based tensions, the film is an attempt to recover largely unsymbolised history, and its focus falls squarely on the solidarity that unites the assorted women inmates. Another director who learnt her trade by practising it is María Miró, who worked with the Colectivo de Cine de Madrid (Madrid Film Collective) in the late 1970s on documentaries, and as a photographer with Vicente Aranda and Eloy de la Iglesia, before joining TVE Catalunya in 1983. There she worked on arts programmes before producing her first (and so far only) film, *Els baguls del retorn* (Baggage for the return journey) (1994), a beautifully filmed account, using mostly non-professional actors, of a young displaced Saharan girl's dreams of returning to her home by the sea. Once again, a renewed self is sought in the move from arid centre to more fertile periphery. Cristina Andreu, who acquired her own cinematographic skills at a private school in Madrid, did not work for TVE, and her directorial debut was a burlesque episode in a collective film, *Delirios de amor* (Mad about love) co-directed in 1987 with Antonio González Vigil. But her feature film, *Brumal,* – made in 1988 with a mostly female technical crew – bore the imprint of state television's preference for literary adaptations. Mysterious and fantastic by turn, it is based on an atmospheric short story by Cristina Fernández Cubas which evokes a woman's return to her childhood home following the death of her mother. Here, however, geographical displacement does not issue in a new identity, and the past is not recovered through the operations of nostalgia. It remains vague and elusive, as the film's focus shifts from the object of the search to the seeking process itself.

In 1981, 137 full-length feature films were made in Spain. By 1989 this had fallen to 48 (Torres 1995). In 1985 Miró's successor as Director General of Cinematography had abolished the law that required all feature programmes to include a short, further reducing training opportunities for aspiring directors. This was counter-balanced to some extent by support from the newly established regional governments which (particularly in Catalonia and the Basque Country) used film policy to promote regional languages. This encouraged the development of a pool of technical expertise and opportunities and experience for new film-makers. Among directors who took advantage of this expertise are Ana Díez and Arantxa Lazcano. Lazcano studied at the Andoain school for film and video makers in Guipúzcoa, and made one short before embarking on *Los años oscuros* (The dark years) (1993). Set in the oppressive atmosphere of the post-Civil War Basque Country, it is an ambiguous exploitation of childhood and its lingering effects on the adult woman narrator. Like Lazcano, Ana Díez has made only one full-length feature, but its subject matter has assured her a place in most film surveys. Having travelled to Mexico in the early 1980s, she took the opportunity to attend Buñuel's Film Studies Centre and completed a critically-acclaimed documentary before returning to Spain in 1984 where, after working with some of the leading young Basque directors, she completed *Ander eta Yul* (Ander and Yul) (1988). This powerful and controversial film, produced in the Basque language with a mostly Basque technical team, focuses on the tensions between two friends when the drug-dealing activities of one makes him the target of the other, an ETA member under orders to kill traffickers.

Spain's entry into the common market in 1986 meant that EEC films could not be differentiated from Spanish ones when quotas were established, futher reducing exhibition opportunities for domestic films. In 1989, as the hold of big US distributors tightened and cinema audiences continued to fall, Miró's advance on receipts system was dismantled. Increasing production difficulties, coupled with dwindling demand, led some cinema directors to take refuge in television, as opportunities with expanding regional and private channels grew. One beneficiary of this expansion has been Rosa Vergés. After the critical and popular success of her first film – *Boom boom* (1990), a romantic comedy – she was able to obtain support from Canal +, TV3 and TVE for her second. *Souvenir* (1993) is a blackly comic study of alienation, which charts the experiences of a Japanese boy who loses his way and his memory after arriving in Barcelona.

But the expansion of private TV ate into TVE's profits, and an early casualty (in 1990) was its collaboration agreement with the film industry. Its own film production – and thus its role as a home for displaced film-makers – was also reduced. In 1993 there was a slight increase in Spanish film production but a continuing decline in audiences – almost 70 per cent of whom went to see US productions (Torres 1994, 1995). The Ley del Cine (Cinema Law) of 1994 has sought to reverse this decline by introducing a quota system designed to protect European productions against the US distribution giants, and by offering state support for films which achieve audiences of at least 50,000. Designed to ensure a closer match between what audiences want to see and films actually made, this will tend to favour film-makers with established reputations or large advertising budgets. It will do little to ease the path of aspiring directors, even those who (like Mónica Laguna or Lourdes Bañuelos) already have excellent shorts to their credit.[2]

As the recurring phrase 'first and so far only feature' underlines, one feature does not necessarily make a director. Pilar Távora's only full-length film (after a number of shorts on her home city, Seville) was a 1983 adaptation of Lorca's *Bodas de Sangre* (Blood Wedding). At the time of writing, Gracia Querejeta's output is also limited to a single feature: *Una estación de paso* (Rite of passage) (1992), an evocative account of a boy's troubled emergence into adulthood. Ana Belén already enjoyed a national reputation as a singer and theatre, television and film actress, and had been involved in film production for a number of years, when she made her only feature, *Cómo ser mujer y no morir en el intento* (How to be a woman and come out of it alive) (1991). Based on the best-selling novel by high profile feminist Carmen Rico-Godoy, the film is a satirical manual for women trying to combine a career and an emotional life in an inhospitable environment. Although the film was a popular success it was attacked by critics unsympathetic to feminism, and Belén has declined to repeat the experience. Like her, Icíar Bollaín enjoyed a reputation as one of Spain's leading young cinema actresses – contributing to films as diverse as Chus Gutiérrez's *Sublet*, Víctor Erice's *El sur* (The south) (1983), and Ken Loach's *Tierra y libertad* (Land and freedom) (1995) – and had also written screenplays, produced films, and directed two shorts before making her first feature in 1996. The engagingly naturalistic *Hola, estás sola?* [sic] (Hi, are you alone?) charts the attempts of two easy-going 20 year olds, La Niña (Silke) and Trini (Candela Peña) as both try unsuccessfully to establish a relationship with La Niña's estranged mother and with a young Russian construction worker. The film's warm popular and critical reception suggest that, unlike Belén, Bollaín will follow this up in due course. However, it is increasingly difficult for directors at the beginning of their careers to finance (particularly less bankable) projects – especially if they do not enjoy the profile and contacts, for example, of a Bollaín. Eva Lesmes, for example, made her first short in the early 1980s but did not make her directing debut until 1996 with *Pon un hombre en tu vida* (Put a man in your life), in which a man and a woman accidentally swap bodies and genders. Similarly, some eight years elapsed between Isabel Coixet's first feature – a stylish Barcelona-based study of the so-called X Generation, *Massa vel per a morir jove* (Better to die young) (1988) – and her second, an English-language US co-production (*Things I never told you/Cosas que nunca te dije*).[3] Chus Gutiérrez made her feature debut in 1992 with *Sublet*, based on her experiences in a sucession of kitchen and cleaning jobs as she worked her way through film school in New York. Funding problems nevertheless held back her next project, *Sexo oral* (Oral sex) (1994), a witty documentary on contemporary sexuality, and it was not until 1996 that a follow-up feature *Alma gitana* (Gipsy soul) was released. A considerable popular and critical success – on which more shortly – it deals with the clashing of cultures as a gipsy girl and non-gypsy boy fall in love in the face of family opposition.

Some of these women directors would describe themselves as feminists. Many others would not, however, and would not wish their efforts to be appropriated for a history or genealogy of women. Although the two terms are often used interchangeably, objectors' reasons are easier to understand if a distinction is maintained between them. Equality feminist histories are designed to highlight the achievements of previously undervalued women in order to affirm all women's equal worth in relation to men. But, as noted in chapter 1, there are many (especially, but not only, younger) women who question the privileging of biological sex and the tendency of some practitioners to elide 'female' with 'feminist'. Pilar Miró is not alone, for example, in seeing feminism as 'algo trasnochado' (rather out of date), insisting that her work be seen as films rather than 'women's films' and resisting attempts to elevate her leading characters into feminist heroines or (in the case of *La petición*) anti-heroines. But genealogies attract a rather different type of criticism. This is because they seek to address the obliteration over time of the mother-daughter relationship not in order to demonstrate an (equal or unequal) relation to men, but in order to reaffirm women's existence on their own terms. As in the case of media criticism, the equality feminist model when applied to film content tends to assess film images on the basis of their supposed likeness to life. This may be linked to the use of films as an archive of documents on women's lives, for example, or as symptoms or indices of lived reality (Alonso Dávila 1995). More often, film is seen as significant to the extent that its representations help to condition that reality, through the construction of women as images or characters and, in particular, as audiences. Hence the significance that Pilar Aguilar attributes to the paucity of women protagonists, which she attributes to the fact that (particularly in classic or dominant film) protagonism is associated with action and women generally are not. Two of the key functions she attributes to women in film are as its passive 'alma' (soul/ spirit) or as spectacle (Aguilar Carrasco 1995). In 1960s Spain this spectacle was often based on US models: Rocío Durcal was transformed into a Spanish Deanna Durbin, for example, by director Luis Lucía. He also helped convert the young Marisol into Spain's answer to Shirley Temple. But the most intense combination of 'alma' and spectacle can arguably be found in the performances of flamenco artistes like Sara Montiel, Lola Flores and Carmen Sevilla. More inward looking than US-modelled forms, this type of spectacle was also more backward looking to the extent that it responded to the regime's promotion of a mythologised vision of Spain's past. By the mid-1970s, however, as the timid 'apertura' (opening up) continued and the relaxation of censorship was increasingly exploited, the nature of film spectacle and women's place in it had changed significantly. Among the acres of female (and occasionally male) flesh exposed in Spanish films of the period was that of both Carmen Sevilla and Marisol. But arguably the most striking example of body as pure spectacle can be glimpsed in the short but intense career of María José Cantudo. Catapulted to celebrity in Spain's first full-frontal nude shot – in Jorge Grau's La trastienda (The back room) (1975) – dismissed as a non-actress by critics, her voice dubbed, Cantudo stands as one of the most wholly visible and thoroughly negated figures of Spanish cinema.

Particularly in dominant cinema – and rather like dance sequences in classic musicals – women's bodies continue to invest and arrest the narrative's resolution with unresolved tension. The face caught in a static, closed frame, for example, or the camera lingering on body or clothing, temporarily blurring the background. This deferral heightens the pleasure of the resolution when it comes and, to this extent, makes spectacle a structural necessity in certain types of narrative. The same function – as a moment of structural or other resistance to be overcome – is served by the figure of woman as 'aguafiestas' (a spoilsport) or as endangered (Aguilar Carrasco 1995: 101). In the first case – familiar from a range of classic westerns and thrillers – a woman's unsuccessful attempts to discourage a man from performing a rash act emphasise his independence from her and (by insisting on his awareness of the risks involved) maximise his valour. In the second case her activities or difficulties are the motive for the risks that will be taken by the hero, as in José Luis Garci's classic noir-type thriller El crack (The crack) (1981), which is organised around the private detective's quest for a financier's missing daughter. This model is stripped down to its structural essentials in Bigas Luna's 1978 classic Bilbao, which revolves around the attempts of an obsessive collector to add the eponymous prostitute to his personal collection. In both films the female character is reducible – as daughter or as fetishised object of desire – to the property of an active male (Kinder 1993).

In the 1980s and 1990s, however, as career women became more socially visible, the films of Belén, Molina and Miró began to provide representations of women characters with their own qualities and life projects. Earlier challenges to the tendencies noted by Carrasco could also be found in male-directed films like Erice's El espíritu de la colmena (The spirit of the beehive) (1973) and Saura's Cría cuervos ... (Raise crows ...) (1976) – both featuring the young Ana Torrent. But these films use female characters more metaphorically, exploiting the hallucinating gaze of a traumatised young girl to comment on the legacy of the Civil War and the regime (Hopewell 1986).[4] By contrast, women characters in feminist-identified films like Belén's tend to be viewed metonymically, as individual members of a class. Despite the fact that directors like Miró actively resist such identification, some critics see a feminist critical perspective as the only way of systematically challenging the role of dominant film in perpetuating the prevailing sex-gender system. With this in mind, Begoña Siles Ojeda advocates searching in films made by women for specific qualities which might give rise to female, and (she claims) ultimately feminist, discourses on film (Siles Ojeda 1995). In particular, she insists on the need to expose the shadowy process by which subjects are constructed through film, and the values assigned to them on the basis of their gender. Her psychoanalytically-informed analysis characterises men as active subjects whose gaze constructs women as the passive support of male desire and as the threatening (potentially castrating) site of sexual differentiation. This construction process is not simply a reflection of the vision or psycho-sexual dynamic of particular male directors or technical staff, she maintains: it has become enshrined over time in a range of socio-technical practices and values that may equally be assumed by women directors. To watch a film, Siles maintains, is to identify with this gaze and thus to accept its construction of the female as object. Unlike male spectators, however, women cannot distance themselves from the object of their adopted gaze: they see versions of themselves endlessly reflected back at them. And making their position even more uncomfortable is the fact that these images tend to be fragmented and fetishised. Fetishisation occurs as the male gaze attempts to supplement the missing maternal phallus (to mask the ever-present threat of castration) or more or less sadistically to dominate the potentially castrating female. Women are thus, once again, spectacles in the sense that they are: the objects of this gaze; the means by which the seer sees; and the speculum or mirror in which the masculine subject can see himself in fantasised completeness. To this extent, Siles maintains, women figure as the object of male desire but not as a subject in their own right. And only by casting light on the darkest corners of this process and the binary oppositions that underpin it – masculine subject/feminine object, possessing/not possessing the phallus – can they be made explicit and challenged.

Equality feminist models tend to focus on women's equal access to film direction and other creative and technical posts, or on their equivalent protagonism in the films produced. What Siles is advocating is a way of looking at women on screen that is not conditioned by the dynamic of male desire.[5] But while her critique can be applied to examples of dominant film, it is less powerful where the work of more radical film-makers is concerned. While the gender-stereotypical basis of much commercial film-making in Spain and elsewhere remains in evidence, the broad social changes from which feminism sprang, and in which it has played a key role, have meant that the 'male gaze' has never been less homogeneous and less dominant. As Paul Julian Smith has noted, some of the liveliest of recent skirmishes on the borders of gendered identity and desire have figured in the work of male directors (Smith 1992, 1994, 1996). For Siles, however, and despite her broad emphasis on gender rather than biological sex, the feminist search for '"otro" espacio de deseo' (an 'other' space of desire) can only be carried out through a revaluation of women directors. But she does not speculate on how she or we might recognise this 'other' space.[6] If in Molina's La Lola, for example, the camera lingers in passing on a male body, are we glimpsing the possibility of an 'other' desire or a specular image or reversal of an all too familiar one? Something like an answer emerges from Molina's earlier *Lo más natural*, in which the dominant, socially-sanctioned narrative of an older man's affair with a younger woman is reversed, with far-reaching implications. The assumption that the sanctioned version is 'only natural' and its reversal somehow perverse is de-naturalised by the film's ironic reiteration of the phrase. By highlighting the fact that seemingly natural relations and events are, in fact, socially-constructed, Molina is able to make a much wider point about women and nature. She questions, for example, the assumption that men are rational subjects with a range of optional and evolving predicates, while women are only natural, with innate and static properties which are inaccessible to social change. In the process, by undermining notions of the natural conceived as 'conformidad con el orden regular' (conforming to the normal order of things) she jams the mechanism by which this binary scheme is filled out with dramatic significance (Selva and Solà 1995: 202).

In *Alma gitana*, Chus Gutiérrez achieves a similar effect by making the familiar dichotomies so permeable, overlapped and over-determined that they effectively cease to function. Schematically, the gypsy girl Lucía is marginalised in relation to outer (non-gypsy) social groups by her ethnicity, and in relation to the inner (gypsy) groups by her gender. Both she and her 'payo' (non-gypsy) boy-friend cross the boundaries of traditionally acceptable behaviour within their groups, and are able to do so precisely because these boundaries are breaking down. Despite restrictions on girls' careers in more conservative sections of the gypsy community, for example, Lucía is able both to work and to pursue a non-gypsy education. Meanwhile, her boyfriend is himself identified with 'gypsy soul', and with the spectacle so often associated with it in Spanish film, through his flamenco dancing and that of his (now dead) mother. His desire for the other, though framed here in a traditional heterosexual love story, is thus traced through a 'payo'/gypsy genealogy in which the affirmation of the mother enables him to act as both spectacle and protagonist. In this dual role he is able to resist the traditionally-legitimated attempts of Lucía's father to block her developing autonomy and social protagonism.

Although *Alma gitana* has contributed to the vogue for romanticised and abstract representations of gypsy culture – from which it partly sprang – its implications are much wider. The permeability of ethnic and gender boundaries in the film is linked, via its insistence that the 'other' is part of us, to the rapidly evolving multiculturalism of Madrid and many other large cities in Spain – a multiculturalism heteroglossically underlined in characters' regional Spanish, Latin American, African, US and other accents. In *Hola, estás sola?* Icíar Bollaín links this to its wider philosophical (and economic) implications as the young girl, La Niña, pairs up with a Russian immigrant construction worker who has little money and no Spanish. He stays briefly at the flat she shares with a girlfriend until the girls go away for a period and lose track of him. Traditionally, Antónia Cabanilles has observed, '[l]a mujer [...] ha sido hablada' (woman has been spoken); here, however, it is the man's language which figures as exotic, marginal and unintelligible (Cabanilles 1989: 13). Despite the absolute impossibility of linguistic exchange, the openness and tolerance of all three characters makes rudimentary communication possible. The girls, in particular, quickly reach an understanding: though both desire him in different ways they do not jeopardise their friendship by competing for him, nor put off their travels to be with him. The film ends as, reunited after a brief argument, the two girls decide to continue their journey together. Unlike Thelma and Louise they do not precipitate themselves from a male world in which they have no place. Instead the narrative is grounded in an acceptance of otherness (whether linguistic, cultural or generic) on its own terms, as a part of identity, and without sacrificing solidarity.

More directly than in film, however, changing relations to language, identity and otherness can be traced in women's writing.[7] Before poststructuralist critiques of identity helped put the notion of literary generation into question, Spanish writers and their work were routinely divided into a succession of schools or movements which, taken together, formed an apparently unbroken literary tradition. This impossible identity was secured largely by over-generalising and decontextualising texts, or by making each a symptom of something else.[8] Particularly interesting is the extent to which whatever resists this (never innocent) categorisation is consigned to such catch-all headings as 'Other tendencies' or 'Writing by women' (López 1995). And in each case, the apparently unambiguous authority of the dominant category is attested by its marginalised supplement. In recent years, a progressive loss of faith in rigid literary divisions (and taxonomies in general) has made this strategy increasingly questionable. In the immediate postwar period, however, direct and indirect censorship marginalised whole areas of cultural production as part of Franco's attempt to create a pure, exclusively Spanish culture. Aided by the Falangists in charge of the universities, it sought to block the circulation of all texts – particularly foreign texts – thought likely to undermine the population's identification with the regime. It has been argued that the fear of the direct censorship that cut, suppressed, or delayed the distribution of supposedly subversive material led certain women writers – Elena Quiroga, for example, and arguably Carmen Laforet – to cultivate stylistic indirectness and thematic ambiguity in order to convey their more radical points (Pérez 1988). At the same time, however, the more mediated pressure exerted through Falange's women's section (SF), other official and quasi-official channels, the middle-class family and wider social relations, and officially-sanctioned literature each in varying degrees contributed to a climate of self-censorship which would, in some cases, have come to be second nature. And if the profoundly restricted experience of many younger middle-class women – especially in the 1940s and 1950s – gave them little objective cause to self-censor it does not appear to have relieved them of the associated guilt or anxiety (Martín Gaite 1994). This, and the regime's identification of women with uncontroversial domestic matters, may explain the censors' less detailed attention to postwar women's writing (Zatlin 1992).

The almost obsessive search of some women writers and film-makers in the 1970s and 1980s for an alternative identity can be seen against this background. While writers like Rosa Chacel and Mercé Rodoreda undertook this search in exile, others struggled in an atmosphere of repressive internal isolation, which only occasional translations of blander foreign publications were allowed to trouble. A limited analogy can be drawn here between the 'bricolaje' and making-do that characterised the postwar years of hunger and writers' adaptation of existing materials to eke out their limited cultural capital. One striking and, in the 1940s and 1950s, exceptionally popular example of this was the 'novela rosa' or sentimental romance. By the efforts of such prolific exponents as Luisa Alberca Lorente and Carmen de Icaza this genre, which can be traced back to nineteenth-century 'folletines' (serialised melodramatic novels), came to define the parameters within which postwar women novelists worked in Spain. Among its stock characters are: a usually beautiful and always virtuous young woman; an older, more experienced man with whom she falls in love; and a less virtuous or less beautiful woman to whom the man is on the point of committing himself. The ending – like those of 'culebrones' – involves an inevitably felicitous union as the man finally recognises the superior claims of the more virtuous girl (Amorós 1968). This pattern continually reaffirmed the regime's only route to personal pleasure for women, and confined it ever after to the domestic sphere (Martín Gaite 1994).

As Francisca López notes, the reader's imaginative transition from fictional to non-fictional world is eased by the narrative's minute detail, its precise chronology, and its blend of real and fictional characters (López 1995). By no means all women completed this transition. But even those who, like the young Martín Gaite, came to question the inevitably happy ending did not necessarily stop seeing the love, marriage and maternity that preceded it as women's *raison d'être* (Alemany Bay 1990). By the mid-1950s, however, some writers – Martín Gaite in *Entre visillos* (Between the blinds) (1957), for example, Laforet in *La mujer nueva* (The new woman) (1955), and Carmen Kurtz in *La vieja ley* (The old law) (1956) – were beginning to use the 'novela rosa' frame to highlight the restrictions imposed on women (and particularly provincial women) under Franco. Given the nature of these restrictions, until a space emerged from which more women could see and reject them their criticism would remain (in general) fairly oblique. But oblique as it was this challenge to National Catholicism, the regime's only legitimate discourse, represented a challenge to the regime itself. The fact that it could be traced in the writing of SF members like Mercedes Fórmica – whose *Instancia de parte* (On behalf of the third party) (1955) took issue with the regime's treatment of married women – was thus doubly significant. With its testimonial account of the prewar years this novel was one of a number in the mid 1950s to adopt a more documentary realist approach. As the decade advanced, and the regime's economic and political problems became more evident, realist texts were increasingly used to highlight social phenomena masked or misrepresented by the official media. The fact that most critical women writers continued to challenge the discourse of the regime more obliquely, however, led to charges for evasiveness from some proponents of social realism.[9] The assumption that the private was somehow separate from and secondary to the social – a particularly questionable one in the Franco years – was a fundamental weakness of much social realist writing. From the mid-1960s, as the influence of French structuralist theory and the so-called boom of Latin American writing took hold among the rising generation of Spanish writers, this very restricted notion of realism began to fall from favour.

By the end of the decade, the effects of modernisation (including the increased availability of key European films and cultural and philosophical texts in translation), the May 1968 'évènements', and the growing accessibility of television had all helped to open Spain up to the international social and cultural influences which the regime had tried, with decreasing success, to exclude. Younger writers mediated between these new and more traditional influences, helping to break down barriers between elite and popular cultural forms (Labanyi 1995a). This was a crucial stage in Spain's developing social and cultural heterogeneity, which would hit its peak in the 1970s. In poetry, writers like Ana María Moix (born 1947) were creating novel combinations of aestheticised form, flip tone and pop cultural elements and her two early novels – Julia (1970) and Walter ¿por qué te fuiste? (Walter, why did you go?) (1973) – were heavily influenced by filmic techniques. While the subject of the first – an intense, quasi-autobiographical account of a young girl's desire to retrace the personal crisis that leads to her suicide attempt – links her to the existential novels of the 1950s and early 1960s, the multiple perspectives, erotic charge and self-referentiality of her second links her to the newer experimental current. To this extent she is a key transitional figure (Brooksbank Jones 1995a).[10] If elite culture was becoming more permeable and mass culture was evolving rapidly with the growth of consumerism, popular culture was also changing. And if foreign influences were usually felt first in cities, urban influences were themselves increasingly felt in more rural areas. Local 'fiestas' and folkloric gatherings were increasingly shunned by young people more interested in urban events, for example; doctors were progressively displacing or supplementing the traditional 'curanderas' (women healers); traditional alliances of property were increasingly deemed inferior to love matches; first communions became more elaborate rites of passage, while mourning became less rigorous (Shubert 1990). The cultural dominance of urban centres, the technologisation of health, the elevation of romance over social and economic functionality, the promotion of the celebratory, and the first stage of what Anthony Giddens terms the sequestration of death are all familiar aspects of modernisation. What is striking is the speed at which they occurred in Spain. In this context the very limited successes of social realism – and of the often forbidding experimental texts that largely displaced it – is not so surprising. The incorporation of pop elements in the work of young writers like Moix was designed to speak to the new generations. The pool of potential readers remained very small, however, and the vast majority of Spanish readers continued to prefer their diet of kiosk literature (Carr 1982).

Moix's generation was also influenced by other, and more immediately literary, sources. In particular, these included the work of Mercé Rodoreda (some of whose work Moix translated) and Rosa Chacel. Through her links with the so-called 1927 generation Chacel had been associated with the development of Spanish modernism until her self-imposed exile during the Franco years. But the extensive body of work she published in exile and on her return to Spain, its implacable mnemonic reworking of her exile identity, its intimist tone and formal complexity all achieved particular resonance among younger writers for whom (as Moix notes) she represented a monumental bridge back to writers who had preceded or laboured through the darker years of Francoism (Moix 1994). Like Chacel, Rodoreda had been associated with vanguardist writers (in this case the so-called Sabadell group) before she left Spain. Although her work became the focus of particular identification among young Catalan women writers, the large sales of La plaça del diamant (Diamond Square) (1962) in Castilian and other translations testify to her success in making the daily lives of individual women triumphantly visible. At the same time, by seeming to recover outside of Spain what could not be represented within it, she helped to lay some of the ghosts of the Civil War.

Geographical and temporal displacements produced by the war thus led to a generational one, by helping to counter the traditional impulse of young writers to 'matar a papá' (kill daddy). By the mid-1970s, Rodoreda and Chacel were working at the peak of their reputation alongside Moix, Lourdes Ortiz, Marta Portal and other young writers. Meanwhile, once banned plays were now being performed in Spanish theatres and, as in the cinema, an official desire to demonstrate the regime's liberalisation to foreign visitors was being exploited with the inclusion of scenes of near or total (and usually female) nudity in the metropolitan diet of bourgeois comedy. Once again, the domestic economic changes the regime was produc-ing came increasingly into conflict with the bougeois Catholic values

that sustained it. This conflict became more open in the last years of
the regime, as opposition activism and the rise of feminism gave
some women an active role in determining Spain's democratic
future. This taste of social protagonism had a profound effect on
many of those involved and, once the euphoria of the Transition had
subsided, a number of women were prompted to rework these
experiences in their writing. Rosa Montero's *Crónica del desamor*
(Chronicle of disenchantment) (1979), Lidia Falcón's *El largo esperar
callado* (The long, silent wait) (1979), Montserrat Roig's *L'hora violeta*
(The violet hour) (1980) and Mercedes Soriano's later *La historia de no*
(The story of no) (1989) all in their different ways sought to recover
what were represented as collective experiences, helping to raise
feminist consciousness, dramatising the debates of the time and
exploring their history. Since the 1960s, young Spanish writers had
been less inclined than their parents to work out their commitment
in their writing. The growth in women's testimonial and auto-
biographical or quasi-autobiographical writing ran broadly counter
to this tendency. In particular, as organised feminism fragmented,
the left lost its impetus, and party politics began to be perceived as a
matter of management rather than commitment, feminist and other
testimonial writing helped to reconfigure the notion of collectivity
(Davies 1994). It did so partly by offering readers an opportunity to
work through experiences that were not culturally affirmed
elsewhere and, with it, the possibility of a more or less pleasurable or
uncomfortable identification. These texts were produced in and
contributed to a climate which gave younger women in particular a
measure of self-confidence and a sense of increased empowerment.
The early work of writers as diverse as Soledad Puértolas, Elena
Santiago, Lourdes Ortiz, Cristina Fernández Cubas, Carmen Gómez
Ojea, María Xosé Queizán, Carme Riera and Adelaida García Morales
was published between 1974 and 1985. And while not all were
writing from a feminist perspective, each was contributing to the
establishment of a transitional cultural space which would be
exploited in their own and others' later work.[11]

Some of their writing was marked by the continuing influence of
French narrative theory and Latin American experimental writing:
Ortiz's *Luz de la memoria* (Light of memory) (1976), for example, or
Puértolas' *El bandido doblemente armado* (The doubly armed bandit)
(1980). But others were characterised by a revived interest in plot-
driven and superficially more realist narratives. There was a wide

sense, however, that the teleology that structured traditional plots and the associated faith in the authority of the writer her- or himself could no longer be taken for granted. The new thrillers and detective novels, for example, were marked by a loss of certainties and (in some cases) a search for socio-cultural bearings. The rapid growth of socio-cultural heterogeneity at national and regional level, its increased visibility in the mass media, and its flattening out by the effects of the globalising cultural market-place all had complex and contradictory effects (Graham and Labanyi 1995). As Graham and Labanyi note, Spaniards were experiencing simultaneously periods that elsewhere in Europe had been successive. The resulting sense of disorientation became progressively more evident at a time when economic crisis and women's increased social protagonism were unsettling women and men alike. In Ortiz's *Picadura mortal* (Fatal sting) (1979), for example, the woman investigator can be seen as marking both the possibilities of this newly won protagonism – the power to interpret events, to reconfigure evidence, to assign blame or exonerate – and the search for a point from which to exercise it. The popularity of pastiche as a way of remotivating traditional genres is linked at one level to the perceived failure – to change society, for example, or to find and radicalise a significant readership – of both realist and experimental writing. Its charge of conditional, quasi-ironic nostalgia for the past and anxiety about the future also make it characteristically millenarian. At the same time, it highlights the extent to which the rejection of (Francoist and patriarchal) models involved working with and against the discredited materials. The popularity of pastiche also underlines Spaniards' complex relation with authority and tradition in post-Franco Spain. The metafictive text's supposed resistance to critical readings, for example, is itself a product of critical readings with their own resolutely ambiguous relation to authority. These complexities are reflected and compounded by a widespread, postmodern-inflected refusal to continue policing the borders of the literary, for example, or to assert the authority of the author. Given these parallels, it is unsurprising that the notion of the postmodern – defined as a loss of faith in authoritative narratives – has enjoyed so much relatively uncritical attention in Spain. Unsurprising, too, that writers like Rosa Montero and Esther Tusquets who question the notion of the author as self-present origin are so reluctant to offer definitive interpretations or explanations of their work (Montero 1995; Nichols 1989).

UNIVERSITY OF
WOLVERHAMPTON
ARRISON LEARNING CENTRE

24/11/03

09:00 pm

Women in contemporary Spain
code: 7621310815
Date: 01/12/2003 23:59

hank You for using Self Sevice Issue
lease keep your receipt and return or
renew by the due date.

verdue books are fined at 40p per day
week loans. 10p per day long loans.

In this context, women writers' rejection of the homogenising discourses of the regime had especially complex ramifications. Franco was the definitive patriarch of their mothers' generation – a generation which broadly, and faute de mieux, came to identify with centrally-legtimated values and roles which their daughters would later reject massively. Feminist attacks on the 'ama de casa' figure in the 1980s and the force of demands for contraception which began a decade earlier signal the difficult relation with mothers and motherhood and perhaps also the displacement of a familiar patriarchal, patricidal impulse. Women who rejected Francoism were to this extent more thoroughly orphaned than their male counterparts. The importance of bridging figures like Chacel and Rodoreda can be seen against this background. So too can the persistence of dynastic narratives like Rodoreda's Mirall trencat (Broken mirror) (1974) and Roig's Ramona adéu (Goodbye, Ramona) (1972). As Biruté Ciplijauskaité has observed, the consciousness-raising potential of the 'espejo de las generaciones' (generational mirror) technique lies chiefly in its tracing of continuities and changes in relations between women over time (Ciplijauskaité 1994). In Ramona adéu this charting process includes changes within as well as between individuals and the building of a community of women (Davies 1994). In Mirall trencat, by contrast, the dynasty decays, the mirror breaks, the dialogue gives way to ghostly monologue. If Roig's community remains more vital and more dynamic, it is partly because she integrates social/testimonial and personalised elements, mimicking autobiography and insisting on its fictionality in order to construct herself as a unified subject (Davies 1994; Wing 1995).

In a brief but excellent 1995 essay, Jo Labanyi has characterised the search of writers like Roig for a women's identity independent of Francoist and of patriarchal models as an essentially modernist one (Labanyi 1995b). In the process she obliquely demonstrates the power of the prefix 'post' to suggest a complete break with all that precedes it, homogenising the past while projecting itself into posterity. A postmodern insistence on the heterogeneity, provisionality and negotiated status of identity, for example, obscures other non-essentialising but also non-individualistic possibilities. Of particular interest is Renato Ortiz's conception of identity as constructed in interactions with other identities which are themselves constructed from different perspectives over time, their competing claims based not on appeals to authenticity but on social plausibility (Ortiz 1996).

This account would help to explain the diverse approaches to identity in Spanish women's writing. For if Spain in general experienced two successive time-frames simultaneously in the 1970s and early 1980s, many women emerging from years of isolation in the regime's model family arguably experienced three. Ortiz's notion of relative social plausibility can also account for the resistance to postmodern attitudes among many of Spain's predominantly left-aligned feminists, sensitive as they are to the political implications of denying a collective basis for their demands (Amorós 1994). Whether or not practitioners accepted postmodern claims, however, once the possibility of an authentic, knowable self that might be recovered or realised was put into question, anxiety around identity and the status of the subject became a feature of contemporary culture (Villanueva 1992; Christie *et al.* 1995). This anxiety prompted writers to hide or seek themselves in narrative mirrors that either highlighted the irredeemable fragmentation of the self or (as in the case of Roig) conjured the possibility of its reunification. Back in 1978, for example, Martín Gaite's *El cuarto de atrás* (The back room) had affirmed the constructed nature of autobiography, identity and subject alike, and the wider socio-historical references are first and foremost building blocks in that construction process (Ciplijauskaité 1994). The element of mystery, which both structures the central character's quest for identity and underlines its illusoriness, also figures in more recent writing by women. The mystery that obstructs the obscure search for origins in *El columpio* (The seesaw) (1995), for example, and much of the earlier work of Cristina Fernández Cubas can be seen as the trace of what always resists incorporation or interpretation. A less foregrounded but equally pervasive sense of mystery informs *La tía Agueda* (Aunt Agueda) (1995) and earlier novels by Adelaida García Morales, where it evokes the remoteness and unknowability of the other – male – subject.

The search for alternative identities – or new discursive conditions in which these might emerge – also remains ongoing. It can be traced in mid-1980s texts such as Paloma Díaz-Mas's *El rapto del Santo Grial* (The seizing of the Holy Grail) (1984), Gómez Ojea's *Los perros de Hecate* (Hecate's dogs) (1985), and Queizán's *O segredo da Pedra Figueira* (The secret of Figueira Rock) (1985), which reconfigure myths to place women at their centre (Pérez 1988; Ordoñez 1991). What is at issue here is arguably not just the recovery of lost truths but an extension of the Imaginary, or repertoire of affirmative symbolisations, available to women from which a sense of self (whether conceived as tactical or enduring) might be constructed. History, too, is being rewritten. Once again, there is a tension between the search for a more accurate alternative to traditional top-down or androcentric accounts, and a more thoroughgoing critique of historiography as a project. Angeles Caso (in 1993) and Moix (in 1994), for example, have both reworked histories of Sissy of Bavaria. But while Caso's novelised diary invokes her as a subject rather than an object of history, Moix makes her the constantly monitored but always elusive meeting-point of multiple perspectives.

One area in which the potential for extending women's symbolic repertoire has attracted particular attention since the late 1980s is in representations of sexuality, linked to the growing market for 'literatura erótica' (erotic literature) by women. While some exponents (such as Ana Rossetti and Lourdes Ortiz) had previously worked in other areas, Almudena Grandes and Mercedes Abad are among those who made their names in this field. Judith Drinkwater has suggested that the writing currently marketed as women's erotica is, rather, men's erotica with a woman's signature (Drinkwater forthcoming). In particular, she notes, turning the voyeuristic gaze on to a fragmented male body, like the sadistic or masochistic overtones that often accompany the encounters, tends to reverse dominant male models without displacing them. If what is proposed in erotic writing by women is the active appropriation of a discourse in which women have figured as the objects of other's desires, then what Drinkwater traces is, superficially, a form of 'equality eroticism'. Its banality is linked to the requirement to be instantly recognisable and marketable as erotica, and is an effect of repeating (with different pronouns) a mode of writing with a marked teleological impulse which tends by its nature to be repetitive. As suggested in relation to Josefina Molina's film *Lo más natural* in the right context such reversals can be telling. Elsewhere, however, the result figures as an imitation which actively reinforces the potency of the original. But, as Drinkwater notes, it has to be possible for women writers to explore questions of sexuality – at the very least as one aspect among others of their daily lives and functional identities. Neither appropriations of the body as so-called pornographic or marketing signifier, nor publishers' promotions of a particular version of the erotic alter this fact, although they certainly complicate it.[12] At the margins of the mass-selling market-place something like

an 'erotics of difference' is being elaborated – in the work of
Barcelona-based Cristina Peri Rossi, for example, more ambiguously
in the work of Esther Tusquets, and (as noted in chapter 4) among
lesbian-identified women who believe that heterosexual sex cannot
escape patriarchal paradigms.

Although Tusquets' work in particular has received considerable
attention from anglophone critics, this developing area, and feminist
criticism in general, has a relatively low profile in Spain (Vásquez
1991; Molinaro 1991). A fairly recent study of critical practices in
contemporary Spain (which was written for a North American
audience) starts by noting that Spanish academic criticism has
traditionally been undertaken in philology departments as a primarily
linguistic activity (López *et al.* 1994). The volume is designed to
indicate how the entry of new teaching staff in the democratic period
and the modernising of curricula have helped to transform this state
of affairs. The fact that most of the essays included are resolutely
linguistically-oriented and that there are no references whatever to
feminist criticism highlights the limits of this supposed transformation. Although feminist literary theory was reportedly filtering into
Spain from the late 1970s, as late as 1984 feminist criticism remained
largely confined to equality feminist 'images of women'-type
approaches (Ordoñez 1987, 1991; Nichols 1992). As noted in earlier
chapters, although versions of difference feminism have been treated
with considerable suspicion by most academic feminists, a number
of factors have encouraged a rather more receptive climate in recent
years. Most importantly, there has been Spain's growing integration
into Europe and larger international academic and publishing
networks, and increased opportunities for Spanish academics to study
abroad. With a few notable exceptions, however, the effects of this
integration and of work done in university-based Women's Studies
Institutes have not yet been widely felt in mainstream curricula. The
fact that these institutes tend to favour philosophical, historical or
sociological approaches to gender issues both reflects and com-
pounds the conservatism of much academic cultural criticism in
Spain in the absence of a strong feminist or cultural studies current.[13]
Apart from the work of notable individual researchers like Antónia
Cabanilles (Professor of Literary Theory at Valencia University and
leading specialist in French feminisms), the clearest exception to this
is in Barcelona, where the Autonomous University recently launched
an important new forum for work on Spanish and other women's

writing: *Lectora: Revista de dones i textualitat* (Woman Reader: Journal of Women and Textuality) (1995).[14] The first issue contains contributions from leading feminist critics like Neus Samblancat and Neus Carbonell (the editors, both of whom have Ph.D.s from Indiana University), and writer and Professor of Spanish Literature Carme Riera.

The more or less even growth of outlets like *Lectora* for feminist research and of the material to sustain them is crucial for the development of any academic field. Where the development of women's writing more generally is concerned, however, the publishing industry has played an increasingly important conditioning role since the last years of the regime. It was at this time that a new generation of independent publishers arose whose translations of leading-edge European and US writers brought Irigaray and Lacan among others to Spanish audiences for the first time. Many of these independent publishers were based in Barcelona where – despite the demise or take-over of many in the intervening years – the majority of Spain's key publishers are concentrated today. Women enjoy a relatively high profile among these companies. Imelda Navajo is Managing Editor for Planeta's bookshops, for example, while Beatriz de Moura is one of the founder members of Tusquets, a company now part-owned by Planeta – which is itself part of a larger publishing group that includes two other leading literary publishers, Seix Barral and Destino. But the undisputed doyenne of Spanish publishing is still Esther Tusquets. Head of the once fiercely independent Lumen – 80 per cent of which has now been sold to Plaza and Janés – her family has been publishing in Barcelona since 1960. As well as publishing her own novels, the company is also responsible for the Femenino Lumen series which publishes work by other women writers such as Moix and Elena Santiago. Anagrama's Narrativa Hispánica series, introduced in the late 1970s to promote indigenous narrative, has also published work by key women writers including Martín Gaite, Paloma Día-Mas, Adelaida García Morales and Belén Gopegui. With the exception of Martín Gaite (whose most recent novel had a first edition of 40,000 copies) even Anagrama's print runs rarely exceed the 10,000 copies mark, beyond which a novel qualifies as a 'best-seller' (Blanco 1996).

This concentration of publishing houses in a few (increasingly multinational) hands and growing emphasis on economies of scale and mass sales have encouraged publishers to slash their lists and put more money into marketing fewer, and more obviously bankable titles. Literary awards like the Premio Anagrama (Anagrama Prize) may initially have sought to encourage writing in specific areas, but more recently their proliferation has as much to do with raising a publisher's market profile. A prize can bring new writers of high quality apparently overnight success – as happened with Belén Gopegui's extraordinary first novel, *La escala de los mapas* (The scale of maps) (1993) – but they are increasingly used to promote favoured writers or allies. Like fairs, and in particular the massive Madrid Book Fair where trends are packaged and exploited if not engineered, they are primarily an arm of literary marketing.

Regardless of the quality of individual writers, the 'boom' in Spanish women's writing in the 1980s was itself partly a marketing phenomenon, and one that helped to condition what was written and what offered to publishers, as well as what was finally published. Nowhere is the relation between writing and markets clearer than in the contemporary 'novela rosa'. In 1994, the two principal publishers of the genre, Edimundo/Corin Tellado and the multinational Harlequin, were reportedly selling half a million novels per month in Spain alone, each combining the familiar pseudo-realist techniques with the suppression of any elements that might jar with the idealised settings and highly formulaic romantic plotlines (Cristóbal 1994a). The tendency of producers – including younger writers with little or no recollection of the Franco years – to underplay recent changes in women's broader social status and changing role have attracted scathing criticism from equality feminists.[15] As with the 'culebrón' (TV soap), however, groundbreaking work by Tania Modleski, Janice Radway and others outside of Spain has challenged the notion that romance novels mobilise a 'monolithically pernicious and disabling ideology' which reinforces patriarchy (Pearce and Stacey 1995: 13). For the reasons suggested in chapter 5, this is a key debate in cultural studies, and one which has yet to be worked through in Spain. The rehabilitation of romance under the sign of pleasure has been eased in practice, however, by postmodern-inflected consumerism, through the operations of which nostalgia and other ambiguous pleasures can be reframed and thus simultaneously enjoyed and rejected – though the ratio of enjoyment to rejection may vary. In Rosa Montero's *Te trataré como a una reina* (I'll treat you like a queen) (1983), for example, the bolero functions as a focus for pleasurable yearning and romantic fantasy. Intercut and undermined by the journalistic account of a crime and thriller elements, however, in a text that insists on the jarring features which 'novelas rosa' omit and that discounts happy endings from the outset, the bolero's limitations could not be more mercilessly exposed. The novel was written at the height of the post-transitional 'desencanto' (disillusionment), when earlier desires and expectations were still fresh in the minds of those who now felt themselves betrayed by the new democratic reality. Although Montero's novel is not simply the expression of a certain generational malaise, this might help to explain why romantic fantasy has to be punished – and thoroughly punished. There is no such punishment in the contemporary 'novela rosa'. And although it is less impervious to change than some critics suggest – encounters are no longer entirely asexual, for example – pastiche, irony and other strategies for having one's cake and eating it have no place here. Instead, consumers devour their bland but undoubtedly pleasurable fare, while publishers grow fat.

Bankability is a key determinant in which women's writing is published, but it is not the only one. The globalising of literary markets has been accompanied by a growth in more locally-based publishing with support from national and, in particular, regional government. Thus, work that conforms with certain – usually linguistic – requirements can become part of the local cultural capital or patrimony with which regional governments are seeking to substantiate their claims to cultural depth and specificity (García Canclini 1995; Labanyi 1995b). Within regional Institutes for Women or their equivalents, this policy is encouraging the sponsoring and in some cases the direct publication of creative (as well as critical, theoretical or empirical) writing by women (Co-ordinadora Una Palabra Otra 1994). The mass selling 'novela rosa' seems at the other end of the cultural spectrum from regional language texts produced in tiny editions. Yet such is the flexibility of the current publishing market that these affirmations of the local and the specific may be adopted, translated into Castilian Spanish, win national prizes and sell in relatively large numbers (Villanueva 1992). In the process, texts which are valued precisely because they are assumed to embody or otherwise affirm their locale become what Néstor García Canclini terms 'de- and re-territorialised': the seemingly natural relation of culture to geographical and social territories is lost and a new, partial, territorial relation is established (García Canclini 1995).[16]

These shifts and the hybrid forms they help to produce contribute to the vitality of mass and popular culture today. This vitality is not reducible, as some critics suggest, to the delirious irrationality of consumerism (Conte 1990). But where books are concerned, reading has certainly been reconfigured, partly through the operation of publishing markets, as a mass leisure activity. And while mass sales of so-called 'literatura light' (consumer literature) have brought book prices down, the number of books published each year in Spain continues to fall. Writing in 1992, for example, Darío Villanueva noted that Spain had one of the lowest book-buying rates in the EU, with only 13 per cent of adults buying a book each month (Villanueva 1992). But if readership overall is falling, the proportion of young women who regularly read a book is holding up better than that of young men (Gil Calvo 1993). With their increased educational opportunities and desire for cultural capital, their admission to the workplace and associated travelling time, women have become a new, large and potentially lucrative market. The books they read on the metro and elsewhere may well be by women, but they are as likely to be comic books, photo-novels or textbooks. Or they may be canonised literary texts which have become mass sellers on the back of a film or TV adaptation, or contemporary 'classics' incorporating traditional, pop and mass cultural elements.

Some of these women write themselves, or will write. When they do, according to Myriam Díaz-Diocaretz and Iris Zavala, their texts will be shaped in a dialogue with the factors, references and omissions that shape their daily experiences and interactions: the graffiti messages and advertising slogans they read on the metro walls, for example, social rituals, official discourses, technology and media messages, and oral cultural forms (Díaz-Diocaretz and Zavala 1993). In turn, work produced in negotiation with this 'texto social' (socio-text) will help to modify the context in which future negotiations take place. Useful though it is, it could be argued that the notion of dialogue underplays the disorderly pleasures, tensions and conflict, the endless shuttling back and forth involved in these interactions. In particular, more could be said about the inflection and refraction of the socio-text through women's biographies, their family and other relationships, the personal as well as the public spaces in which they live out their experiences, their psyches, memories and bodies – bodies as the locus of desires and pleasures but also of aches and pains, hunger and material weight. A study like this can begin to gesture towards these negotiations. It is for women like Belén Gopegui – in *Tocamos la cara* (Touching faces) (1995), for example – to draw them together, shape them into the possibility of collective projects for women and men and new kinds of solidarity.

1 Helena Cortesina not only starred in the silent film *Flor de España o la leyenda de un torero* (Flower of Spain or the legend of a bullfighter) (1921) but also co-directed it with José María Granada – despite which he is usually named as sole director. Cortesina was followed by Rosario Pi, who made two 'españoladas' – films with a strong Spanish folkloric element, typical of the period: *El gato montés* (The mountain cat) (1935) and the co-produced *Molinos de viento* (Windmills) (1937). Spain's third woman director, Margarita Aleixandre, made her directorial debut with *Cristo* (Christ, or The passion) (1953), a documentary history of the passion through paintings. This was followed by *La ciudad perdida* (The lost city) (1954), an Italian co-production based on the novel by Mercedes Fórmica, attacked by censors for its supposedly improper treatment of its central relationship between a fugitive and his young middle-class hostage. Her third film, an españolada entitled *La gata* (The she-cat) (1955), is remembered chiefly for being Spain's first film in CinemaScope and Eastmancolour.

My comments on women's cinema are particularly indebted to Torres (1994, 1995), Hevia (1994) and Selva and Solà (1994, 1995), but for reasons of space they are specified in the text only when cited directly. What promises to be an invaluable overview of women in Spanish film by Rikki Morgan (a chapter in a book on Spanish film co-written with Barry Jordan, forthcoming from Manchester University Press in 1997) is still in progress at the time of writing.

2 Mónica Laguna's critically acclaimed shorts are *Sabor a rosas* (Scent of roses) (1989) and *Quiero que sea él* (I want it to be him) (1990). Lourdes Bañuelos debuted with *No estamos* (We are not here) (1988), followed by *La cita de Lola* (Lola's date) (1989).

3 I am indebted to Rikki Morgan for bringing these two films to my attention, and also a scene in Molina's *Lo más natural*, mentioned below.

4 Some actresses have also come to prominence in this period as the so-called muse of a specific director: Maribel Verdú and Victoria Abril with Vicente Aranda, for example, and Abril subsequently with Pedro Almodóvar, Carmen Maura also with Almodóvar, Emma Suárez with Julio Medem and so on.

5 For an extended discussion of the use of women as a signifier of aspects of patriarchal discourse see Marsha Kinder's *Spanish Cinema: The Politics of Family and Gender*, Berkeley, University of California Press, 1989.

6 One possibility arises from Marta Balletbo-Coll's Barcelona-based first feature *Costa Brava* (1994), which came to my attention after this volume had gone to press. This English-language romantic comedy, which won Best Film Award at the San Francisco Lesbian and Gay Film Festival, traces the developing relationship between a Catalan performance artist (played by Balletbo-Coll) and an Israeli engineer, as the two women struggle to balance their professional and emotional lives.

7 Since this area of Spanish women's activities is the least unfamiliar to most academic anglophone readers, the focus here is restricted to more general observations, and to narrative. On postwar women's writing see, for example, Brown (1991), Ciplijauskaité (1994), Condé and Hart (1991), Davies (1993, 1994), Falcón and Siurana (1992), Galerstein (1986), Hart (1993), López (1995), López and Pastor (1989), Manteiga et al. (1988), Nichols (1989, 1992), Ordoñez (1991), Pérez (1984, 1988), Valis and Maier (1990), Zatlin (1987), and the special editions of ALEC (Society of Spanish American Studies 1987) and Bulletin of Hispanic Studies (Mackenzie and Severin 1995). More

generally, see Christie *et al.* (1995), Gascón Vera (1992), Landeira and Valle (1987), Sanz Villanueva (1991) and Villanueva (1992). There are also excellent studies of individual writers, some of which are referred to in the course of this chapter.

8 Having entered the literary scene at the age of 23 with *Nada* (Nothing) (1945), for example, Carmen Laforet has remained a fixture in overviews of the period less on the basis of what her novel said than for its role as a symptom of the genesis of neo-realism, say, or a new postwar anxiety or collectivity. As will be clear from the preceding pages, the most self-conscious overviews can hardly avoid this tendency.

9 A more direct challenge came from the realist novels of Concha Alós and from Dolores Medio, whose *El pez sigue flotando* (The fish keeps floating) (1959), and *Funcionario público* (Public servant) (1956) have ensured her inclusion among social realists.

10 For biographies and bibliographies of most of the writers mentioned in this chapter see Linda Gould Levine, Ellen Engleson Marson and Gloria Feiman Waldman's invaluable *Spanish Women Writers: a Bio-bibligraphical Source Book*, Westport, Greenwood Press, 1993.

11 Throughout the 1980s, as the most egregious gender-based discriminations and inequities were eradicated, women's education and work opportunities continued to expand, and the market for women's narrative began to open up, women's writing became increasingly professionalised. Today, many of the best-known figures work in publishing or journalism (including Rosa Montero, Ana María Moix, and Montserrat Roig, Esther Tusquets and Carmen Rico-Godoy) or as university teachers (among them Marina Mayoral, Nuria Amat, Carme Riera and Paloma Díaz-Mas).

12 They may, for example, be encouraging the conflation of what Marta Portal characterises as the erotic pleasures of writing with the pleasures of erotic writing. Or promoting the channelling of a need to represent desire in general into a single, ready-packaged and bankable form. Almudena Grandes, for example, whose novel *Las edades de Lulú* (The ages of Lulú) (1989) is often credited with initiating the vogue for woman-authored erotica, has recently stated that she was at the time less interested in writing about physiological sex than about desire itself (cited Alameda 1996).

13 In López and Pastor's 1989 volume of essays on women and literature (from Granada University's Women's Studies Seminars 1987-88), for example, the focus of all but two of the essays is either pedagogic or historical. The two that deal expressly with contemporary feminist criticism are by Carme Riera and Antónia Cabanilles, on whom see below.

14 Significantly, the Autónoma has both a woman professor of Spanish Literature (in Carme Riera) and a woman head of the Philology Department.

15 The example of the genre's most successful exponent, Corin Tellado, is no doubt a factor in this. In rather bizarre contrast with the romantic vision of the artist starving in a garret for his [sic] aesthetic principles, this extremely wealthy widow turns out two tales per week of youthful virtue unfailingly rewarded by the love of a strong, seemingly cold but finally passionate older man. She freely acknowledges that the novels' oblique sexual references are inserted into her manuscripts later and without reference to her by editors if and when the formula seems to require it (Cristóbal 1994a).

16 This is clearly reminiscent of Anthony Giddens's notion of dis- and re-embedding, but in a recent conversation García Canclini indicated that he was unfamiliar with Giddens' work in this area.

Afterword

A S THE SAYING goes, some things are written. Today, International Women's Day, is an improbably auspicious moment to conclude a study of Spanish women and to reflect on the limits and possibilities of solidarity. The volume began by obliquely insisting on limitations, with it references to the increasing instability of the term 'woman'. Without overplaying the 'ouroboros tendency' in Hispanic writing I want to close by questioning the remainder of my title. Unlike 'Spanish Women', 'Women in Contemporary Spain' delimits the field of study with reference to time and place rather than national identity. It was chosen partly because the notion of national identity is questioned more or less directly throughout the volume. This reflects, among other factors, the evolution of regional and local identifications: while the popular mobilisations of the 1970s were directed chiefly against Madrid, the environmental and other campaigns of the 1990s are more likely to target regional or local administrations. But national identity is under pressure not only from internal forces. The dynamics that condition relations between internal groups or movements and central government are increasingly being intersected by other European and globalising lines of force. It is with this complex new dynamic, which is helping to transform women's lives from Spain's metropolitan centres to its decreasingly remote rural heartlands, that this study concludes.

Many of the advances won for Spanish women over the last decade have been foreshadowed in or supported by European initiatives, and the influence of EU policy is set to increase significantly as the integration process advances. Spain's centre-right government is working doggedly and with some notable successes – plummeting long-term interest rates, falling inflation – to achieve the conditions necessary for economic convergence. At the time of writing so-called core EU member countries remain to be convinced that these successes are sustainable. If they remain unconvinced Spain may be obliged to unify later as part of a Mediterranean group – an identification that the government is anxious to avoid. In either case, however, despite the anxieties of many citizens and the repeated stalling of social dialogue the drive towards integration seems unstoppable. In the meantime, European law and policy-making continue to affect more aspects of the daily lives of Spanish women and men. It is thus reassuring to hear that the EU's Fourth Action Programme (1996-2000) undertakes to place equality of opportunities at the core of all relevant policy issues. However, the force of this undertaking is heavily dependent on the definition of relevance used. Moreover, and as the preceding pages repeatedly demonstrate, even if every policy led to a law with an unambiguous equal opportunities dimension the outcome would not necessarily be material equality. The benefits of EU membership for Spanish women are evident throughout this volume but, as the European Parliament's own working parties acknowledged in 1996, it has not prevented an increase in sexual trafficking of women among member countries, for example, or in Internet pornography featuring women. Meanwhile, rising unemployment and other socio-economic repercussions of convergence strategies in EU member states may actively reduce rather than enhance opportunities, parti-cularly for working women.

As well as conditioning national policy development, EU programmes are targeting regions increasingly directly with funding and other initiatives that tend to view regions as socio-economic and cultural entities independent of national boundaries. Local initiatives, such as women working with prostitutes in the Basque Country, can also benefit from direct European social funding. However, the forces shaping women's lives regardless of national, regional and local boundaries do not all emanate from the EU. Women are also being addressed in their locales and even in their homes by globalising cultural, technological and economic forces. Spanish links with Latin American women, so much in evidence today, have been developed through travel and tourism opportunities, the media, business and educational networks, and communications technologies undreamt of in Franco's Spain. These forces enable International Women's Day to assert a transcendent commonality on the basis of gender while emphasising differences between groups of women. In practice this involves contrasting a metropolitan vision of Spanish women with media images of Peruvian peasant women, for example, or impover-ished residents of São Paulo's shanty towns. Yet these differences are made manifest against a common background that is not reducible to gender. Throughout Latin America, and throughout the world, each country (however unevenly 'developed') has its globalised zones where affluent, Westernised and usually younger people enjoy the benefits of global modernity and international consumer culture. A relatively wealthy professional woman from São Paulo's Zona Sul or Lima's Miraflores district may have more in common with her Madrid equivalent than with her peasant or shanty-dwelling co-national. They may shop in stores bearing the same names, watch the same TV programmes (though not necessarily at the same time), eat at the same chain of restaurants, see the same films, read the same magazines, use the same bank, have the same images decorating their walls, work for the same company and voice the same complaints about the double shift. This does not mean that each woman understands or evaluates the signs of cultural modernity in exactly the same way, since the material conditions in which they take effect are very different. However, when a traveller finds herself surrounded by Benetton signs, Marlbro men or Marilyns in the anonymous space of Lima, São Paulo or Madrid airport they assure her that she is in some sense 'at home'. Like its Latin American equivalents, Madrid airport is also part of a locale. As well as international hotels and highways this locale, Barajas, has the family homes and sidestreets, bars and local foodstores conventionally associated with roots and identity. Yet these family homes may include the city house of an Iberian Airways employee who has a holiday flat on the Mediterranean coast, who spends much of her professional life in other countries, and whose sister, brother or child may be studying with a sporting scholarship in Connecticut or on an EU-funded Erasmus exchange in Nottingham, whence the customary pleas for money may arrive daily by e-mail.

These examples underline the current complex shifts in territorially-based identities. But this does not mean that Spanish women today are no longer Spanish, or that their locale (wherever it might be) is somehow wired up directly to 'the global'. It means that they are not only Spanish, that intersecting local, national, European and globalising forces have their effects on individual women's lives. One or more of these forces may be dominant at a given time. It depends on whether they switch on local or national/international news, for example, as to whether these women worry about the collapse of a local refuse tip, the latest policy statement by the Minister for Environment, the after-effects of Chernobyl, or global warming. And as these examples demonstrate, the most local event does not always have the most direct effect on their lives. Rather as relationships in a Valencian village may be transformed by a lottery machine in Madrid, a bank employee will check the Nikkei, Dow Jones and Dax indices as well as the closing figures for the Madrid stock exchange. And in the era of so-called flexible production a car worker in northern Spain may see her social status and financial security transformed by a trade agreement signed in Mexico, for example, as the job imported five years ago from the Rhine Valley is re-exported to Puebla.

It is easy to overplay this interconnectedness and its novelty. Despite Franco's best efforts, Spain's borders were not wholly impermeable even in the postwar years. What is at issue here is the acceleration of this process and its implications for national territorial allegiance in particular, as regional identities gain in strength. For the moment at least, however, the nation remains a geopolitical fact, even as national government strategies contribute more or less directly to the development of new heterogeneities within and across nations and within a globalising, broadly homogenising frame. Despite some of the claims made for it, this frame is not necessarily a democratising one. As well as tourist images of smiling Bolivian peasants, International Women's Day confronts us with Guatemalan women labouring for poverty wages in pesticide-drenched fields as they cultivate unseasonal blooms to grace European living-rooms. It reminds us that interconnectedness creates spaces for new forms of domination as well as new solidarities, and that the solidarities it gestures towards are at best virtual ones. Among the growing band of women who cultivate flowers in Andalusia there may be some who express solidarity, however fleeting and unfocused, with their Guatemalan counterparts today. Yet these Spanish women, who work in very different conditions and with regional and EU support, may one day deprive some of those Guatemalan workers of their livelihood. To this extent virtual solidarities are a useful rallying-point, but they cannot be made material simply by an annual surge of goodwill and are powerless against the material effects of transnational flexible production. This book was written in the belief that such solidarities are a useful supplement or starting-point, but no substitute for informed engagement.

Appendix: list of abbreviations

AEDENAT	Asociación Ecologista de Defensa de la Naturaleza (Ecological Association for the Defence of Nature)
BUP	Bachillerato Unificado Polivalente (Baccalaureate)
CCOO	Comisiones Obreras (independent Workers' Commissions)
CDS	Centro Democrático Social (Social Democratic Centre)
CIU	Convergència i Unió (Convergence and Union)
COU	Curso de Orientación Universitaria (University Orientation Course)
CP/AP	Coalición Popular/Alianza Popular (People's Coalition/People's Alliance)
CRECUL	Comité Reivindicativo y Cultural de Lesbianas (Committee for Lesbian Rights and Culture)
EC	European Community
EEC	European Economic Community
EGB	Educación General Básica (General Basic Education)
EOC	Escuela Oficial de Cinematografía (Official Film School)
EU	European Union
FLM	Frente de Liberación de la Mujer (Women's Liberation Front)
FP	Formación Profesional (vocational training)
IM	Instituto de la Mujer (Institute for Women)
IU	Izquierda Unida (United Left)
LGE	Ley General de Educación (General Education Law)
LODE	Ley Orgánica del Derecho a la Educación (Right to Education Law)
LOGSE	Ley Orgánica de Ordenación General del Sistema Educativo (General Educational Reform Law)
LRU	Ley de Reforma Universitaria (University Reform Law)
MDM	Movimiento Democrático de Mujeres (Democratic Women's Movement)
MLM	Movimiento para la Liberación de la Mujer (Women's Liberation Movement)
NGO	non-governmental organisation
ONCE	Organización Nacional de Ciegos Españoles (Spain's National Organisation for the Blind)
PCE	Partido Comunista de España (Spanish Communist Party)
PEPA	Plan de Educación Permanente de Adultas (Continuing Education Programme for Adult Women)

PF   Partido Feminista (Feminist Party)
PNV   Partido Nacionalista Vasco (Basque Nationalist Party)
PP   Partido Popular (People's Party)
PSOE   Partido Socialista Obrero Español (Spanish Socialist Party)
RNE   Radio Nacional de España (Spain's state-controlled radio
            network)
RTVE   Radio-Televisión Española (Spain's state-controlled
            broadcasting organisation)
SF   Sección Femenina de Falange (Women's Section of Falange)
SMI   salario mínimo interprofesional (national minimum wage)
TF   Teología Feminista (Feminist Theology)
TVE   Televisión Española (Spain's state-controlled television network)
UCD   Unión de Centro Democrático (Union of the Democratic
            Centre)
UN   United Nations
UNED   Universidad Nacional de Educación a Distancia (National
            Distance Learning or 'Open' University)
UNESCO   United Nations Educational, Scientific and Cultural Organisation

Bibliography

Abad, Isabel (1994), Opciones constitucionales de los modelos de representación y participación política, in Forum de Política Feminista, *Mujeres al poder: Elecciones 1993*, Madrid, Forum de Política Feminista, 35-47.

Abril, Nati (1995), Las categorías sexo/género en la construcción del discurso periodístico, in Ortega *et al.*, *Las mujeres*, 151-60.

Abril, Natividad (1992), Modelos femeninos propuestos desde la publicidad, la radio y la televisión, las revistas femeninas y la prensa vasca, in Ricardo Oleaga (ed.), *El ama de casa hoy*, Vizcaya, Eroski, 180-205.

Adán Revilla, María Teresa (1995), Rituales de agresión en subculturas juveniles urbanas: 'Hooligans', 'Hinchas', y 'Ultras', *Cuadernos de Realidades Sociales*, 45/6, January, 51-3.

Aguilar, Yolanda (1996), Lo veo todo negro, *Cambio 16*, 6 May, 68-71.

Aguilar Carrasco, Pilar (1995), Conferencia, in Ortega *et al.*, *Las mujeres*, 97-102.

Alameda, Sol (1996), Almudena Grandes: la literatura y la vida, *El País Semanal*, 31 March, 28-33.

Alba Pérez, Teresa (1993), Untitled contribution, *Emakunde*, 11, 9.

Alberdi, Inés (1986), La educación de la mujer en España, in Borreguero *et al.*, *La mujer*, 70-80.

Alberdi, Inés (1996), Nuevos roles femeninos y cambio familiar, in García de León *et al.*, *Sociología*, 41-68.

Alberdi, Inés, Flaquer, Lluís, and Iglesias de Ussel, Julio (1994), *Parejas y matrimonios: actitudes, comportamientos y experiencias*, Madrid, Ministerio de Asuntos Sociales.

Alemany Bay, Carmen (1990), *La novelística de Carmen Martín Gaite*, Salamanca, Diputación de Salamanca.

Aler Gay, Isabel (1995), De pretexto privado al contexto cívico de la información: las mujeres y la opinión pública, in Ortega *et al.*, *Las mujeres*, 163-76.

Alonso, César, and Hernández, Mili (1994), Entrevista con Elena Vázquez, *Entiendes ... ?* [sic], 29, May-June, 18-19.

Alonso Dávila, Isabel (1995), El cine como representación. *Españolas en París: una representación de la emigración femenina a Francia en los años 60*, in Ortega *et al.*, *Las mujeres*, 183-90.

Alted Vigil, Alicia (1991), Las mujeres en la sociedad española de los años cuarenta, in Instituto de la Mujer, *Las mujeres y la Guerra*, 293-303.

Alvarez, Natividad, *et al.* (1977), *Aportaciones a la cuestión femenina*, Madrid, Akal.

Alvarez Durante, María Luisa (1994), ¿Ecofeminismo o feminismo ambiental: aportes para un debate?, *Revista 8 de Marzo*, 14, 2-11.

Alvarez Junco, José (1994), Movimientos sociales en España, in Enrique Laraña and Joseph Gusfield (eds), *Los nuevos movimientos sociales: de la ideología a la identidad*, Madrid, CIS, 413-42.

Alvarez Lires, Mercedes, and Soneira Vega, Gloria (1992), ¿Tienen marca de género las matemáticas?, in Moreno, *Del silencio*, 306-31.

Amorós, Andrés (1968), *Sociología de una novela rosa*, Madrid, Taurus.

Amorós, Celia (1986), Evolución del feminismo en España, in Borreguero *et al.*, *La mujer española*, 41-54.

Amorós, Celia (ed.) (1994), *La teoría feminista*, Madrid, Comunidad de Madrid, Dirección General de la Mujer.

Ardèvol, Elisenda (1986), Vigencias y cambio en la cultura de los gitanos, in San Román, *Entre la marginación y el racismo*, 61-108.

Asamblea de Mujeres de Bizkaia (1994), Las mujeres, la ecología y el progreso: algunas reflexiones sobre las propuestas ecofeministas, in Federación de Organizaciones Feministas del Estado Español, *Jornadas Feministas*, 257-70.

Asociación de Mujeres Gitanas ROMI (1994), Problemática de la mujer gitana, in Federación de Organizaciones Feministas del Estado Español, *Jornadas Feministas*, 51-4.

Astelarra, J. (ed.) (1990a), Introducción, in Astelarra, *Participación política*, ix-xiv.

Astelarra, J. (ed.) (1990b), *Participación política de las mujeres*, Madrid, Centro de Investigaciones Sociológicas.

Astelarra, Judith (1986), *Las mujeres podemos: otra visión política*, Barcelona, Icaria.

Baca Lagos, Vicente (1995), El análisis de las representaciones sociales de los géneros y los Estudios de la Mujer en España, in Martín Serrano, *Las mujeres y la publicidad*, 96-130.

Ballarín Domingo, Pilar, Gallego Méndez, María Teresa, and Martínez Benlloch, Isabel (1995), *Los estudios de la mujer en las universidades españolas 1975-91: libro blanco*, Madrid, Instituto de la Mujer.

Barrio Rodríguez, Emilia (1993), Ecofeminismo: nuevos valores, *Mujer Trabajadora*, 7, 4-6.

Bayón, Miguel (1996a), Desciende la edad de los consumidores, *El País*, 16 June.

Bayón, Miguel (1996b), El 'éxtasis': la gran amenaza para los adolescentes, *El País*, 16 June.

Bellosillo, Pilar (1986), La mujer española dentro de la iglesia, in Borreguero et al., *La mujer española*, 109-26.

Blanco, María Luisa (1996), Las letras españolas parlen catalá [sic], *Cambio 16*, 24 June, 64-9.

Bonder, Gloria (ed.) (1995), *Mujer y comunicación: una alianza posible*, WAC/ Centro de Estudios de la Mujer, Buenos Aires, Centro de Estudios de la Mujer.

Borreguero, Concha, Catena, Elena, De la Gándara, Consuelo, and Salas, María (1986), *La mujer española: de la tradición a la modernidad (1960-1980)*, Madrid, Tecnos.

Brooksbank Jones, Anny (1994), Contemporary Spanish feminism, *Journal of the Association of Contemporary Iberian Studies*, 7:2, 60-5.

Brooksbank Jones, Anny (1995a), Women, politics and social change in contemporary Spain, *Tesserae*, 1:2, 227-94.

Brooksbank Jones, Anny (1995b), Spain's Institute for Women, *The European Journal of Women's Studies*, 2, 261-9.

Brooksbank Jones, Anny (1995c), The incubus and I: unbalancing acts in Moix's *Julia*, in Mackenzie and Severin, *An Issue of Gender*, 73-85.

Brown, Joan L. (ed.) (1991), *Women Writers of Contemporary Spain: Exiles in the Homeland*, Newark, University of Delaware Press.

Busquets, Dolors, Fernández Nistral, Teresa, and Sastre, Genoveva (1992), ¿De quién y para quién son las matemáticas?, in Moreno, *Del silencio*, 228-42.

Bustamante, Enrique (1995), The mass media: a problematic modernization, in Graham and Labanyi, *Spanish Cultural Studies*, 356-61.

Bustelo, Carlota (1994), El movimiento de mujeres: un elemento clave, in Forum de Política Feminista, *Mujeres al Poder*, 77-84.

Cabanilles, Antónia (1989), Cartografías del silencio: la teoría literaria feminista, in López and Pastor, Crítica y ficción literaria, 14-23.

Camacho, Ana (1995), Mujeres: por la puerta de servicio, El País, 8 January.

Campo Alange, Condesa de (1967), Habla la mujer: resultados de un sondeo en la juventud actual, Madrid, Aguilar.

Camps, Victoria (1994), The changing role of women in Spanish society, RSA Journal, 142: 5452, 55-63.

Cañas, Gabriela (1996), La titular de Asuntos Sociales antepone la integración a la defensa de la familia, El País, 5 May.

Capel Martínez, Rosa María (ed.) (1986), Mujer y sociedad en España (1700-1975), Madrid, Instituto de la Mujer.

Carr, Raymond (1982), Spain: 1808-1975, Oxford, Clarendon.

Castaño, Cecilia, and Palacios, Santiago (eds) (1996), Salud, dinero y amor: cómo viven las mujeres españolas de hoy, Madrid, Alianza.

Castillo del Pino, Carlos (1993), La obscenidad, Madrid, Alianza.

Centre d'Estudis Demogràfics (1990), Estructuras familiares en España, Madrid, Instituto de la Mujer.

Cervera, Montserrat , Morón, María, Pérez, Carmela, Pinto, María Jesús, and El Safareig [sic] (1992), Reflexiones sobre el movimiento feminista de los años 80-90, mientras tanto [sic], 48, 33-50.

Christie, Ruth, Drinkwater, Judith, and Macklin, John (1995), The Scripted Self: Textual Identities in Contemporary Spanish Narrative, Warminster, Aris and Phillips.

Ciplijauskaité, Biruté (1994; 1st pub. 1988), La novela femenina contemporánea (1970-85): hacia una tipología de la narración en primera persona, Madrid, Antropos.

CIS (1991), Las mujeres españoles: lo público y lo privado, Madrid, Ministerio de Asuntos Sociales, Centro de Investigaciones Sociológicas.

Co-ordinadora Una Palabra Otra (1994), Espacios en espiral: dossier cine, literatura y teatro de mujeres, Co-ordinadora Una Palabra Otra, Barcelona.

Col.lectiu de Dones joves Desobediencia [sic] (1994), Mujeres jóvenes: iguales ¿en qué? feministas ¿para qué?, in Federación de Organizaciones Feministas del Estado Español, Jornadas Feministas, 223-38.

Comas, Amparo (1991), La prostitución femenina en Madrid, Madrid, Dirección General de la Mujer.

Comisión Antiagresiones de Madrid (1994), Soy puta: y ¿qué?, in Federación de Organizaciones Feministas del Estado Español, Jornadas Feministas, 223-6.

Comunidad de Madrid/Médicos del Mundo (1995), *Guía de recursos de la población inmigrante en la Comunidad de Madrid*, Madrid, Comunidad de Madrid.

Condé, Lisa P., and Hart, Stephen M. (1991), *Feminist Readings on Spanish and Latin American Literature*, Lewiston, Edwin Mellen.

Conte, Rafael (ed.) (1990), *Una cultura portátil: cultura y sociedad en la España de hoy*, Madrid, Temas de Hoy.

Control (1994), Acciones judiciales contra publicidad sexista, *Control*, 379, March, 70-2.

CRECUL (1994), *Mujeres y Punto: Revista del Comité Reivindicativo y Cultural de Lesbianas del Estado Español*, June.

Cristóbal, Ramiro (1993), El sexo fuerte, *Cambio 16*, 27 December, 20-6.

Cristóbal, Ramiro (1994a), Letras en rosa , *Cambio 16*, 8 August, 60-3.

Cristóbal, Ramiro (1994b), Mujer y publicidad: crónica de una violación, *Cambio 16*, 3 October, 28-34.

Cristóbal, Ramiro, and Lechner, Lolita (1996), El culebrón del 2000, *Cambio 16*, 27 May, 88-90.

Davies, Catherine (ed.) (1993), *Women Writers in Twentieth-Century Spain and Spanish America*, Lewiston, Edwin Mellen.

Davies, Catherine (1994), *Contemporary Feminist Fiction in Spain: The Work of Montserrat Roig and Rosa Montero*, Oxford, Berg.

De Felipe, Ana, and Rodríguez de Rivas, Lilo (1995), *Guía de la solidaridad*, Madrid, Temas de Hoy.

De la Peña Herrero, Mercedes (1995), El ama de casa en la publicidad, in Ortega *et al.*, *Las mujeres*, 111-9.

De Miguel, Amando (1991), *Cien años de urbanidad*, Madrid, Planeta.

De Miguel, Amando (1993), *La sociedad española 1992-3*, Madrid, Alianza Editorial.

De Miguel, Amando (1994), *La sociedad española 1993-4*, Madrid, Alianza Editorial.

De Miguel, Amando (1995), *La sociedad española 1994-5*, Madrid, Alianza Editorial.

De Onís, Mercedes, and Villar, José (eds) (1992), *La Mujer y la salud en España: informe básico*, Madrid, Instituto de la Mujer.

Del Arco, Miguel Angel (1993), Las mujeres declaran la guerra a la publicidad machista, *Tiempo*, 6 December, 111-12.

Del Campo, Salustiano (1991), La nueva familia española, Madrid, Eudema.

Del Valle, Teresa (1993), La obscenidad como propuesta cultural, in Castillo del Pino, La obscenidad, 141-56.

Delgado, Gema (1996), Mujeres con mando en plaza, Cambio 16, 3 June, 22-31.

Delgado, Juana (1990), Discurso y contenido, Poder y Libertad, 14, 28-9.

Díaz Salazar, Rafael, and Giner, Salvador (eds) (1993), Religión y sociedad en España, Madrid, Centro de Investigaciones Sociológicas.

Díaz-Diocaretz, Myriam, and Zavala, Iris M. (eds) (1993), Breve historia feminista de la literatura española (en lengua castellana). Teoría feminista: discursos y diferencia, Madrid, Anthropos.

Dirección General de la Mujer (1992), Interrupción voluntario del embarazo en la comunidad de Madrid, Madrid, Comunidad de Madrid, Dirección General de la Mujer.

Drinkwater, Judith (forthcoming), 'Esta cárcel de amor': erotic fiction by women in Spain in the 1980s and 1990s, Letras Femeninas.

Durán, María Angeles (1988), De puertas adentro, Madrid, Instituto de la Mujer.

Durán, María Angeles (1993), El nivel de satisfacción en las relaciones familiares, Amaranta: Revista de la Asamblea Feminista de Madrid, 24-30.

Durán, María Angeles, and Gallego, María Teresa (1986), The Women's Movement in Spain and the new Spanish democracy, in Drude Dahlerup, The New Women's Movements: Feminism and Political Power in Europe and the USA, London, Sage, 200-16.

EEC (1991), Igualdad de oportunidades en la radio televisión europea: guía práctica, Brussels, EEC.

El Mundo (1993), Anuario El Mundo, Madrid, El Mundo.

El País (1996), Anuario El País, Madrid, Ediciones El País.

EV [sic] (1994a), Ellas se defienden, Cambio 16, 19 December.

EV [sic] (1994b), La rebelión de las senadoras, Cambio 16, 19 December.

Evans, Peter (1995), Back to the future: cinema and democracy, in Graham and Labanyi, Spanish Cultural Studies, 326-31.

Fagoaga, Concha (1993), Género, sexo y elites en los medios de comunicación, in Ortega et al., La flotante identidad, 97-118.

Fagoaga, Concha (1995), Modelos de género en la cultura mediática, in Ortega et al., Las mujeres, 129-38.

Fagoaga, Concha (1996), El género en los medios de comunicación, in García de León et al., Sociología, 351-61.

Falcón, Lidia (1990), Pornografía: ni libertad, ni sexualidad, Poder y Libertad, 14, 38-46.

Falcón, Lidia (1992), Mujer y poder político, Madrid, Vindicación Feminista.

Falcón, Lidia, and Siurana, Elvira (1992), Mujeres escritoras: catálogo de escritoras españolas en lengua castellana (1860-1992), Madrid, Consejería de Presidencia, Dirección General de la Mujer.

Federación de Organizaciones Feministas del Estado Español (1994), Jornadas feministas: juntas y a por todas, Madrid, Dirección General de la Mujer, Comunidad de Madrid.

Feministas Autónomas de Madrid (1990), La pornografía, Special issue of Revista FAM, 1.

Fernández de Angulo, Javier (1995), La mujer en los medios de comunicación: prensa, in Ortega et al., Las mujeres, 79-84.

Fernández, Loli (1992), Ser mujer y ser gitana, Amaró Gaó, 8, 6-7.

Fernández, Loli (1994), La mujer gitana, Crítica, 814, March, 27-30.

Fernández Villanueva, Concepción (1989), La mujer en la universidad española: docencia, investigación y poder. Datos y aspectos cualitativos, Revista de Educación, 290, 161-70.

Foessa (1994), Informe Foessa 1994, Madrid, Fundación Foessa.

Folguera, Pilar (ed.) (1988), El feminismo en España: dos siglos de historia, Madrid, Fundación Pablo Iglesias.

Folguera, Pilar (1993a), Relaciones privadas y cambio social 1940-1970, in Folguera, Otras visiones, 187-211.

Folguera, Pilar (ed.) (1993b), Otras visiones de España, Madrid, Editorial Pablo Iglesias.

Forum de Política Feminista (1992), Por una política feminista, Madrid, Forum de Política Feminista.

Forum de Política Feminista (1994), Feminismo y estado del bienestar, Madrid, Forum de Política Feminista.

Franco Rubio, Gloria Angeles (1986), La contribución de la mujer española a la política contemporánea: el régimen de Franco (1939-1975), in Capel Martínez, Mujer y sociedad, 391-431.

Fundación Solidaridad Democrática (1988), La prostitución de las mujeres, Madrid, Instituto de la Mujer.

Galerstein, Catherine L. (ed.) (1986), *Women Writers of Spain: an Annotated Bibliographical Guide*, Connecticut, Greenwood Press.

Gallego, Juana (1990), *Mujeres de papel: de ¡Hola! a Vogue: la prensa femenina en la actualidad*, Barcelona, Icaria.

Gallego, Soledad (1995), Conferencia, in Ortega *et al.*, *Las mujeres*, 85-8.

Gallego, Teresa (1994), Intervención, in Instituto de la Mujer, *Foro internacional*, 21-6.

Gallego Méndez, Teresa (1983), *Mujer, Falange y franquismo*, Madrid, Taurus.

Garaizábal, Cristina (1990), ¿Matamos al mensajero?, *Poder y Libertad*, 14, 34-7.

García, Esther (1995), La mujer en la producción de cine, in Ortega *et al.*, *Las mujeres*, 103-6.

García Canclini, Néstor (1995), *Hybrid Cultures: Strategies for Entering and Leaving Modernity* trans. C. Chiappari and S. L. López, Minneapolis, University of Minnesota Press.

García de León, María Antonia (1991), *Las mujeres políticas españolas (un ensayo sociológico)*, Madrid, Comunidad de Madrid, Dirección General de la Mujer.

García de León, María Antonia, García de Cortázar, Marisa, and Ortega, Félix (eds) (1996), *Sociología de las mujeres españolas*, Madrid, Editorial Complutense.

Garrido, Luis J. (1993), *Las dos biografías de la mujer en España*, Madrid, Instituto de la Mujer.

Gascón Vera, Elena (1992), *Un mito nuevo: la mujer como sujeto/objeto literario*, Madrid, Pliegos.

Gil Calvo, Enrique (1990), Permisividad y emancipación, *Catorce Treinta*, 2, 25-9.

Gil Calvo, Enrique (1993), *La era de las lectoras: el cambio cultural de las mujeres españolas*, Madrid, Instituto de la Mujer.

Gil Ruiz, Juana María (1996), *Las políticas de igualdad en España: avances y retrocesos*, Granada, Universidad de Granada.

Giménez, Nicolás (1994), La postura gitana ante la integración, in Luisa Martín Rojo, Concepción Gómez Esteban, Fátima Arranz Lozano and Angel Gabilondo Pujol (eds), *Hablar y dejar hablar (sobre racismo y xenofobía)*, Madrid, Ediciones de la Universidad Autónoma de Madrid, 283-93.

Gispert, Concha (1990), Políticas públicas a favor de las mujeres, in Astelarra, *Participación política*, 241-51.

Glattstein Franco, Sarah (1995), La mujer como objeto y sujeto de la comunicación, in Ortega et al., Las mujeres, 75-8.

Goetze, Dieter, and Solé, Carlota (1994), El dificultoso camino de la emancipación femenina en España, in López-Casero et al., El precio, 113-48.

Gould Levine, Linda, and Feiman Waldman, Gloria (1980), Feminismo ante el Franquismo: entrevistas con feministas de España, Miami, Universal.

Graham, Helen (1995), Gender and the state: women in the 1940s, in Graham and Labanyi, Spanish Cultural Studies, 182-95.

Graham, Helen, and Labanyi, Jo (1995), Spanish Cultural Studies: An Introduction, Oxford, Oxford University Press.

Grau Biosca, Elena (1993), De la emancipación a la liberación y la valoración de la diferencia. El movimiento de mujeres en el Estado español, in Françoise Thébaud, Historia de las Mujeres, vol. 5, Madrid, Taurus, 171-93.

Grupos de Mujeres de la AEDENAT (1994), in Federación de Organizaciones Feministas del Estado Español, Jornadas Feministas, 251-7.

Guerra, A. and Tezanos, J.F. (1993), La década del cambio: diez años de gobierno socialista 1982-1992, Madrid, Sistema.

Guerra Gómez, Manuel (1993), Los nuevos movimientos religiosos (las sectas), Pamplona, Ediciones Universidad de Navarra.

Guerrero Serón, Antonio (1996), Nivel educativo de la población femenina española como proceso de construcción social, in García de León et al., Sociología, 69-91.

Gutiérrez, Purificacíon (1990), Violencia doméstica. Respuesta legal e institucional, in Maquieira and Sánchez, Violencia, 127-40.

Haimovitch, Perla (1990), El concepto de los malos tratos. Ideología y representaciones sociales, in Maquieira and Sánchez, Violencia, 81-104.

Hart, Stephen (1993), White Ink: Essays on Twentieth-Century Feminine Fiction in Spain and Latin America, London, Tamesis.

Hevia, Helena (1994), Realizadoras de largometrajes del estado español: biofilmografías, in Co-ordinadora Una Palabra Otra, Espacios en espiral, pages unnumbered.

Heywood, Paul (1995), The Politics and Government of Spain, London, Macmillan.

Hooper, John (1995), The New Spaniards, London, Penguin.

Hopewell, John (1986), Out of the Past: Spanish Cinema since Franco, London, British Film Institute.

Iglesias de Ussel (ed.) (1994), ¿Conflicto generacional o armonía familiar?: los jóvenes en España, in López-Casero *et al.*, *El precio*, 149-80.

Institut Català de la Dona (1994), *El sostre de vidre: situació sòcio-professional de les dones periodistes*, Barcelona, Institut Català de la Dona.

Instituto de la Juventud (1993), *Informe Juventud en España*, Madrid, Instituto de la Juventud.

Instituto de la Mujer (1990a), *La mujer en España: situación social: política*, Madrid, Instituto de la Mujer.

Instituto de la Mujer (1990b), *Plan para la igualdad de oportunidades de las mujeres 1988-1990*, Madrid, Instituto de la Mujer.

Instituto de la Mujer (1991), *Las mujeres y la Guerra Civil española*, Madrid, Instituto de la Mujer.

Instituto de la Mujer (1992), *El trabajo de las mujeres a través de la historia*, Madrid, Instituto de la Mujer.

Instituto de la Mujer (1993a), *II Plan para la igualdad de oportunidades de las mujeres (1993-1995)*, Madrid, Instituto de la Mujer.

Instituto de la Mujer (1993b), *La educación no sexista en la reforma educativa*, Madrid, Instituto de la Mujer.

Instituto de la Mujer (1993c), *Las mujeres en la administración del Estado: explotación de datos secundarios*, Madrid, Instituto de la Mujer.

Instituto de la Mujer (1994a), *Diez años del Instituto de la Mujer*, Madrid, Instituto de la Mujer.

Instituto de la Mujer (1994b), El programa español para participar en la iniciativa 'EMPLEO' (suplemento sobre formación profesional y empleo), *Trabajo en Femenino*, 16, 1-12.

Instituto de la Mujer (1994c), *Foro internacional: mujer, poder político y desarrollo*, Madrid, Instituto de la Mujer.

Instituto de la Mujer (1994d), *La mujer en cifras (Una década: 1982-1992)*, Madrid, Instituto de la Mujer.

Instituto de la Mujer (1995a), *El largo camino hacia la igualdad: feminismo en España 1975-1995*, Madrid, Instituto de la Mujer.

Instituto de la Mujer (1995b), *El voto femenino en España*, Madrid, Instituto de la Mujer.

Instituto de la Mujer (1995c), *No digaís que no hay mujeres abogadas, arquitectas, periodistas*, Madrid, Instituto de la Mujer.

Instituto de la Mujer (1995d), *Observatorio de la publicidad*, Madrid, Instituto de la Mujer.

Instituto de la Mujer (1995e), *Spanish Women on the Threshold of the 21st Century*, Madrid, Instituto de la Mujer.

Izquierdo, María Jesús (1988), 20 años después del Womens [sic] Lib, unpublished paper to conference entitled *20 años después del Womens Lib*, Madrid, 13-15 October.

Jordan, Barry (1995), Redefining the public interest: television in Spain today, in Graham and Labanyi, *Spanish Cultural Studies*, 361-9.

Kinder, Marsha (1993), *Blood Cinema: The Reconstruction of National Identity in Spain*, Berkeley, University of California Press.

Labanyi, Jo (1995a), Censorship, or the fear of mass culture, in Graham and Labanyi, *Spanish Cultural Studies*, 207-14.

Labanyi, Jo (1995b), Postmodernism and the problems of cultural identity, in Graham and Labanyi, *Spanish Cultural Studies*, 396-406.

Landaburu, Gorka (1996), Hay que respetar el derecho al asilo, *Cambio 16*, 12 August, 34-5.

Landeira, Ricardo, and González-del-Valle, Luis T. (eds) (1987), *Nuevos y novísimos: algunas perspectivas críticas sobre la narrativa española desde la década de los 60*, Boulder, Society of Spanish and Spanish-American Studies.

Lesbianas sin Duda (1994), *LSD: non grata*, 1, June.

Llorach Boladeras, Nuria (1995), Superar la discriminación en la vida cotidiana, in Bonder, *Mujer y comunicación*, 19-21.

Longhurst, Alex (1991), Women and social change in contemporary Spain, *Journal of the Association for Contemporary Iberian Studies*, 4:2, 17-25.

López, Aurora, and Pastor, María Angeles (eds) (1989), *Crítica y ficción literaria: mujeres españolas contemporáneas*, Granada, Universidad de Granada.

López, Félix (1990), La sexualidad de los universitarios: un estudio comparativo 1977-1987, *Revista de Sexología*, 42, 1-20.

López, Francisca (1995), *Mito y discurso en la novela femenina de posguerra española*, Madrid, Pliegos.

López, Silvia L., Talens, Jenaro, and Villanueva, Darío (1994), *Critical Practices in Post-Franco Spain*, Minneapolis, University of Minnesota. Press.

López-Casero, F., Bernecker, W. L., and Waldmann, P. (eds) (1994), *El precio de la modernización: formas y retos del cambio de valores en la España de hoy*, Madrid, Iberoamericana.

López Puig, Anna [sic] (1992), La agresividad en la infancia. Estudio empírico comparativo entre los sexos, in Moreno, Del silencio, 35-46.

Lovenduski, J., and Norris, P. (1993), Gender and Party Politics, London, Sage.

Mackenzie, Ann L., and Severin, Dorothy S. (eds) (1995), An Issue of Gender: Women's Perceptions and Perceptions of Women in Hispanic Society and Literature (Special Issue of Bulletin of Hispanic Studies), 72:1.

Mañeru Méndez, Ana (1994), La educación de las mujeres, in Instituto de las Mujeres, 10 años, 81.

Manteiga, Roberto C., Galerstein, Carolyn, and McNerney, Kathleen (eds) (1988), Feminine Concerns in Contemporary Spanish Fiction by Women, Potomac, Maryland, Scripta Humanística.

Maquieira, Virginia, and Sánchez, Cristina (eds) (1990), Violencia y sociedad patriarcal, Madrid, Ediciones Pablo Iglesias.

Marín, Isabel (1994), El Comité Europeo para la Igualdad de Oportunidades en Radio-TV, Mujeres en Acción, 7, 7-8.

Martín Barroso, Clemente (1992), Embarazo, aborto y maternidad entre las adolescentes de la Comunidad de Madrid, Madrid, Dirección General de la Mujer.

Martín Gaite, Carmen (1994; 1st pub. 1987), Usos amorosos de la postguerra española, Barcelona, Anagrama.

Martín Serrano, Manuel (ed.) (1995), Las mujeres y la publicidad: nosostras y vosotros según nos ve la televisión, Madrid, Instituto de la Mujer.

Martínez, Miquel (1992), Els altres matrimonis, Serveis Socials: Full Informatiu, 48, 8-9.

Mazariegos, Josechu Vicente, Camarero Rioja, Luis, Porto Vázquez, Fernando, and Sampedro Gallego, Rosario (1993), Situacion socioprofesional de la mujer en la agricultura, Madrid, Ministerio de Agricultura, Pesca y Alimentación.

Méndez, Lucía (1995), Conferencia sobre la mujer y la prensa, in Ortega et al., Las mujeres, 89-93.

Ministerio de la Presidencia (1994), España 1994, Madrid, Secretaría General del Portavoz del Gobierno.

Ministerio de la Presidencia (1995), España 1995, Madrid, Secretaría General del Portavoz del Gobierno.

Miranda, María Jesús (1987), Crónica del desconcierto, Madrid, Instituto de la Mujer.

Moix, Ana María (1994), El Cervantes se quedó sin Rosa, Cambio 16, 8 August, 64-5.

Molina Petit, Cristina (1986), Feminismo y publicidad: la apropiación publicitaria del discurso feminista, in Universidad de Zaragoza, *Jornadas de Investigación Interdisciplinaria*, Zaragoza, Universidad de Zaragoza, 389-94.

Molinaro, Nina (1991), *Foucault, Feminism and Power: Reading Esther Tusquets*, Lewisburg, Bucknell University Press.

Montañés Serrano, Manuel, García Sainz, Cristina, Ramos Torres, Ramón, Elejejabetia, Carmen, and Hortelano, Juan Carlos (1994), *El trabajo desde una perspectiva de género*, Madrid, Dirección General de la Mujer.

Montero, Justa (1994), Aspectos del feminismo socialista y las políticas del bienestar, in Forum de Política Feminista, *Feminismo y Estado*, 15-22.

Montero, Rosa (1993), El misterio del deseo, *El País Semanal*, 31 October, 16-26.

Montero, Rosa (1995), El camino de las palabras, paper to the *Aspects of Identity Conference*, University of Leeds, 6 May.

Moreno, Montserrat (1992), *Del silencio a la palabra: coeducación y reforma educativa*, Madrid, Instituto de la Mujer.

Moreno, Sebastián (1993), Las lesbianas: del gueto a la provocación, *Tiempo*, 26 August, 100-3.

Moreno Sardá, Amparo (1988), La réplica de las mujeres al franquismo, in Folguera, *El feminismo*, 85-110.

Moreno Sardá, Amparo (1995), Desajustes entre cultura ilustrada y cultura de masas: el orden androcéntrico del discurso académico, in Ortega *et al.*, *Las mujeres*, 139-49.

Morgan, Rikki (1994), Woman and isolation in Pilar Miró's *El pájaro de la felicidad* (1993), *Journal of Hispanic Research*, 2, 325-337.

Nichols, Geraldine, C. (1989), *Escribir, espacio propio: Laforet, Matute, Moix, Tusquets, Riera y Roig por sí mismas*, Minneapolis, Minnesota, Institute for the Study of Ideologies and Literature.

Nichols, Geraldine C. (1992), *Descifrar la diferencia*, Madrid, Siglo XXI.

Nicolás Marín, M. E., and López, B. (1986), La situación de la mujer a través de los movimientos de apostolado seglar: la contribución del franquismo (1939-1956), in Capel Martínez, *Mujer y sociedad*, 365-89.

O'Donnell, Hugh (1996), From a manichean universe to the kitchen sink, *Intellect: International Journal of Iberian Studies*, 9:1, 7-18.

Olivares, Javier (1994), Las bestias humanas, *Cambio 16*, 10 October, 84-6.

Ordaz, Pablo (1996), Carne joven, *El País*, 28 January.

Ordóñez, Elizabeth (1987), Inscribing difference: l'écriture féminine' and new narrative by women, in Servodidio, *Reading for Difference*, 45-58.

Ordóñez, Elizabeth (1991), *Voices of Their Own: Contemporary Spanish Narrative by Women*, Lewisburg, Bucknell University Press.

Ortega, Félix, Fagoaga, Concha, García de León, María Antonia, and Del Río, Pablo (1993), *La flotante identidad sexual: la construcción del género en la vida cotidiana de la juventud*, Madrid, Universidad Complutense/Dirección General de la Mujer.

Ortega, Margarita, Sebastián, Julia, and De la Torre, Isabel (eds) (1995), *Las mujeres en la opinión pública*, Madrid, Instituto Universitario de Estudios de la Mujer, Universidad Autónoma de Madrid.

Ortiz, Renato (1996), *Otro territorio: ensayos sobre el mundo contemporáneo*, Buenos Aires, Universidad Nacional de Quilmes.

Ortiz Corulla, Carmen (1987), *La participación política de las mujeres en la democracia (1979-1986)*, Madrid, Instituto de la Mujer.

Osborne, Raquel (1993), *La construcción sexual de la realidad*, Madrid, Catedra/ Universitat de Valencia/Instituto de la Mujer.

Pardo, Rosa (1988), Feminismo primero, política después, *Poder y Libertad*, 8, 16-17.

Parra, Isabel (1986), El control de la natalidad, in Borreguero et al., *La mujer española*, 61-70.

Paz Benito, Luz María (1993), Mujer y cambio en la década de los ochenta, in Guerra and Tezanos, *La década del cambio*, 699-723.

Pearce, Lynne and Stacey, Jackie (eds) (1995), *Romance Revisited*, London, Lawrence and Wishart.

Peña-Marín, Cristina, and Frabetti, Carlo (1990), *La mujer en la publicidad*, Madrid, Instituto de la Mujer.

Peñamarín, Cristina (1995), Mujer y seducción publicitaria, in Ortega et al., *Las mujeres*, 107-10.

Pérez, Janet (ed.) (1984), *Novelistas femeninas de la postguerra española*, Madrid, Porrúa.

Pérez, Janet (1988), *Contemporary Women Writers of Spain*, Boston, Twayne.

Pérez, Odila, and Trallero, Margarita (1983), *La mujer ante la ley*, Barcelona, Martínez Roca.

Pina, Beatriz, Fumarral, Lola, Yuste, Chini, and Yuste, Pilar (1994), Cristianas al descubierto, in Federación de Organizaciones Feministas del Estado Español, *Jornadas Feministas*, 127-138.

Pineda, Empar (1988), El poder patriarcal en el orden social burgués, *Poder y Libertad*, 8, 14-15.

Pineda, Empar (1994), Rompiendo el silencio, *El País*, 26 June.

Pont Chafer, Neus (1994), Incidencia de la crisis en la mujer, in Federación de Organizaciones Feministas del Estado Español, *Jornadas Feministas*, 7-12.

Prego, Victoria (1995), Radio y televisión, in Ortega *et al.*, *Las mujeres*, 61-7.

Presencia Gitana Equipo de Estudios (1990), *Mujeres gitanas ante el futuro*, Madrid, Editorial Presencia Gitana/Asidiajú Callí.

Principado de Asturias (1995), *Carta para la igualdad de oportunidades de las mujeres rurales de Asturias*, Oviedo, Principado de Asturias, Dirección Regional de la Mujer.

Pujol Algans, Carmen (1992), *Código de la mujer*, Madrid, Instituto de la Mujer.

Puleo, Alicia H (1994), *Conceptualizaciones de la sexualidad e identidad femenina: voces de mujeres en la Comunidad Autónoma de Madrid*, Madrid, Universidad Complutense/Dirección General de la Mujer.

Rabalska, Carmen (1996), Women in Spanish cinema in Transition, *International Journal of Iberian Studies*, 9:3, 166-79.

Radl Philipp, Rita (1996), Los medios de comunicación de masas y sus imágenes femeninas, in García de León *et al.*, *Sociología*, 367-84.

Ramírez, Fátima (1995), La tele es suya, *Cambio 16*, 30 January, 26-33.

Ramírez, Fátima (1996a), Quince años tiene mi desamor, *Cambio 16*, 22 July, 58-9.

Ramírez, Fátima (1996b), Hay que cambiar el neomachismo estúpido y pseudoerótico, *Cambio 16*, 3 June, 30-1.

Rey, Juan (1994), *El hombre fingido: la representación de la masculinidad en el discurso publicitario*, Madrid, Fundamentos.

Rico-Godoy, Carmen (1993), El machismo quiere enterrar al feminismo, *Cambio 16*, 27 December, 24.

Roig, Encarna (1994), *La libertad sexual violada: las agresiones sexuales, sus víctimas y su entorno*, Madrid, Dirección General de la Mujer.

Roig, Mercedes (1989), *A través de la prensa: la mujer en la historia: Francia, Italia, España, Siglos XVIII-XX*, Madrid, Instituto de la Mujer.

Roig, Monserrat (1986), *El feminismo*, Barcelona, Salvat.

Roldán, Asun (1994), Programa de atención socio-sanitaria a las mujeres que trabajan en la prostitución en Navarra, *Revista Iberoamericana ETS* [sic], 8:6, November-December, 487-90.

Rollin, Hilary (1995), Women, employment and society in Spain: an equal opportunity?, *Journal of the Association for Contemporary Iberian Studies*, 8:2, 45-60.

Román, Marta (1995), La reconstrucción del espacio cotidiano (Sección Monográfica), *Mujeres*, 19, 6-7.

Román, Paloma (ed.) (1995), *Sistema político español*, Madrid, McGraw Hill.

Romano García, Vicente (ed.) (19945), *Líneas actuales de investigación sobre mujer y medios de comunicación: análisis y repertorio bibliográfico*, Madrid, Instituto de la Mujer.

Romero López, Marcial (1996), Empresarias y autónomas: riesgo económico e identidad femenina, in García de León *et al.*, *Sociología*, 187-218.

Roura, Assumpta (1993), *Telenovelas: pasiones de mujer: el sexo del culebrón*, Madrid, Gedisa.

Rubery, Jill (ed.) (1993), *Las mujeres y la recesión*, Madrid, Ministerio de Trabajo y Seguridad Social.

Rubio Castro, Ana (1990), El feminismo de la diferencia: los argumentos de una igualdad compleja, *Revista de Estudios Políticos (Nueva Epoca)*, 70, October/ December, 185-207.

Sáez Lara, Carmen (1994), *Mujeres y mercado de trabajo: las discriminaciones directas e indirectas*, Madrid, Consejo Económico y Social.

Sal (1993), Dos hombres, una mujer, *Sal*, 14, 3-19.

Salido Cortez, Olga (1994), Género y poder político: la participación de las mujeres, in Forum de Política Feminista, *Mujeres al poder*, 7-17.

Sampedro, M. Rosario (1993), Una política social dirigida a la mujer, in VVAA [sic], *El espacio posible: mujeres en el poder local*, Quito, Ecuador, Ediciones de las Mujeres/Isis Internacional.

San Román, Teresa (ed.) (1986), *Entre la marginación y el racismo. Reflexiones sobre la vida de los gitanos*, Madrid, Alianza Universidad.

Sánchez López, Rosario (1990), *Mujer española, una sombra de destino en lo universal*, Murcia, Universidad de Murcia.

Sánchez Mellado, Luz (1995), La guerra de la ciudades, *El País*, 14 May.

Sánchez Rodríguez, Miguel Angel (1995), El Parlamento pide al gobierno la Ley de Convivencia, *Entiendes...?* [sic], 33, Jan.-Feb., 10-11.

Santos, Carlos (1994a), Las chicas son guerreras, *Cambio 16*, 15 August, 12-17.

Santos, Carlos (1994b), Los chicos sin las chicas, Cambio 16, 7 November, 14-20.

Sanz Villanueva, Santos (1991), Historia de la literatura española: 6/2 literatura actual, Barcelona, Ariel, 4th ed.

Scanlon, Geraldine M. (1986), La polémica feminista en la España contemporánea 1868-1974, Madrid, Akal.

Scanlon, Geraldine M. (1988), Orígenes y evolución del movimiento feminista y contemporáneo, in Folguera, El feminismo, 147-72.

Sebastián, Julia (1995), La imagen de la mujer en la publicidad: análisis de los mensajes latentes en los anuncios de contenido sexual, in Ortega et al., Las mujeres, 121-6.

Selva, Marta, and Solà, Anna (1994), Acerca de una historia no escrita: las mujeres en el cine (español), in Co-ordinadora Una Palabra Otra, Espacios en espiral, pages unnumbered.

Selva, Marta, and Solà, Anna (1995), Premisas para una discusión sobre mujer y cine, in Ortega et al., Las mujeres, 199-202.

Senado/Instituto de las Mujeres (1994), Las mujeres en el poder político, Madrid, Instituto de la Mujer.

Sendón de León, Victoria (1994a), Feminismo: un extraño holograma, El viejo topo, 74, 65-70.

Sendón de León, Victoria (1994b), Feminismo holístico: de la realidad a lo real, Bilbao, Cuadernos de Agora.

Servodidio, Mirella (ed.) (1987), Reading for Difference: Feminist Perspectives on Women Novelists of Contemporary Spain (Special issue of Anales de la Literatura Española Contemporánea), 12, 1-2.

Shubert, Adrian (1990), A Social History of Modern Spain, London, Unwin Hyman.

Siles Ojeda, Begoña (1995), El 'otro' espacio del deseo, in Ortega et al., Las mujeres, 177-82.

Smith, Paul Julian (1992), Laws of Desire: Questions of Homosexuality in Spanish Writing and Film 1960-90, Oxford, Clarendon.

Smith, Paul Julian (1994), Desire Unlimited: The Cinema of Pedro Almodóvar, London, Verso.

Smith, Paul Julian (1996), Vision Machines: Cinema, Literature and Sexuality in Spain and Cuba, 1983-1993, London, Verso.

Society of Spanish and Spanish-American Studies (1987), Reading for Difference: Feminist Perspectives on Women Novelists of Contemporary Spain, Special edition of Anales de la Literatura Española Contemporánea, 12:1 and 2.

Solé, Carlota (1994), La mujer inmigrante, Madrid, Ministerio de Asuntos Sociales.

Subirats, Marina, and Brullet, Cristina (1988), Rosa y azul. La transmisión de los géneros en la escuela mixta, Madrid, Instituto de la Mujer.

Tamames, Laura and Ramón (1992), Introducción a la Constitución española, Madrid, Alianza.

Tenreiro García, Gracia (1995), El observatorio de la publicidad: una experiencia española, in Bonder, Mujer y comunicación, 34-8.

Threlfall, Monica (1985), The Women's Movement in Spain, New Left Review, 151, 44-73.

Threlfall, Monica (1986), The role of women in the opposition to Francoism and the transition to democracy, paper to European Consortium for Political Research, Gothenburg, 1-6 April.

Threlfall, Monica (1996), Feminist politics and social change in Spain, in Monica Threlfall (ed.), Mapping the Women's Movement: Feminist Politics and Social Transformation in the North, London, Verso, 115-51.

Toharia, José Juan (1989), Cambios recientes en la sociedad española, Madrid, Instituto de Estudios Económicos.

Torres, Augusto (1994), Diccionario del cine español, Madrid, Espasa.

Torres, Augusto (1995), The film industry: under pressure from the State and television, in Graham and Labanyi, Spanish Cultural Studies, 369-73.

Unión de Consumidores de España (1995), Programa de seguimiento y control de la publicidad y los medios de comunicación dirigidos a la mujer, Madrid, Unión de Consumidores de España.

Uría, Paloma (1987), ¿Es posible y/o conveniente una plataforma del feminismo socialista?, unpublished paper to 3a Conferencia de feminismo socialista, Madrid, 20-22 November.

Uribarri, Fátima (1991), ¿Qué hacer con las prostitutas?, Cambio 16, 7 October, 38-40.

Valcárcel, Amelia (1993), Etica y obscenidad, in Castillo del Pino, La obscenidad, 125-40.

Valcárcel, Amelia (1994), El techo de cristal: los obstáculos para la participación de las mujeres en el poder político, in Instituto de la Mujer, *Foro internacional*, 36-7.

Valenzuela, Encarnación (1995) Los jóvenes abandonan al PSOE, *Cambio 16*, 19 June, 18-24.

Valiente, Celia (1995), The power of persuasion: the Instituto de la Mujer in Spain, in Dorothy McBridie Stetson and Amy Mazur, *Comparative State Feminism*, London, Sage, 221-36.

Valis, Noël, and Maier, Carol (1990), *In the Feminine Mode: Essays on Hispanic Women Writers*, Lewisburg, Bucknell University Press.

Valls-Llobet, Carme (1994), *Mujeres y hombres: salud y diferencia*, Barcelona, Institut Catalá de la Dona.

Varela, Pilar (1994), La televisión y la radio: el Comité Europeo para la Igualdad de Oportunidades en Radio-TV, *Mujeres en Acción*, 7, 4-7.

Varela, Pilar (1995), Las mujeres en la opinión pública, in Ortega *et al.*, *Las mujeres*, 69-70.

Vargas, Ana (1995), La palabra en los medios de comunicación, *Mujeres*, 18: 2, 14-15.

Vásquez, Esther (1991), *The Sea of Becoming: Approaches to the Fiction of Esther Tusquets*, Westport, Greenwood.

Vera Balanza, María Teresa (1995), Las bases de una cultura desigual; mujer y prensa en Málaga, in Ortega *et al.*, *Las mujeres*, 191-7.

Vilchez Fernández, Leonor (1994), Feminismo e instituciones, in Federación de Organizaciones Feministas del Estado Español, *Jornadas Feministas*, 179-83.

Villanueva, Darío (1992), Introducción: los marcos de la literatura española (1975-90), esbozo de un sistema, in Darío Villanueva (ed.), *Historia y crítica de la literatura española/Los nuevos nombres 1975-1990*, 9 (General ed. Francisco Rico), Barcelona, Editorial Crítica.

Wing, Helen (1995), Deviance and legitimation: archetypal traps in Roig's *La hora violeta*, in Mackenzie and Severin, *An Issue of Gender*, 87-96.

Zaldívar, Carlos Alonso, and Castells, Manuel (1992), *España fin de siglo*, Madrid, Alianza.

Zatlin, Phyllis (1987), Women novelists in democratic Spain: freedom to express the female perspective, in Servodidio, *Reading for Difference*, 29-44.

Zatlin, Phyllis (1992), Writers against the current: the novels of Elena Quiroga, in Brown, *Women Writers*, 42-58.

Index

'n' after a page reference number indicates the number of a note on that page.

The following abbreviations have been used in the index:
EU   European Union
IM   Institute for Women (Instituto de la Mujer)
SF   Women's Section of Falange (Sección Femenina de Falange)